OUT ON THEIR OWN
Conversations with Irish Entrepreneurs

IVOR KENNY
OUT ON THEIR OWN

CONVERSATIONS WITH IRISH ENTREPRENEURS

GILL AND MACMILLAN

Published in Ireland by
Gill and Macmillan Ltd
Goldenbridge
Dublin 8
with associated companies in
Auckland, Delhi, Gaborone, Hamburg, Harare,
Hong Kong, Johannesburg, Kuala Lumpur, Lagos, London,
Manzini, Melbourne, Mexico City, Nairobi,
New York, Singapore, Tokyo

© Ivor Kenny, 1991
Index compiled by Helen Litton

Print origination by
Seton Music Graphics, Bantry, Co. Cork
Printed by
Colour Books Ltd, Dublin

British Library Cataloguing in Publication Data
Kenny, Ivor 1930–
Out on their own : conversations with Irish entrepreneurs
1. Ireland. Entrepreneurship
I. Title
338.040922

ISBN 0-7171-1771-5

For Maureen
    Dermot
    Geraldine
    Conor
    Judith
    Ivor
    Helen
    Mark
    and
    Maeve

Contents

Acknowledgments

Twenty people helped me to write this book—
nineteen entrepreneurs and my friend and
secretary, Gillian Acton.

I am in their debt.

Introduction

*That some should be rich, shows that others may
become rich, and hence is first encouragement to
industry and enterprise.*

– ABRAHAM LINCOLN, 1864

The purpose of this book is to add to our knowledge of entrepreneurs. The method is the one used for the companion volume, *In Good Company*.[1] The conversations took place in the subjects' homes or, occasionally, offices. They lasted, on average, three hours. I had no misgivings in assuring the subjects that nothing would be published without their consent. The danger in doing so is that a rehashed, unpublishable, anodyne script would be returned, bearing the deadly marks of the public relations consultant. That did not happen with *In Good Company* and it did not happen here. Changes were usually minor and related to matters of accuracy or concern for the sensitivity of third parties. In two exciting instances, changes were made to avoid libel suits.

There is a distinct transmutation between the spoken and the written word — even more so when questions or interjections (which in fact were few and far between) are eliminated from the text as superfluous.

Some subjects felt that what was written read like an ego-trip. There is no way people can talk about themselves without liberal use of the first person singular and, anyway,

1

you, the reader, will form your own judgment. This was a particular phenomenon with *In Good Company*, where every reader I met had a different 'favourite' chapter — and where those who knew well the personages in that book had their likes and dislikes reinforced with even-handed prejudice. Books like this do not change strongly held opinions.

What is an entrepreneur?

In a 1971 review of research, it was concluded that the entrepreneur was like the mythical heffalump who had not been caught or even reliably described.[2] Warren Bennis in a popular book wrote something suspiciously similar fourteen years later when he described leadership as like the Abominable Snowman.[3] Despite these discouragements the authors managed to write long books.

I started with the simple notion that an entrepreneur was someone who built something that was not there before. In the opinion of some scholars I was not too far out: the entrepreneur created and built something new and more effective rather than just continued something which already existed.[4] But scholarship is seldom simple. It was suggested that what was really needed was a theory not of the entrepreneurs' success but of the failure of those around them.[5] That was outside the scope of this volume.

My spiritual progress in the quest for a definition took me from Casson (1982), with unintended alliteration, through Carland (1984)[6] and Carsrud (1986).[7] I ended up with this one:

> Entrepreneurs are people who have the ability to see and evaluate business opportunities; to gather the necessary resources to take advantage of them; and to initiate appropriate action to ensure success.[8]

Even that is not complete if it implies, as it seems to, enduring success. In the time that it took to write this book, several Irish firms, all household names, went out of business. That is hardly to suggest that those who created them were not entrepreneurs. In changing times, *tout passe, tout casse, tout lasse.*

Entrepreneurs are people who make a difference. But are *they* different? Five variables have been identified: abilities/ skills, constructs, expectations, values and plans.[9] What abilities and/or skills do successful entrepreneurs in a particular industry need? What causes them to think and act entrepreneurially? What expectations of success might they have? What are their values in terms of the success of their business and of the wider market economy? Does the entrepreneur develop strategies and plans to ensure that the business will be a success?

The key is in how the entrepreneur perceives and deals with each situation. The successful entrepreneur recognises an opportunity and knows how to exploit it. The unsuccessful entrepreneur may recognise that there is an opportunity, but be unable to do the right thing at the time. In either instance, their behaviour is the manifestation of some cognitive, motivational or affective element.[10]

However, a lot more empirical research is needed before we can measure such latent cognitive variables. The body of research is growing, some of it of varying quality and doubtful application, and little of it accessible to the general reader.[11] It does, however, provide a theoretical framework against which some general conclusions can be drawn *after* the stories these entrepreneurs tell have been recorded. It was critical for the integrity of this book that there was no *a priori* attempt to have them conform to a theoretical framework — with which, in any event, they would have played ducks and drakes. They are individuals and individualists — 'Behold, Esau my brother is a hairy man, and I am a smooth man.'[12] They run the gamut between smooth and hairy even in the businesses they chose: a travel agency, medical research, hotel and leisure activities, money broking, accountancy, hotels and pubs, veterinary medicines, property development and printing and restaurants, textiles, agribusiness and Third World development, publishing, industrial engineering, building, oil exploration, supermarkets, conglomerates, mineral water, quarrying, financing. We gain an understanding of what they are by listening to them talking about what they do.

With one exception they came from comfortable homes. If there was an average in the nineteen, which was not a statistical sample, it would be — 'We didn't want for anything but we did not have an abundance of it.' Parents were supportive, showing trust and confidence in their children, giving them space to develop. For most, not all, the father was the more influential, setting standards and raising horizons. Many were sorry their fathers were not alive to share in their achievements. Some had to go to work before their time because of the death of the breadwinner.

Their educational background varies. Half went on to third level. Of the other half some did not finish second level. Several insisted they were not academic or clever and were bored with study. For those who went to university it seemed to be an experience more pleasant than influential, with the exception of two who completed doctorates, significant steps in their lives. For those who did not go to university there was a residual nostalgia, but not much, and fading. When pressed, all admitted that they were pretty bright. Some showed an entrepreneurial spark in school. For others, it did not show until they matured.

Several commentators have found the values and attitudes in Ireland inimical to entrepreneurship.[13] The familiar reasons are given: a colonial, dependent past; a high need for security — permanent and pensionable; an educational system dominated by an authoritarian Church; a peasant culture that puts a higher value on the professions than on business, and so on, all encapsulated in the word begrudgery. Joe Lee (1989) said: 'Sixty years after independence, fifty years after blanket protection, twenty years after the Committee on Industrial Organisation, fifteen years after the Anglo-Irish Free Trade Agreement, eight years after entering the EC, a native entrepreneurial cadre of the requisite quality had failed to emerge.'[14] As recently as 1984 I said that Irish society is not one which rewards what is new and different. We are not Yeats's swift, indifferent men. The struggle to get cultural legitimacy for enterprise in Ireland is therefore a struggle against odds. We Irish find it hard to stomach the rich. We even find it hard to stomach success. We rejoice in the failure of others.[15]

Now, I wonder. We have a travelled younger generation to whom a colonial past means nothing. They have had the opportunity to compare with other countries the quality of life in Ireland and have found it good. The influence of the Church is waning and the old dependent, prurient system of education is gone. The number of young people trying to get into third level business courses exceeds the number of available places and now outpaces the older professions such as law and medicine. Perhaps most influentially, a *very* small number of Irish companies and a rather larger number of Irish executives have been successful internationally.

A fairly strong theme running through these entrepreneurs' stories is a love of Ireland and its people and a wish to live here. Some of them still see evidence of begrudgery: 'If you fail in Ireland, people always like to be able to issue their condolences. If you succeed, they all wonder what funny business you are up to.' Some compare Ireland unfavourably with America. But they are personally unfazed — not surprising when one of their most consistent characteristics is persistence — 'I never give up', 'If we meet a closed door we just try again.' And they do not care much what other people think of them — 'Satisfaction in the success of my company is essentially an inner one, just for me.' In summary, 'Times are never good or bad — it is only what you are doing that counts.'

Despite an endemically fragile economy, there is evidence that the environment for enterprise in Ireland is changing and for the better. In any event, begrudgery has not been a drag on the people in this book. But then they are the successful ones. And there is the view, supported by international evidence, that entrepreneurs flourish in a supportive environment, not despite a hostile one.[16]

With two exceptions these entrepreneurs eschew politics. Three Northern Ireland participants commented on the political situation there because of its pervasiveness. They would agree with Ken Whitaker in *In Good Company*[17] that the Anglo-Irish Agreement was of very limited value, one of them describing it as a non-event. The northern and southern cultures were quite different; what was needed first in Northern Ireland was a period of peace. If an 'integrated' Ireland were ever to come, it could give a heady mixture — the hard-headed northerner and the creative southerner.

The entrepreneurs are capitalists to a man (and woman).

Apropos of women, the two women entrepreneurs found their gender an advantage — 'The first thing is that you get to be remembered' and 'Men tend to be polite to women.'

Several of the participants felt they had paid a price for their success in the neglect of family and friends. Work took first place in their lives, on occasion displaced by a traumatic event, then reasserting itself and causing some regret as they grew older.

Most were loners. Some enjoyed 'sociability'. All thoroughly enjoyed working hard — some influenced by an inherited work ethic, most because they could not abide idleness. They were self-confident — 'I live for each day and am confident in my own ability.'

Some saw themselves as good managers, had definite views about management and were skilled at it. For some it was a bore, something that had to be done because there was no one else to do it — what they really wanted was to move on to their next project.

None of the characteristics so far discussed would distinguish these entrepreneurs from managers/leaders. Managers work in organisations. They are happy to work for other people.

Entrepreneurs are definitely not — they are essentially unemployable:

- Once the merger was in place, it became a corporation and had to be run on formal lines and that did not suit me at all.
- I had absolute freedom in the business, something that's given to very few.
- I would not now be attracted to being chief executive of anything. That would be a limitation on a freedom I enjoy.
- I have never liked working for people — that has probably been my most consistent thing. I don't like being told what to do.
- I was always prepared to think for myself and I had no desire to take orders. I liked to do both whatever my conscience and my desire dictated.
- When I looked at all those grey faces crammed into the railway compartments, I decided that I was never going to work for anybody else. If I ever made a conscious decision about my life, that was probably it.
- Establishing the company was the way in which I could have my own identity. I wanted to do things my way.
- I was sixteen. I left the next week. I decided to leave with nothing to go to. I was clear in my mind that I wanted to start something on my own. That experience taught me that I really had to work for myself.
- I left the partnership after several years and that was the first instinct I had that I wanted to work for myself.
- We don't yield too easily to Danes. Make your arrangements. I'll be gone in three months. I'm a stubborn bastard.

Against this background of an unremitting need for independence, and that has to include financial independence, some were clear about what they wanted to do: 'I knew from seventeen I wanted to be a chartered accountant.' Others were not: 'I did not have the faintest idea what I wanted to do with my life.' Some had the grand vision: 'The important thing is to get the big play right.' Others: 'I am really quite short-term.'

Their views on luck were polarised between: 'There is this notion that you make your own luck; I don't believe it', and 'You make an awful lot of your own luck.' This is an arid argument that leads nowhere.

What finally distinguishes entrepreneurs from other people is that, whatever their beliefs about luck, about timing and about being in the right place at the right time, *they are the ones who see the opportunities and who do something about them.*[18] And they don't want to stop. The grail beckons, always leading them on because, as one participant puts it, recalling the fable of the frog and the scorpion, it's in their nature. They see things differently from the rest of us. They are out on their own.

Ivor Kenny
Woodview
University College
Dublin
1 October 1990

NOTES

[1]Ivor Kenny, *In Good Company: Conversations with Irish Leaders,* Dublin: Gill and Macmillan, 1987.

[2]P.M. Kilby, *Entrepreneurship and Economic Development,* New York: The Force Press, 1971, 27; Chad Perry, 'After Further Sightings of the Heffalump', *Journal of Managerial Psychology,* 5, 2, 1990, 22–31.

[3]Warren Bennis and Bert Nanus, *Leaders,* New York: Harper & Row, 1985, 20.

[4]J.A. Timmons, L.E. Smollen, A.L.M. Dingee, *New Venture Creation,* Homewood, Ill.: Irwin, 1977.

[5]Mark Casson, *The Entrepreneur: an Economic Theory,* Oxford: Martin Robertson, 1982, 11. Casson went on to define the entrepreneur as 'someone who specialises in taking judgmental decisions about the coordination of scarce resources' (23). That did not get me anywhere at all.

[6]J.W. Carland, F. Hoy, W.R. Boulton, J.A.C. Carland, 'Differentiating Entrepreneurs from Small Business Owners: a Conceptualisation', *Academy of Management Review*, 9, 2, 1984, 354–9: 'An entrepreneur is an individual who establishes and manages a business for the principal purposes of profit and growth. The entrepreneur is characterised principally by innovative behaviour and will employ strategic management practices in the business.' Carland told us what in his view the entrepreneur did. His definition did not purport to tell us why the entrepreneur did it and in at least one characteristic the entrepreneurs in this book did not fit: it would be stretching things to say that they all used strategic management practices — several of them cheerfully made things up as they went along.

[7]A.L. Carsrud, K.W. Olm and G.G. Eddy, 'Entrepreneurship: Research in Quest of a Paradigm', in D.L. Sexton and R.W. Smilor (eds.), *The Art and Science of Entrepreneurship*, Cambridge, Mass.: Ballinger, 1986, 368: 'An entrepreneur is an individual who is willing and able to engage in personal risk taking and responsibility, while at the same time combining the means of production and credit in the expectation of realizing profit and/or other specific objectives such as power and prestige.' We were getting close.

[8]G.G. Meredith, R.E. Nelson, P.A. Neck, *The Practice of Entrepreneurship*, Geneva: International Labour Office, 1982, 3.

[9]E. Chell, 'The Entrepreneurial Personality: a Review and Some Theoretical Developments' in J Curran *et al.* (eds.), *The Survival of the Small Firm, Volume 1: The Economics of Survival and Entrepreneurship*, Aldershot: Gower, 1986, 102–19.

[10]Elizabeth Chell and Jean M. Haworth, *Explorations of the Entrepreneurial Personality*, Paper presented to the Second Workshop on Recent Research on Entrepreneurship, European Institute for Advanced Studies in Management, Vienna, 5–6 December 1988.

[11]An honourable exception is the readable pamphlet by Joyce O'Connor and Mary Lyons, *Enterprise — The Irish Approach*, Dublin: The Industrial Development Authority, Publication Series Paper 7, 1983. See also M.P. Fogarty, *Irish Entrepreneurs Speak for Themselves*, Dublin: ESRI Broadsheet No. 8, December 1973.

[12]Genesis 27:11.

[13]John A. Murray, 'In Search of Entrepreneurship', *Journal of Irish Business and Administrative Research*, 1981, 3, 43 *et seq.*; Patrick O'Farrell, *Entrepreneurs and Industrial Change: the Process of Change in Irish Manufacturing*, Dublin: Irish Management Institute, 1986, 160 *et seq.*

[14]J.J. Lee, *Ireland 1912–1985: Politics and Society*, Cambridge: Cambridge University Press, 1989, 534–5.

[15]Ivor Kenny, *Government and Enterprise in Ireland*, Dublin: Gill and Macmillan, 1984, 17–18.

[16]John Murray, op. cit., 48.

[17]ibid., 301.

[18]See Chad Perry, op. cit., 27: 'The major characteristic distinguishing entrepreneurs from the general population and other groups is not a personality trait like risk-taking propensity but a perception of the relevant risk in the world; that is, the distinguishing characteristic is not an approach or reaction to the world, it is how the world is perceived.'

1

Gillian Bowler

I suppose we are all faced at some time with a choice of whether to stay with the safe options or to strike out. It is in that period when you haven't decided that you know fear. Once you have decided to strike out, all fear disappears. The worst time is just before you make the decision.

Gillian Bowler is Managing Director of Budget Travel Limited.

She was born on 18 November 1952 in London and educated at Carrisbrook School, Isle of Wight.

She is married to Harry Sydner who is also in the travel business.

In September 1987 she sold her company to Granada plc.
She is a former board member of the Irish Goods Council,
Chairman of the Tourism Task Force (Report now completed),
Chairman of the Dublin Heritage Area Development Group,
Board member of the Independent Radio & Television Commission,
Director of the Douglas Hyde Gallery,
Director of Granada Travel,
Former chairman of the Tour Operators Council,
Chairman of the Irish Museum of Modern Art at Kilmainham,
member of Australia/Ireland Economic Committee,
Director of Leisure World (a consortium chaired by Paschal Taggart),
committee member of various charitable organisations,
director of various private companies,
member of the Temple Bar Committee.

She was conferred with an LL.D. (Honoris Causa) by the National Council for Educational Awards.

I think I was competitive as a child. I went to school at age four. In those days we used to do mental arithmetic — I don't know if they do it now. There was a boy in my class called Clive and he was very good at arithmetic. I usually won in English and other subjects, but with arithmetic it was a real contest with Clive. I imagine that if I were competitive at that age, it's likely that I would want to carry on with it later in life. I like coming first. I was the same with sport even though that is more of a team effort. I was on net-ball and hockey teams for the school and we competed throughout the south of England. Winning was very important. Life was not destroyed when we lost, but whenever we went into a game it was terribly important that we would win. There was a definite difference in coming home the victors and in coming home the losers. The schools I was in all encouraged competitiveness — not necessarily to come first, but to come near the top and always to do your best.

Funnily enough, my parents did not encourage competitiveness at all. They would say things like, 'You can only do your best' and 'You mustn't work too hard', which, I imagine, is the opposite of normal parents encouraging kids, for example, to do as well as they can in their exams. My parents were very laid back about academic and sporting achievement. Of course, if I came home and was proud of something, then they would be proud of it too, but there was never any pressure to perform.

I think when I won I was just pleased for me. Of course I told my parents, but I didn't want to dash home and tell them, them or anyone else. It was the winning in itself that was important.

I had to leave school when I was thirteen because I got a fairly rare form of nephritis, a kidney disease. There are two kinds of nephritis — one is where you go on a kidney machine, which means that your body can't handle proteins and they turn to poison in the body. The kind I had was where you just lose protein and your kidneys cease to function. Initially I was in hospital near my parents' home and then I was sent a long way away which involved a half-day's journey, so I only saw my parents once a week. It was a small renal unit. I was really on my own or occasionally sharing a twin room with a girl studying at the university and once or twice much older people. It was a restricted circle. On and off, I was ill for about two years, much of the time confined to bed. It was not a nice experience: I was sick constantly; I could not eat or drink; I was just vomiting all the time. Eventually they told my mother I was dying and they were sending me home.

Then they decided to try an experimental drug and I remember crying because I was so looking forward to going home. I was so miserable. I had not been told I was dying.

I was lying there very late one night and the chief consultant came in and he said to me, 'You have to fight.' I remember that. Even though it was purely physical, it was not psychosomatic at all. The next day I made a big effort to tell myself that I would fight it. They were keeping me for another six weeks to try the new drug. And, in fact, as you can see, I got better. When I came out at age fifteen, I was four stone ten.

I didn't want to go back to school and start off with a whole new bunch of friends. I think that, when you spend some time in hospital, you become institutionalised, spoiled probably. My only conversations had been with people who were much older than me: nutritionists, dietitians and consultants. When I was getting better, I used to follow them around and find out how the kidney machine worked and things like that. The thought of going back to school became less real, going back to people who were thirteen or fourteen — I had missed that period. So I sat an entrance exam for a nearby regional college. You had to be sixteen or seventeen to enter. They let me in early and I got a couple of A Levels there through a six-months' course. They were the easy subjects, English language, literature, secretarial stuff and accountancy.

I have often been asked if I regret the lack of education. My parents' plans and mine would have been for me to go to university. I would love to have gone to Oxford — I had an image of it as a wonderful place. I have frequently said that to succeed in business you don't need a university education — in some ways it can be a hindrance rather than a help. Somebody suggested to me that that might be sour grapes, and there may well be an element of that. But I still feel that when you get to start off work early, you learn an awful lot that you can never learn in a classroom about business and about making money. On the other hand, I think that education is like manure. If you feed a brain with education, it grows faster, but in pure terms of making money, there's a lot to be said for the early start.

I did not take a conscious decision to make a lot of money — a lot of life is not conscious decisions. It's the particular turning it takes. The turning my life took was that to go to university, I should have to have gone back and done those two years of school that I had missed. I have a residual regret about having missed what is probably a romantic notion of university life. Of course, if I had gone to university, it would not have been anything like that.

There is an erroneous idea that academic life is shielded from real life. Academic people I've met have been as political and as back-biting as I've ever seen, and some of them are quite dim outside their own field — it's difficult to have a conversation with them, well, not all of them!

However, I read a lot — I read everything. If I were stuck in a bathroom and there was a telephone directory, I'd read it. I would have about three books going at the same time: poetry, biography and something else that would be in short chapters that would be a five-minute break. I need the comfort of two or three going at the same time. I hate historical romances or long sagas. I'm not strong on history at all but I am interested in art. I am starting now to read modern, contemporary history — political biographies. If I have a good book I don't put it down until four o'clock in the morning and I wake up in bits the next day. I went to a villa in Mallorca and took fifteen books with me and discovered to my joy that the walls were lined with books — the owner runs a publishing company. I was like a child let loose in a sweet shop. They had a great book on Margaret Thatcher which was interestingly bitchy but with very good insights as well. I read it through in three hours.

This sounds very immodest, but I had the best secretarial skills in the class. I was still very competitive. Because I was good, particularly at shorthand, the college principal telephoned a friend of hers who was Clerk of the Town Council. I got a job which, in the Isle of Wight at that time, would have been considered good and safe and sure. At the end of my first day in it, I was bored rigid.

The Town Clerk used to have coffee with me and the other three girls in the office and the assistant Town Clerk. One of the girls said to him one day that she was bored, that there was nothing to do. He said, 'You should make your own fun.' I asked him if I could hire the Town Hall. I was earning about £4 a week at the time. I hired the hall for £15 and a band for £50. The Civil Service Trade Union was NALGO and, four days before the dance, they came along to me to tell me that I should not be allowed to do it. The clerk said I should but that I would have to give half the proceeds to NALGO, if there was a profit. If there was a loss, I had to carry it all myself. I was only sixteen and it was hard to argue. I was told that if I continued to argue, I could not have the hall. As I had already paid £50 for the band, I could not afford not to go ahead with it. The dance made £100 — I got to keep £50, with NALGO getting £50. That was my first experience of working on my own. I left the next week.

I went to London, to an employment agency in Bond Street, and they told me that there was a company upstairs that needed someone. They were called Greek Island Holidays. They asked me if I could start straight away. I was very lucky in that it was a tiny little company. They had two male equal partners who were as different as chalk and cheese. They had a brilliant salesgirl who was living with and is now married to one of the partners. And they had a receptionist who was a blonde bombshell — and me! In a short while, I was selling for them and going abroad. I was never a rep. but I would do some of the contracts abroad. They had no winter holidays and I started up Canary Island holidays for them. I opened an office in Manchester and one office in Dublin. I was eighteen. When I came to Dublin I liked it and I met Harry. I did not fall in love with him at first sight. I went back to London but I found it shallow and uninviting. There was nowhere I could go in the company without kicking the owners out. I decided to leave — with nothing to go to. The partners wouldn't believe I was going, but I left and wrote brochures freelance from my flat in London and bought and sold seats from there. There was a lot of money in that at the time. It was possible to make up to £1,000 a week with little effort. It was short-term gain with no long-term future.

I enjoyed it for a while and then, quite by chance, I met Harry again in Corfu. I had gone out on a brochure-writing expedition for a company, for which I was charging them £800. Harry said, 'I haven't met you for ages and I'd like to see you again.' I said, 'Fine. I'll see you next week.' I packed up and came to Dublin.

I was clear in my mind that I wanted to start something on my own, but I felt that at first I had to understand the business environment in Dublin.

I got a job with Jan Kaminski in the travel business. I worked with him for all of two hours. I was allowed to answer the phone but only to say, 'Can you hold on please?' Jan had a great ability to laugh at himself and he has always laughed with me at my *short* time with him. Years later he said that he alternated between its being a pity and being lucky that he did not keep me on, because I would have stolen all his trade secrets. I told him that he didn't have any trade secrets worth stealing. That experience taught me that I really had to work for myself.

I spent about a month working for Harry in his agency in Ballyfermot. I didn't like that either. I found it boring. I had already been doing things that were more interesting. That's when I opened Budget Travel. It wasn't a major decision though everybody thinks it was.

I picked the name Budget because I wanted it to denote value for money but without having to use the word, 'cheap'. In retrospect, I still think it was the right name. We have had an image since of being specialist as well, but I don't think the two images contradict each other. We have combined the name, 'Budget', with a specialisation on Greece and with up-market holidays, and it works. The vast mass of our market is concerned about price even if it's to an up-market destination like the South of France. A person at any level buying a holiday does not want to feel that they are being ripped off. They want to feel that they are dealing with an honest, good-value company. If it's a holiday costing £1,000 or £100, the principle remains the same.

People may be a little suspicious of travel agents and, in the early eighties before bonding was introduced, there were a lot of company collapses. That was where semi-state travel companies had an advantage, because people would feel that they, at least, were reliable. That advantage has gone now.

The early days of Budget were in a one-room basement with a rent of twelve pounds a week which, thank God, was paid in arrears.

It was no big deal. Nowadays it would be a much bigger undertaking because there would be financial guarantees and people have become more sophisticated. This was 1974, the beginning of the recession. That was probably very good for me because a small company can get a niche foothold in a recession that a big company cannot. In fact, for a small company, it's easier than in the boom years when the big companies are expanding rapidly.

I did not find the first year tough in any way. We carried two or three hundred customers. The second year we produced a little brochure, eight pages in black and white, and

I was probably prouder of that than I was of anything that had gone before. We carried about eight hundred people. That was enough to make a living: I was an owner-manager, I was doing everything. Then I had one person in to help me. The third year, I employed somebody again, and the fourth year we moved to larger offices. The growth was a fairly steady pattern.

It got more fun after the first five years. Harry joined Budget in 1983 and also kept on his own agency. By then Budget had become big enough to need him. Budget never made a loss. We ploughed back all the money in the early years to make the business grow.

I wanted to be the best and the most profitable travel agency. I don't think that being the biggest necessarily means being the most profitable. There is no point whatsoever in having a tour-operating business in which you have 100,000 passengers and you lose £100,000. If you could have 50,000 passengers and make £50,000 — which would you rather have?

Making money is not the most crucial element in life but it is a goal that one would want to achieve simply for the sake of comfort and security. It's much nicer to have some money than not to have it. I don't believe it is the reason why one works eighteen hours a day seven days a week. If that were true then many people who have made sufficient money for the rest of their lives would stop. We could all get to a level where it would be very easy to say, 'Well, I'll retire now. That's it.' I have never known anybody who had sufficient enterprise to start a business and earn good money who wanted to stop. It takes more strength of character to say, 'Stop. I have enough.' than to keep on going.

I would find it very, very hard to do nothing. Of course, I have enough money now to live comfortably but money is something other than what you spend. It is a measure of the success of your company. If you create a company, then profits are important because they are the sign that the company is thriving and set for continued growth. If profits are going down, one is not doing what one should be doing, taking corrective measures.

Satisfaction in the success of my company is essentially an inner one, just for me — I never wanted to publicise my profits. However, I would like Budget Travel generally to be seen as a successful company. This may seem a contradiction, but I don't have any need to go out and say X company is number two or three and we are number one. I need to know for myself where we stand in ranking.

The business I'm in is a service one and publicity is good for the company. I have had a fair amount of publicity over the years. It would be a lie to say that if there is a nice article praising me or Budget Travel, that I could not care less. I do. If I exploited the PR I was getting, I think it is true to say that the PR people exploited the fact that I was a woman. There was a sort of mutual exploitation. That did not bother me, not even remotely. I certainly think it's true that if I had been a man, I would not have got half the amount of interviews in the press that I got. I certainly would not have been phoned up and asked what I wore in bed!

When a journalist rings you up, they can be doing an intelligent think-piece or a jokey piece or they can ask you a question like what you wear in bed. I think the first thing you've got to remember is that they, too, are doing a job. They have probably been at an editorial meeting which has decided that they are going to run a piece because they have nothing else to put on that page. I really don't find questions, no matter how stupid they are, intrusive. If I did not want to answer, I could say so. But I have very rarely been put in that position. I never feel any resentment that people may be asking me a question only because I am a woman, or that I am invited to something because I am a woman, or that I am the token woman on a board. I don't mind if I'm a token woman!

I am secure within myself and Harry says that I am self-confident, but I am giving you the impression that I don't care what other people think of me, and that would not be true. I care very much what my friends think about me. I would be very upset if I thought somebody thought badly of me for some reason that was wrong and I would dwell on it quite a bit. But I would never get upset about where I was seated at a dinner table. And if somebody is giving me an advantage because I am a woman, I'll just accept it. It would be very stupid to turn it down.

If you phone people up, they are more likely to talk to you because men tend to be polite to women. Purely as a matter of courtesy, they will take the call to tell you no.

I have mixed views about people living and working together. In theory, it's probably not a good idea. It's almost inevitable that you bring the office home with you. I'd like to be able to say that Harry and I do not bring the office home with us but, truthfully, we do. We certainly have heated arguments at work and can equally do so at home, but it doesn't affect the love in the relationship. We are more honest and probably therefore more hurtful in the working relationship. We are blunter with our opinions about one another's ideas than you would be with someone with whom you had only a working relationship. Then you would be more sensitive and polite; you would enter into areas of conflict with a lot more delicacy. There is an awful lot of truth in our relationship — but that is because we know we can handle it. With Harry I can say, 'That really is an awful idea', and vice versa, while with someone with whom you just had a working relationship, you might have to approach things obliquely, saying, 'Have you thought about doing it this way?' The closer the friendship, the more honest one is.

Everybody has a weak point and there are some people you would be careful with. I think I'm good with people on the surface. On a personal level — with friendships — I sometimes feel I don't put enough time into them. I have friends who are very good, who are brilliant with their own friends — they make a point of seeing them every week.

They are great at writing letters or keeping in touch. I'm bad at things like that. I would get stricken with guilt and do an overkill for a few days and then get busy again for a couple of months. I'm not in constant touch with friends, which is bad. You could say it was preoccupation with the business but, really, everybody can make time for anything if they really want to.

I would not know what my staff *really* think of me. What people really think and what they appear to think are sometimes two different things. I think different people see me in different ways. My secretary, Liz Herssens, would see me differently from the guy who does the post. Colleagues I've worked with on other boards would see me in a completely different way again. Budget is a friendly company. It's all first names and there is no standing on ceremony. I'm accessible — people walk into my office without knocking. We have board meetings, but if there was a majority in favour of a certain action which I, together with Harry, thought was wrong, I would certainly use all my powers to go in the direction I thought was right. You have to go with what you think is right. But that would be on areas where I would know the business better than other people. However, in practice it's never been an issue. If I were taking advice on a legal or accounting matter, I would employ the best I could get and take it.

Back to Budget, which took a quantum leap in 1980 when it nearly doubled in size. Up to 1980 it had been a specialist operator in Greece. Then we brought in a French brochure with, for the first time, colour photographs. The year after that, Spain — Ibiza, because it was a young person's market and our business at that time seemed to be more towards the younger person, though that changed over the years. I now have brochures that are aimed at young people and others that are aimed at middle, professional people. In 1981, we bought premises in Baggot Street, a whole building with four floors — the first time we did not have rented accommodation. (We sold that last year and moved to even bigger offices.) If you asked me where my real affection was, it was in that office in Baggot Street where the real growth came. That's where all the major excitement was and I still pass that building and feel nostalgic for it.

Perhaps a little of the excitement has gone out of the business now because I've been at it so long and I know it so well and I want to do other things — combine other things with what I'm doing, is what I should say. We have now grown to the stage where it is necessary to make another quantum leap or do something else.

Granada happened in 1987. They had a leisure division and they decided to invest money in travel. I believe the experts told them that they could not have a substantial involvement in leisure without being involved in travel. Leisure — and travel — were going to be the fastest growing sectors in the foreseeable future: tourism is going to be the second largest business in the world. Granada bought a number of companies in England and then they employed an English market researcher to do some research in Ireland. We came out the best in terms of service, quality and profitability, profitability in so far as they would know about it — they had not seen our figures. Our load-factors were certainly the highest and in most areas we were the strongest. They approached me and we talked. I did not feel overjoyed at selling, but in thinking about it at that time, I knew we needed a partner to help us expand and grow. Otherwise it was going to get boring: you can't stay the same size forever. The other thing about staying the same size is that then it becomes defensive instead of opportunistic. You are protecting the past rather than expanding the future — not a position that anybody readily enjoys. It was a good deal: we got in £4.50 m. following an earn-out, which is now successfully over. I had mixed feelings: I did not want to part with the ownership of Budget, but the decision was made and I believe it was the right one.

Granada were good in the sense that they were a very large company with large resources. They have a lot of clout and, despite the bureaucracies of a big company, they have not interfered in any shape or form with the running of Budget. They have not had to, because the profits have been very good and rising.

In order to work for somebody else you need to have a very wholehearted respect for them and for their ability.

Meanwhile, I've got involved with Paschal Taggart and the bowling business. We are opening two centres in Tallaght and in Cork. The development is seen as mainly Ireland and Europe. We have put quite a bit of money in. Bowling is taking in $20 b. a year in the US. I've also set up a little financial (of sorts) company: that's interesting but not time consuming and, so far, it's been financially rewarding.

I suppose we are all faced at some time with a choice of whether to stay with the safe options or to strike out. It is in that period when you haven't decided that you know fear. Once you have decided to strike out, all fear disappears. The worst time is just before you make the decision.

John Meagher of *Independent Newspapers* told me a story about the frog and the scorpion. The scorpion wants to cross the river. He asks the frog for a lift. The frog says, 'Why should I do that? You scorpions sting and kill and I don't want to run that risk.' The scorpion said, 'Don't be stupid. If I sting and kill you then we both sink and I die too.' The frog thought about that and said, 'You're absolutely right.' The scorpion hops on the frog's back and half-way across stings him. As they are both sinking, the frog says with his last gasp, 'Why did you do that?' And the scorpion replies, 'I couldn't help it. It's in my nature.'

That sums up beautifully why on earth somebody should enter the fray and expose themselves to stresses and strains if they don't need to financially. The answer is, 'Because it's in my nature.'

I have never thought that I have a long life to live — not that, for a minute, I think that I have a short life to live! I just think that it is a mistake to put things off on the basis that you have plenty of time. But I still think I am a dogged person. If I don't achieve my goal instantly, that doesn't mean that I will give up. I will always have it in the back of my mind and work patiently towards it. I am extremely persistent, single minded, determined. If I don't get what I want in year one, I won't have forgotten it in year five. I never stop trying. However, if you have an idea that turns out to be a lousy one, that's different. In terms of long-term plans about where you want to be or what you want to do, I would not give up.

I am remarkably secretive about where I want to be and what I want to do and I don't know why. There is no reason for it. I want to enjoy business.

I don't know that I am being totally honest with you. I don't much like to reveal the private side of myself. But, truthfully, and the thing that I would say is, that I want to continue working and I want to continue succeeding. I don't want life to become boring, work-wise. My home life is very happy and content. But on a work level I would not like it to stay still: I would be stultified. I don't want it to get content and flat. I want to be interested.

I don't think I want overt power, if that's the right word. Power means different things to different people. I don't want the kind of power that is in any way obvious. I am not hung up on status. I would be irritated if somebody were rude or patronising or bad mannered. I like privacy and I'm not particularly a social animal, yet I am gregarious.

This house, you say, is beautiful, but it is a private house, a serene house. With it I am not making any public statement. It is not designed to impress. Harry and I also have a country house which is very simple. This house is a bolt-hole, a haven — I need it. I need a home and I need a base for my sanity: one of the things I value more than anything is serenity, time spent not working. I value that enormously. I like evenings in — I would hate to be on the cycle of constantly having to go out. I get millions of invitations to functions of various kinds and I almost always say no. It may be selfish and not particularly good for business. I like just sitting here and reading and not talking, and I'm quite happy not to see a soul for a couple of days. Even when Harry is away, I enjoy being alone. If I was contracting in the south of France and it took me a day or thirty-six hours, I would spend three days on my own and be perfectly happy, eating and going to bed early — I love that.

I do like to have control of my own life. Prior to the period in hospital when I was a child, I had vague ambitions and ideals — they were unformed at the time. Shortly after I went to hospital I got rid of any idea of wanting to be a doctor, an obvious sort of ideal. After hospital, I certainly had less ambition for about a year. I was a bit dulled. I was not as eager and as energetic. It was largely physical and a bit emotional — I was happy just to be home and alive. If you've had an awful fright, have come close to death or have nearly lost someone dear to you, that's the time you say, 'The only important thing in life is . . .' and you get back to very fundamental things. And no matter how much you say that you will never forget and that you will always be thankful for what you've got, after a year or two, you say, 'Well, that's great! But I would not mind trying for this, this, and this.' It's like people asking for forgiveness from sin. They say, 'I promise I'll never do it again', and that becomes a dulled promise after a while. The instinctive character takes over. I think that, certainly for a while, I was just pleased to be amongst the family and alive and well, and I took simple pleasure in simple things.

When you look back, things that were awful at the time are less awful now — they tend to fade. There were, I suppose, three awful things in my life: one was being very ill in hospital — I still remember it as being very unpleasant. It was nice getting out. The second was a very worrying time at work, where the company was making money, it had expanded rapidly, but I was worried about cash-flows — I was happy that the business was fundamentally sound. It was just a question of finding the cash to finance very rapid expansion. That taught me a lot about financial control and cash-management. It was a very worthwhile lesson: planning your cash-flow. That was a bad period — there was constant worry and stress. Sure, there were times that you would feel like giving it all up, like running the car into the wall. They would last all of thirty seconds. Then you would say, 'God forgive me. I didn't mean it.' The third was a close friend of mine dying: she had been ill for a long time but it was still an untimely death. I was sad about that, but I was also sad during the course of her illness. But I do miss her and that's important.

I don't have many friends that I share hopes and fears with —I don't suppose anybody does. But, even with them, I would keep my business affairs very private. I would find it very difficult to express real business hopes and fears to other people. But on every other level I can be perfectly honest with friends.

I would hope there are still a million peaks to be scaled. I would hate to think that they are all in the past. I prefer to think of life as just starting.

2

Austin Darragh

*Milestones are either stepping stones or millstones.
You have to decide for yourself whether the milestone
you have reached will be a stepping stone to something
new that may be even greater or a millstone that
pulls you down to the depths.*

Austin Darragh is a physician.

He was born in Dublin on 27 April 1927. His father was Alexander C. Darragh, a mathematician. His mother was Frances J. McDonnell. He was the sixth child in a family of nine, four boys and five girls.

He was educated at the Catholic University School, Dublin and Trinity College Dublin — M.B., B.Ch., B.A.O. (1954), M.A. (1955) and M.D. (1963).

He is married to 'Terry' Roddy. They have five children: Marese (39), Paul (37), David (32), Adrienne (31) and Ruth (30).

He established Leo Laboratories in Ireland in the mid-1950s. In 1964 he established his independent clinical research unit in Ireland. He brought his company, the Institute of Clinical Pharmacology, to the New York Stock Exchange in 1984.

In 1989 he entered a joint venture with Aer Rianta and other private investors to establish The European College of Aeronautics at Cork Airport and is currently chairman.

He has had a number of appointments as lecturer in Irish universities.

In 1964 he founded the Irish Cancer Society to which he was elected President during its Jubilee year in 1988.

He has been Adjunct Professor of Medicine and Pharmacology in New York Medical College since 1983.

He is a Fellow of the Royal Society of Health.

He was made an Honorary Fellow of the Institute of Biology of Ireland in 1988.

He is President of the National Council of the Blind.

He is Vice-Chairman of the Mater Hospital Foundation.

He is the author of more than one hundred and twenty scientific publications.

He is Master of the Ballymacads.

There have been many milestones in my life. The one that stands out way beyond any other was the kidnapping and mutilation of my son-in-law, John O'Grady, and the permanent disabling of a fine human being, Detective Sergeant Martin O'Connor, who almost lost his life freeing John from his captors. That happened in October 1987 and it epitomised for me our capacity for hate and jealousy and outright cruelty. I also saw the power of prayer and the ability of good to overcome evil.

It became clear subsequently that I was the intended target and almost certainly would not have survived. But any relief I might have felt has long since been replaced by a sense of guilt for what happened to John, to Martin, to John's whole family and to Father Brian D'Arcy who helped us so much. For all of them, their remaining years have been tainted by Dessie O'Hare, the so-called Border Fox, who has voluntarily compounded the sentence of the court and has condemned himself to fester in solitary confinement. Surely there must be a more humane way for society, conscious of the clear lessons of biology, to deal with such a cancer?

The kidnapping was a direct consequence of the misperception of my financial success projected by the media. I hold journalists responsible to a large degree for having a criminal mind deluded into believing that immense wealth was available to me and to my family to meet the ransom demands.

I started in 1987, Ivor, because only in that way can you understand where the story leads to. But let me now go back to the beginnings, thirty years to 1957.

I believe that intelligence is the ability to guess right and secondly to see order in apparently random things. This has been rather succinctly stated in an article in *The New Scientist* as the fundamentals of intelligence. The ability to guess right has been terribly important in the evolutionary process — for example, guessing the right herbs to eat and the right leaves to avoid. That determined whether people survived or not. This was not judgment. Judgment is something you make on known facts. This was pure guess.

I don't think there is anything terribly unique in a doctor being an entrepreneur. There have been quite a few doctor-entrepreneurs in this country. I can think of people like Dermot Roden, who, as a property entrepreneur, has had many developments; Dr Bryan Alton — responsible for the Mater Pools; Professor Richard Conroy — oil exploration; Mr Jimmy Sheehan, F.R.C.S. — the Blackrock Clinic and inventor of many excellent artificial joints for hips, knees and elbows; George Fegan who had many business enterprises and yet was a brilliant surgeon — indeed some of his skills as a surgeon were used to bring about the fusion of seven Dublin hospitals to be the Federation of Dublin Voluntary Hospitals. Funnily enough it was through that federation that George brought about the closure of Sir Patrick Dun's Hospital — which he congratulated me on reopening!

Anyway, I think these two components of intelligence were what helped me a little bit. My father was a mathematical genius — many people who were his students in Dublin will vouch for that. His mathematical genius escaped me — I was confined to twenty — ten fingers and ten toes. (I was nearly confined to seventeen with a recent hunting accident!) However, I inherited some of his ability to work with geometric figures. I can work out the angles and see the connections between apparently discrete points. It has helped me to put together structures that other people would not necessarily see coming together as logical.

Like most thinking people I like to be able to fix myself in time and space. I suppose I'm most comfortable thinking about myself as a Third Wave creature in terms of Alvin Toffler's Three Waves: the first being the agricultural wave, the second being the industrial wave and the third being the post-industrial wave. Today, in the Third Wave, we have come back to the phase of the producer being also the consumer. I would find it very difficult to understand all the phenomena going on around us if I did not see myself in the setting of this Third Wave. I have asked myself what has determined my ability to function as a Third Wave physician. There are three things which recur: one is the word flotation, the second is the name John O'Grady and the third is Sir Patrick Dun's — or Saint Patrick Dun's as it is also known. John Francis O'Grady (not my son-in-law whom I spoke about when we began), was a close friend of mine and managing director of a pharmaceutical company in Ireland, Abbott. He eventually went to Squibb where the managing director was Kott Scheunert. Scheunert was the man who had the great vision to see Ireland as a strong force in pharmaceuticals. We are now the twelfth largest pharmaceutical exporting country in the world — we weren't in 1954 when Scheunert came here. He saw *then* what Ireland could be.

In 1957 he was having his car filled at a petrol station in south Dublin. Nearby he saw the grass being cut by a machine which floated on a film of air. Being a curious man he went to investigate, fell over a low wall and burst a varicose vein. Through John O'Grady I went to see him in his room in the Russell Hotel. When we had fixed the varicose vein we started talking. He told me he was going to take his fifty per cent stake out of Squibb in Ireland because they weren't going to manufacture. There was a pile of brochures on his dressing-table. He asked me to go through them to help him pick a company for which he could get the agency in Ireland. I took the brochures home and flicked through them and one stood out: Leo of Copenhagen. It was a company with an interest in research, particularly hormones, which I considered in those days to be the future of medicine, and also in the development of semi-synthetic antibiotics.

I went back to Kott and recommended Leo. He agreed and asked me to be his medical adviser on the project and we entered into negotiations. We got the agency for both Ireland and the UK with a view ultimately to attacking the coming Common Market.

We had premises in Fleet Street and I went out to Captain's Road in Crumlin to look at a factory which was closing. It

33

was the State Express 333 tobacco factory. It was magnificent, totally air-conditioned with humidity control. It was one of the most fantastically constructed pharmaceutical factories that one could imagine. In the foyer there was a spiral staircase and in those halcyon days the spiral staircase was the symbol of the pharmaceutical industry. I got photographs taken and found that it was possible to do a deal for £120,000 with the Ardath Tobacco Company who owned the factory. I went to Copenhagen to talk to the owner of Leo, Mr Knud Abilgaard. The deal looked good — even in those early days there were substantial IDA grants available — and I found myself leading the negotiations because Kott's English was not great and his knowledge of pharmaceuticals was more on the selling than on the manufacturing side.

The first snag we encountered was that the Fasenfeld family, Antigen of Roscrea, had been given exclusive rights to manufacture drugs for the Irish market. Fair enough, because they had supplied the country with essential drugs all during the war. But the time had now come to reappraise matters.

The Danes would not negotiate at anything less than seventy per cent export, thirty per cent domestic sales. At the end, that's what it came down to, but not until after a lot of politicking including resistance from the Department of Health. That was 1959/60.

Once the factory became operational they needed someone with the technical skills to manage it and I became director of clinical research not only for the Irish plant but for Leo in Copenhagen. In those early days of the pharmaceutical industry, physicians were thin on the ground. There was a feeling that you deviated from the path of medical rectitude when you became involved with the pots and pans of the pharmacy. This was a bad situation: a bad relationship between the medical profession, the pharmaceutical industry, academic medicine and, indeed, clinical medicine, apart from pure physicians. They just did not have any common ground to talk to one another. You had the strange situation that the pharmaceutical industry was engaged in the development of the ammunition that the physicians would use with patients and yet there was no significant dialogue between the parties involved. They were polarised in their antipathies towards one another.

That situation lasted while there was an availability of funds from governments or from semi-charitable organisations like research councils. When that dried up the physicians had to talk to the pharmaceutical industry. The universities that were the quickest to perceive the change were the ones that benefited most and the massive injection of funds from the pharmaceutical industry developed all kinds of research institutes.

The paucity of doctors who were prepared to work in the pharmaceutical industry probably provided me with a unique opportunity: I was the only medical person in the entire Leo organisation which had companies and agencies in eighty countries world-wide. On the basis, I suppose, of good qualifications, I found myself the director of clinical research for Europe and then I found myself on their seven-man development team in Copenhagen. It was as a member of that team that I learned the benefits of brain-storming with fellow scientists, without notes being taken and no attribution of ideas: both good and bad ideas were the products of the seven. Something you said might trigger a thought in somebody else's mind — if you had not triggered that idea then the other person might not have come forward with this Nobel Prize-winning idea. The intellectual property was common.

Then I became involved in setting up clinical trials in the United States for Leo. From 1963 onwards I got some sense of the size of the United States and made contacts which have stood me in good stead since. I found myself in a very interesting phase of post-graduate education, being helped and financed to stay at the new frontiers of therapeutic development. This would not ordinarily have been available to me as a young physician, now with a family. I was then encouraged by the company to pursue higher degrees. In those early sixties I was interested in the action of drugs and in hormonal problems: one disease in particular interested me in Ireland and that was toxaemia pregnancy. The Master of the Rotunda at that time was Professor Alan Browne. There was another colleague there, Con Cussen, as Assistant Master, who had been there when I was a student. Between the Master and Con Cussen, it was decided that I would be awarded the first clinical research fellowship in the Rotunda to study the possibility that regulating water-load in the patient might be a way of controlling the progress towards the eclampsia which is the end-point of toxaemia. A pre-eclampsia clinic was set up and I acted as one of the medical officers there. In the disease, the mother develops high blood pressure, she develops kidney damage, she develops an extraordinary amount of fluid retention, as a result of which, because of the high blood pressure, the foetus can be imperilled. At that time the mortality rate in eclampsia could be as high as seven out of ten. Working with diuretics, which promote the discharge of urine (and Leo had been very advanced in their development), we started to look at the benefits of oral diuretics, coupled with salt restriction and dietary measures to control weight-gain. Eventually I published a paper in 1963, at a conference in Vienna, which reported on the experience of 1,000 patients at the Rotunda. I then used additional work for my M.D. thesis in Dublin University. It was interesting that my M.D. thesis was on the action of a drug, but also on the endocrine or hormone system which was one of my big interests.

Then, equipped with my higher degree, I had a greater range of choices open to me. With the ordinary M.B. degree you would be precluded from getting into the consultant hierarchy. Because I had been in the pharmaceutical industry and outside the normal pathway for clinical training, I was outside the establishment way to train people. I certainly would not be in a position to get membership of the College of Physicians, which would have been an alternative route to getting a higher degree. The M.D. thesis and examination were, in fact, a harder way because one was being examined by hard-line establishment physicians. However, to be fair to Professor Fleming in Trinity and his British colleagues whom he invited to examine me, they could see that there was something opening up in the manipulation of disease processes by molecular interventions. That was the thing that pulled me along into the whole field of pharmaceutics.

By way of a historical footnote, when I came out of my oral examination in Trinity, I knew that I had got my M.D. and it was the night of the Rotunda dinner dance in the Gresham. We went there to celebrate and were stunned to hear that John F. Kennedy had been assassinated.

The M.D. was a key step towards where I am today.

At that time also, working in Leo, I had the good fortune to meet a Dr Ploug, who had discovered an enzyme in urine which could dissolve clots. It was called urokinase. It digested fibrin which was the basic network which formed a clot. It was of great interest to me: it had to be investigated as a possible remedy for cardiac infarction. Working in Trinity at that time was a profoundly clever man, R.A.Q. O'Meara, Professor of Pathology. R.A.Q. O'Meara noticed that when tumours metastasised they always had a halo of fibrin around them. The conventional view of the fibrin was that it was part of the defence mechanism of the body. O'Meara, as many great people in the past, turned the conventional wisdom on its head and asked if the fibrin might be a weapon of aggression by the tumour cell. The tumour needed to irritate the tissues around it like a speck of sand in your eye. O'Meara asked if we could dissolve fibrin would we restrict the ability of the tumour to flourish. I mentioned to Dougie Thornes, another very clever man who was working with O'Meara, that I had access to the urokinase and could we try it. The safety of urokinase had by then been well established in Denmark.

With Bill Chance in St Luke's Hospital, we got permission to see a dear old lady who was in a terminal condition. She had a huge fungating cancer of her left breast. It was too big for surgery and was, we thought, stuck to her pectoral muscles and it was too fungating for radio therapy, because it would have released so much toxic material that she would have succumbed. Fungating means spreading out like a cauliflower. She received, each day, a million units of the urokinase at a cost of $1,000 a day — which came out of my research budget. Sure enough, the tumour shrank to the size of a walnut so that it could be excised. She had follow-up radiation therapy and she lived for a further two years. It was a fascinating experience.

Working also at that time in Trinity in the Medical Research Council of Ireland, was another great Irish scientific intellect, Vincent Barry, who developed a line of drugs which are very helpful even today in the treatment of leprosy. He was also working in the cancer field from another angle, from the chemo-toxic standpoint. I had been discussing with Vincent whether some of his drugs could be developed commercially by Leo, so that he would have access to funds to keep his research going. In this I saw myself as much a facilitator as anything else. Also, I felt I was doing my job as the person on the spot, looking for opportunities for the pharmaceutical company that employed me.

Vincent Barry was upset because he had lost a grant from an American foundation which had decided to discontinue extra-mural funding. I felt it was quite wrong that Irish research should have to depend on external charity. Together with six friends, one of whom had the bitter experience of losing his wife from cancer, the seven of us set up the Conquer Cancer Campaign. We were fortunate to secure the patronage of Mr C. J. Haughey, who was then a junior minister, and Mr Eamonn Andrews. I had done some broadcasting on the then Radio Eireann and knew Fred O'Donovan who was with Radio Eireann and with the Eamonn Andrews Studios. He introduced me to Frank O'Doherty, who had been raising money for the Mater Hospital in Belfast. I did a very good deal with Frank. I paid him, I think, a basic salary of £5,000 and kept increasing his percentage bonus the more money he raised. I was criticised for this, but it all ended up in the very fine institution we have today, the Cancer Society. We still kept the Conquer Cancer Campaign separate from the authoritative Irish Cancer Society. The group who joined me at that time were Lady Wardell, Jack O'Riordan, who was the director of the National Blood Transfusion Service, Eric Webb, Joe Donoghue and Dillon Digby. These, with Fred O'Donovan, were the seven.

The reason we stuck at seven was that one in seven people in Ireland would die of cancer. Last year we had our Silver Jubilee and, thankfully, all seven were there. That was one activity which was carefully structured to provide funds for R.A.Q. O'Meara and Vincent Barry.

At one stage we had some surplus funds and I went to the Irish Medical Association to offer them £10,000 to set up a cancer information service. They told me that information for patients was no concern of theirs. I went back to our Executive and told them that we had a moral obligation to start our own information service. I took on the task of honorary director. We toured the country with fit-ups in schools and parish halls. Recently a Sister Stanislaus, back from Nairobi, reminded me how one night she had to sew an important button back on my trousers which I had burst lugging the camera equipment into St Michael's Hospital. We were accused of engendering panic but we said no, fear is a very healthy defence mechanism against disease, but fear without knowledge of how to defend yourself leads to panic. Fear that is accompanied by knowledge of how to cope with the threat of danger is very worthwhile. Then you can eliminate the cause of the fear.

When, for two years, I was in general practice in Dundrum and Enniskerry, I saw the families coming to Nutgrove from the centre of the city and suffering far more from asthma and hay-fever than the indigenous families who had adapted to the countryside. I became fascinated by the amount of allergies I was seeing. I got permission to establish in Sir Patrick Dun's, the first allergy clinic in Dublin. I went to London to St Mary's to be trained in allergy testing. I was very impressed by the way they approached the treatment of allergic disorders. I worked on in that clinic even when I became involved in the pharmaceutical industry, but rather pathognomonic of the medical establishment at that time towards the pharmaceutical industry, a senior consultant physician, who was instrumental in getting me the appointment as the consultant allergist, told me he did not know if he and the board would be comfortable with me continuing to see patients while I was involved in the industry.

I am telling you this, warts and all, and not in strict chronological order — I want you to know what it's like when somebody does something outside the norm. The great strength of the medical profession and the great security for patients is that the profession should be slow to accept changes. The good physician is the last person to discard proven therapies. He should be the last to embrace new therapies. The medical profession does its best for the patient by being very critical of change. So I agreed to train a successor for the allergy clinic and then I would step down. I think at the back of the attitude might have been some notion that I was becoming a door-to-door salesman for shoddy medicines. A pharmaceutical physician had never been heard of. But if you don't like to take on the pressures of doing something new, you should not try to climb the mountain. Perhaps I like jumping the ditches — that's why I still hunt! The challenge is there. It gets the adrenalin going and, perhaps, the less you know about the other side of the ditch the better!

Actually, the man who took over from me, Dr Neville Boland, made a much better fist of the allergy clinic than I ever would have. Neville is still today the one Eastern Health Board allergist certified by the American College of Allergists. I am still an officer of the Eastern Health Board. I see patients for the Eastern Health Board and run clinics.

In looking at allergies, it became clear that the mind had a lot to do with the way people responded to certain external forces. Forgetting now about Nutgrove and the difference between the town and the country, I felt there was some psychological function that controlled the endocrine functions. Endocrine is the glandular system which secretes its material directly into the bloodstream, as distinct from exocrine which is the sweat glands and the mucous glands which deposit their secretions on to a surface: it could be the surface of the bowel or the surface of the skin. It was Huxley who took the term endocrine and gave it a better name, hormone, meaning a messenger. He said that these substances which come from various glands like the thyroid, the adrenal, the testis, are messenger molecules. These molecules tell other tissue to perform a task. The word endocrine is only an anatomical, not a dynamic, description. My fascination was with molecular medicine. How the heck could the mind, which was abstract, influence bodily functions? Let me now go to Drogheda and Mother Mary Martin of the Medical Missionaries of Mary.

Mother Mary Martin was the entrepreneur *par excellence*. She took resources of low yield and converted them into resources of high yield. I got to know her through Dougie Thorn, who was doing a cancer clinic in the Lourdes Hospital in Drogheda. Mother Mary was a great visionary, she could foresee trends. She saw the ecumenical trends in the Catholic Church before there was any talk of ecumenism. She was the first person to remove the altar rails which separated the congregation from the sanctuary. She was the first person in the history of the Church who had what I call 'broken file' to go to Communion. People had to go to Communion from all sides, not pew by pew, so that the poor devil sitting there in mortal sin would not be identified! She was simple, caring and humane. She also introduced the short commissions: she accepted women into the Order only for three years. Only after three periods of three years did they make final vows. It meant that young women who had a vocation at a particular time did not have to commit themselves for life to something which they might not want to honour after the passage of time.

She had what I see as the two cardinal rules of management: one, make things happen and, two, use resources efficiently.

She immediately grasped the significance of the development of drugs. She saw there would be a great opportunity for doing good in the mission fields with these magic molecules. She felt that to win both the bodies and souls in the mission fields, we needed more medicines, more effectively administered, with less toxicity. At this time there was a dilemma in the Church because 'the pill' had been discovered by Pincus and you could control fertility by chemically castrating a woman. This was not, and still is not, consistent with the moral teaching of the Church.

The pill is a chemical rather than a surgical castration — even though its effects are only temporary. There had to be a better way than interfering with the natural process. I described that interference like going down to the ESB station with a bomb to turn the lights off in your house. There must be a better switch that you could find closer to the function that you wanted to control. I was quite clear where I was going: I wanted to define psycho-endocrine functions and through psycho-endocrine functions to find methods of controlling various bodily functions — the one which was most eminently of interest was the reproductive function. So Mother Mary Martin and I had to go to Armagh to meet Cardinal Conway to explain the nature of the work I proposed to initiate. At that time I wrote a paper called 'What Shall We Tell Our Sons?', explaining to men what precisely they were doing to women when they invited them to take the pill. We explained to the Cardinal that what we would be doing would be looking at the hypothalamic-pituitary-ovarian axis and at the mental processes that affected the hypothalamus. The Cardinal said fine, but where were we going to get the money. I told him that the pharmaceutical industry was now interested in getting into the mind through, for example, tranquillisers and anti-depressant drugs, but they were starved of research. Our work would lead into other channels which we could make available to them and they, in turn, could fund what would be a very expensive operation. The Cardinal gave our work his blessing.

I was now doing two functions for Mother Mary: firstly, as a management adviser because the Order had expanded considerably. The administrative processes needed to be consolidated and refined. And secondly, she also wanted this avant-garde research which would promote excellence among her colleagues and would produce drugs which would be beneficial in the mission fields.

The blood level of progesterone could be used to study the menstrual cycle and determine the exact time of ovulation. I needed 30 cc of blood each day to measure the progesterone. Even heroic nuns and nurses could not let me have that without being exsanguinated. I had a lot of patients at the time and some of them were in the blood-stock industry. One, in particular, Captain Tim Rogers, was very advanced in horse-breeding. I discussed my work with him one night and he said that he would be very interested in knowing if the progesterone level in his mares was going up. He said he would build me a laboratory on one of his stud farms and I could take all the blood I liked from his mares. He wanted a measure sensitive enough to tell him when the progesterone level was at a height that would indicate pregnancy. At that time pregnancy could only be determined manually at 42 days. There was no ultrasound or anything like that. We actually developed a progesterone method that could determine pregnancy at 18 days. People were then beginning to ask, 'What the hell is Darragh doing? He's a bloody vet!'

Throughout the thirty years that I was involved with drug research, I was fortunate to be invited to work with a number of valuable new therapies for many clinical problems. However the perfection of the progesterone test gave unique satisfaction to our team. Being now able to pinpoint the time of ovulation and monitor the progress of pregnancy, we were well placed to study a series of new drugs designed to treat the great human tragedy of infertility.

Our work resulted in helping to create more than fifty new lives and brought immeasurable happiness to the parents. I am amply rewarded: each Christmas I am sent photos of these 'miracle' babies.

Having established the safety and efficacy of each new drug, the contract research clinician has, of necessity, to move on to the next project.

We got very lucky. I sent a letter to Hoffman La Roche in Switzerland, amongst many others, saying we had clinical research facilities available. A Dr Reggiani came over, liked what he saw and said, 'We'll give you a five-year contract, take all your spare capacity, give you £50,000 a year, and we'll buy all your equipment. If you need more staff we'll take them on.' I now had a contract, Mother Mary was busily building me a new unit — so we now had two laboratories, one at the Ballyowen Stud out in Lucan, and one in Drogheda. We were able to provide a service to Tim Rogers and do our work in the hospital as well. The La Roche contract went on from 1964 right up to 1980, contract after contract. It was a love-hate relationship. You had to maintain a certain professional independence while at the same time you had an undoubted measure of financial dependency. To keep those two things in balance and to maintain your ethics was a most important dimension. But I have to say, in fairness to Hoffman La Roche, that they never ever put any unethical demands on us. If we had any challenge to our ethics, it came from within ourselves. There might have been circumstances where you could fall into the trap of bias, where you would be prejudiced towards the outcome of the experiment because you wanted it to come out that way. You have to have a system of checks and balances which ensure that bias is not woven into the interpretation of the research or the methodology. Early on we developed a great commitment to quality control, quality assurance, independent peer group scientific review. We are now talking about a group which had grown to maybe twelve people. By the time my laboratory was ready in Drogheda, I had my staff trained through an old contact, Victor Wynne, in St Mary's Hospital in London. From the beginning we were committed to the highest level of expertise.

I had come to terms with the fact that the role I had to play was to create a launch-pad. I did not have the scientific training to reach, myself, the scientific heights that were there to be scaled. But by creating the launch-pad, succeeding generations of research physicians would not have to go through the same years of tedious setting-up or finding funds. I would see the analogy with a space-station. The people who build it are perfectly happy when their task is accomplished and from it people voyage into farthest space beyond their comprehension. That's what I tried to do in Drogheda in those early days. It is also what I fervently hope will be the outcome of the restoration of Sir Patrick Dun's Hospital.

However, in my capacity as management adviser to Mother Mary Martin, I told her one day that she had the largest cottage hospital in the world — 300 beds — and only a heartbeat away from having no surgical and no medical service. There was one consultant physician and one surgeon. These views did not endear me to the hospital establishment. The Fitzgerald report came out, suggesting that the Lourdes Hospital would be down-graded to a sort of local hospital. Any ambition it had to become a major specialist hospital would be inappropriate. At that time I had dreams that the College of Surgeons in Dublin might get sense and sell their acres in St Stephen's Green and Bird Avenue, and build a splendid campus on the banks of the Boyne. There was already a sixteenth-century charter, granted at the Parliament of Waterford, which passed only two important acts: one, setting a charter for the University of Drogheda, the other, Poyning's Laws. The main teaching hospital would have the only tropical medicine department in the country.

It could be a great Catholic medical university. It could be the greatest medical campus on this island.

At this stage also there was the O'Malley Report proposing the fusion of UCD and TCD, and St Kevin's was proposed as the teaching hospital for both. O'Malley died and the plan died, but not before Dr Ivor Browne had invited me to join the expanded Department of Psychiatry and to bring in with me a psycho-endocrine centre. I was to go first to St Brendan's, then to St Kevin's, which became St James's — the proposed common UCD/TCD campus. The Dublin Health Authority — predecessor to the Eastern Health Board — gave us space in St Kevin's Hospital. My job was to find the money to build the unit there. We went to the Bank of Ireland, armed with a Hoffman La Roche contract of £50,000 a year for five years.

From that we guaranteed £10,000-plus a year back to the bank to build a prefab.

In 1963 I came under pressure from Leo to move to London to head up the London operation. I wanted to know why the pressure was coming on. I was told by the owner of Leo that because I had founded the Irish Cancer Society, the medical profession was very unhappy and would not buy Leo drugs so long as I was medical director of Leo and involved in the Irish Cancer Society. Abilgaard put the gun to my head: 'You either close out the Irish Cancer Society or come to London and get out of Ireland where you are gumming up the works.' I looked at him very coldly and I said, 'Dr Abilgaard' — I had just got him his doctorate in Trinity — 'Before you ever appeared on the scene, I was able to provide four square meals a day for my family, and when you are gone from the scene, I shall still be able to provide four square meals a day for my family. You may not be acquainted with what happened at the Battle of Clontarf. We don't yield too easily to Danes. Make your arrangements. I'll be gone in three months.'

I left Leo three months later and put my home in Killiney on the market. I moved to rented accommodation in

Killincarrig in Delgany. At least I had the money now from the sale of the house to pay for the rented accommodation and feed the family while I worked my way through this particular problem. Having established Leo in Dublin, in the UK, having found them a factory, got them launched in America, I left Leo with thirteen days' holiday pay. The word was that I had left them with a golden handshake worth millions. I was not prepared to take the dictates of the Irish medical profession about what I would do with my life; nor was I prepared to take from a Dane dictates about what I would do with my family. I'm a stubborn bastard in many ways. I had sold my house in Killiney on three acres for £9,000 on what subsequently became Sunset Boulevard.

Next thing, I found myself commuting on a daily basis from Killincarrig to Drogheda. I wrote off two cars driving up and down to Drogheda and Tim Rogers told me I was a lunatic. He had a house on the stud farm in Maynooth and he gave it to me at a nominal rent. This was certainly a compensation for the family, and I only had to commute from Maynooth across Dunboyne into Drogheda.

This brought me to St Brendan's Hospital and St Kevin's Hospital. I was seeing patients in St Gabriel's in Cabinteely, in Mount Carmel and in St Joseph's, Raheny. Endocrinology was my main medical specialisation but my research was in pharmacology. Pharmacology was a mystery to a lot of doctors because it was very poorly taught. The mystique surrounding the evolution of new drugs was something they never penetrated nor did they want to. Doctors are still prepared to work with drugs with a knowledge that is totally outdated. The consequences are plain to see. Fifteen per cent of all hospital beds are filled with patients suffering from therapeutic misadventure. That's a terrible indictment of a profession that has not grasped the nettle of the anachronism that they license a doctor for life while the half-life of a medicine in the pharmacopoeia today is about five years. Before the discovery of the sulphonamides in 1935, the pharmacopoeia had hardly changed in two thousand years.

There has been more change in the pharmacopoeia since 1935 than in the preceding four thousand years.

Back to Leo where I left a top-of-the-range salary, pension scheme and car. What offended the Irish medical profession was not that I was doing back-street abortions or had become some sort of quack, but that I had helped found an organisation — The Irish Cancer Society — that was teaching patients how to save their own lives. So I said to myself, 'Screw Leo', and that was the stimulus to launch into a new career applying all that I had learned.

In Drogheda, Mother Mary Martin was comatose. There was the Fitzgerald Report. There was transition in the hospital itself. There was transition in the O'Malley concept for St Kevin's. There was an invitation into a hospital with a future as a teaching hospital to which I could transfer my grants from Hoffman La Roche. I had funding from the Bank of Ireland in College Green on the basis of the Roche contract.

In 1971, while we were building the ramp for the prefabs in St Kevin's, there was a cement strike. We had to buy tons of cement across the border for cash, negotiate the deals personally, and bring the cement down to have it on site for the builders the next morning. We started building in February and it was opened on 9 September 1970.

Erskine Childers, who was Minister for Health, was going to perform the opening ceremony. We had been operating for a little while and, on the night before the opening, we discovered that the toilet in the women's cloakroom was blocked. For some inexplicable reason, the women had continued to use it for all their bodily functions — all. When the sanitation squad came from the hospital, they wouldn't touch it. They said it was a plumbing problem. The plumbing department said it was a sanitation problem, and now we were getting to five or six in the evening and this stuff was running down the hall. It was all over the place. I phoned my dear wife and told her I would not be home, I had a little job to do. Using wire coat-hangers I extricated a hand-towel of some considerable size from around the bend in the toilet. I washed the floor and tidied the place and went home around midnight smelling of roses! The next morning I called the staff together. They were quite astounded to see that the place had been cleaned up. I told them that I would never ask anybody to do a job that I was not prepared to do or not competent to do myself: 'I will be able to do any job that you can do, so you will never be able to hold me up to ransom.' Mind you, science has considerably advanced since then and there are several jobs, including the use of computers, that I could not do! In cleaning lavatories, I can still hold my own.

The next eight years rolled by in those prefab buildings. Things were uneventful until 1977. We were doing very well and we had good research funding, now at about £75,000 or £80,000 a year. We had a staff of about twenty-five. The hospital had become a TCD enclave because, following Donogh O'Malley's death, UCD had withdrawn from the idea of a merger and coming on to the St Kevin's/St James's campus. I think they were pushed in this by St Vincent's Hospital. And Ivor Browne and I were part of the psycho-endocrine unit of UCD. It irritated people that we had the money to do anything or to buy any equipment we wanted. We were regarded as the worst possible example of ill-gotten gains.

In 1977 a significant thing happened which again alerted me to make a change. Dr Reggiani of Hoffman La Roche was approached in some way by St Vincent's Hospital to take the contract away from me and to place it in the metabolic set-up in St Vincent's. To their credit, the President of UCD, Tom Murphy, and the Dean of the Faculty of Medicine, D. K. O'Donovan, were embarrassed about this. D. K., I know, liked me as a person and we had travelled very pleasantly together to Denmark, but he did not rate me as an endocrinologist. No way. People in Roche were told how unacceptable I was to establishment medicine in Ireland and that the Hoffman La Roche image would be gravely tarnished if they continued to associate their research programmes with me. There had been a bit of character assassination involved.

I went to Switzerland and spoke to the CEO and the head of research of Roche. I explained the Dublin market to them. North of the Liffey was Mater territory, south of the Liffey was Vincent's territory, both of them hospitals for UCD. If you did something for the Mater you would lose Vincent's and vice versa. Secondly, I told them that they would upset the balance of power, because St James's Hospital was developing as a Trinity medical school. It wished to see itself developing as a centre of excellence in endocrinology and we had the strongest lab in Dublin. The only time St James's recognised our existence was when they were going to be inspected by the Royal Colleges or when they had a deal going with Comhairle na nOispidéal. Then they would count in our staff and space. In the heel of the hunt, Roche wrote to Tom Murphy and said they were quite happy with what I was doing. They proposed to leave things as they were, and the guy in Roche who was engineering the decision was fired. So far as I could understand, the top management in Roche were being told that I wanted out and, to precipitate things, a leak was made to the *Irish Medical Times*. The headline was 'Darragh to Lose Psychoendocrine Funding'. There were grounds to sue but I don't go in for that kind of thing.

Tommy Hardiman was then chairman of the National Board for Science and Technology, and he told me I should develop a strategic plan so that I would not be dependent on the funding from Hoffman La Roche and, at the appropriate juncture, to offer to buy them out and to service them as a contractor group. I did that and bought them out in 1980 for £130,000 and a contract for two years at £1m. a year. That was the level of work we were doing for them.

So, in 1980 we started as the Institute of Clinical Pharmacology Limited. We took over the twenty-five staff, the prefabs and the responsibility for any redundancy payments.

We started to become a commercially driven exercise rather than an academic one.

In 1982, I decided to go to America where we were getting a lot of business. In 1983, I was invited to take a chair in pharmacology in New York Medical College. The new Dean there had just stepped down as Commissioner of the Food and Drugs Administration in Washington, Art Hayes. He wanted me to initiate the clinical pharmacology activities on the campus. I still have a chair there and have tried to develop joint activities between Dublin University and New York Medical College.

You know, Ivor, so many positive things have happened that it's not worth while indulging in any petty recriminations. I remember being asked in an interview by a Mrs Brown for the *Irish Medical Times,* 'How do you cope with your enemies in the Irish medical profession?' and I answered her by saying, 'I don't allow myself the luxury of enmity.' I have disciplined myself to regard opposition for what it is — opposition. Enmity is a malignant emotion that destroys anybody who allows it to take root. Opposition is a fundamentally beneficial force. There is no worthwhile activity in the whole universe that does not have opposing forces. It is what allows the fingers of the gifted pianist to play the piano. It's what holds the entire constellations in place. It stops the lift from plunging and the door from slamming. Without opposition you waste. The astronaut deprived of gravitational pull loses fifteen per cent of his muscle power per week. Opposition is something to be cherished and used appropriately. The tragedy in Ireland is that we continue to harbour feelings of enmity towards any opposition and then we engage in character assassination, something which is so much a feature of our political scene. Instead of welcoming opposition as a means of refining our thought processes, we engage in hatred — something we see so clearly in Northern Ireland and something which drives our young people from these shores. I have no enemies that I recognise — there are people who may not like me and who may oppose me, and now that some success has come my way, enmity has been replaced by jealousy!

We were now way past the point where I needed a new building instead of the old prefabs in St James's, both for the staff and the work they did, and to bring clients to. I needed £3.60 m. to build a 36,000 square feet building. The banks were looking for 2.8 times cover. That must have included my wife's wedding ring. The Dublin old-boy network must have been working against me. And then this tall Irish-American chap sent over by the IDA arrived into my office, told us we were doing splendid work and that it was probably time to go public. The rest is history. I was talking to some analysts subsequently in the Waldorf Astoria Hotel in New York and they asked me why we didn't have any venture capital organisations in Ireland. I told them that we didn't even have a banking system. We had an organised cartel of loan-sharks. None of the shares was taken up in Ireland — they were all taken up outside Ireland. I asked them did they not realise that Ireland would still be a pagan country today if Jesus Christ had been an Irishman.

(The above conversation took place on 8 October 1989. It was resumed on 16 August 1990.)

In the first week of May 1990, recognising the inevitability of a short-term, cash-flow crisis, which would crash the company completely internationally, I advised the board of directors of ICP that we should respond to the urgings of the Bank of Ireland to invite them to put in a receiver. The business depends totally on its credibility with its client companies. Central to that credibility is the issue of perceived viability. Our work has a very significant role in the timeliness of a new drug getting through to the market-place. If we could not fulfil our part of the contract, it would have a grave financial impact, possibly measuring hundreds of millions of dollars, on the client company. Pharmaceuticals quickly become obsolescent. If your molecule does not reach the market at the right time, that market might have disappeared. From sheer economic pressure, a pharmaceutical company that could not be sure that we would be around for the period of the contract, which could be from one to three years, was going to take their business elsewhere.

Once we had decided to put the company into receivership, it was of paramount importance that we got through the process as quickly as possible. Literally a matter of hours — from Thursday evening at five o'clock till Friday night at eleven o'clock — was all it took to have a significant measure of agreement about a potential take-over. It must have been one of the fastest ins and outs of a receivership, somewhat to the chagrin of the people involved, because it would not have enhanced their fees.

Unfortunately all this has its casualties, largely the staff in Ireland who will not work again in the pharmaceutical industry. The same fate did not befall the people in the US or, to a large extent, in the UK. They were all offered jobs — whether they took them or not is another matter. If things had gone differently with the receivership in Ireland, there would have been less mayhem among the employees here.

I know there is no way that I can go back into drug research. It's not the kind of activity where you can re-establish your own personal or professional credibility when something like this happens. There are no second chances. It's a very unforgiving world. The reality of that is inescapable. And this, apart from the fact that one of the necessary conditions for the purchase of the assets of ICP was, that I would not compete for the next ten years. I don't really think that I will be in a competitive situation after the next ten years!

However, serendipity came to the rescue in that I was able to salvage some of my life's experience. I have a network of contacts and friendships from Finland to Sardinia and through the Middle East, in Kuwait and Saudi, in Tehran, in Malaysia, in Hong Kong, in China and in Japan. The opportunity came through Tommy Frist Senior who is one of the great physicians of the twentieth century. From a humble general practitioner office in Nashville, Tennessee, he built Hospital Corporation of America with $5 b. annual turnover and $400 m. profit, and he still maintained the largest general practitioner service in Tennessee. He still practises medicine, though with fourteen other physicians. Through Tom Frist Senior there are a number of opportunities for me to become involved again in medical research of a non-pharmaceutical kind — so that I would not be in a compete situation. There would be no conflict with Besselaar who bought ICP.

The new technology of aqua-dynamics sees one or two new patents a week being registered. When one talks to business people about aqua-dynamics, it's best not to talk about the range of things involved, because it begins to savour of snake oil or black box. If Faraday or Edison had called a press conference to talk about a new energy called electricity and were able to say, 'We shall be able to light this room, cook you a meal and preserve the afters by a process called refrigeration', there would have been a stampede for the door.

The most urgent areas in the nineties will be energy, economy and environment. In aqua-dynamics, we have a product and an energy which can conserve fossil fuels, can improve the operating efficiency of things such as boilers, cooling towers, refrigerants, air conditioning etc. On the other hand, it can significantly reduce carbon dioxide emissions. Detroit Diesel are looking to see if it can improve the efficiency of diesel engines. So there are a number of yet-to-be-developed opportunities.

The immediate commercial application is to prevent scaling and corrosion inside pipes and tanks. This can, among other things, make a big contribution to saving water — perhaps not so important in this country — but this country is not our market. On the Continent, every glass of water you drink has passed through at least three people's kidneys and global warming is causing much quicker evaporation. It is a development not just of commercial interest but of strategic importance.

One's friends of the moment will remind you of your success, but if you are to succeed again, you constantly need to remind yourself of the roots of your failure. The roots of my failure would be that I am basically a physician. I am not by nature interested in the systematic running of a business. That requires great attention to facts and figures and hard objective assessments. Medicine is still predominantly an art form, with science underpinning it.

I believe there is a sharp distinction between a physician and a registered medical practitioner and a doctor. Physicians do not have to be either doctors or registered medical practitioners: Christ was a good physician and he was neither. Many doctors and registered medical practitioners were not attracted to medicine by a true vocation — many people have entered medical school simply because they got the required number of points in the Leaving Certificate. They did not see themselves as entering into a commitment to their fellow human beings. We have seen the consequences of that — for example, the deterioration in the relationship between the patient and the physician which has led increasingly to litigation. I don't think a sympathetic, well-meaning, earnestly-endeavouring physician has ever been taken to the courts. The ordinary decent person feels offended if they are treated by the physician as a child or a fool. I have had to say to a patient, 'I don't know' or 'I shall have to seek further advice' or 'This particular remedy does not seem to be working.' The only reaction I got was that the patients knew that they were participating with me in finding a solution to their medical problems.

I am vocationally a physician and have struggled through the years to keep conversant with medicine. I have a relationship with a core panel of patients. I have been available to my colleagues as a consultant. Of necessity, I did not become involved in acute medicine because I would not always be available. I was simply a background resource. Now, while I'm still physically and mentally active, I am glad that I can go back to serving those patients who would choose me on the advice of their own doctors.

If a business is to succeed, it must have highly professional management. Our business evolved from a non-industrial, non-commercial, academic background. We were physicians and scientists who suddenly found ourselves jettisoned into the role of senior international managers. The primary lesson I learned was that if you would make a business of science, first learn the science of business. It is a science, not an art. I had to empathise so much with my patients that I found it very hard not to empathise with my managers. When they were clearly deficient in skills, I would try to sympathise with them instead of taking the drastic managerial action of kicking them out of a job. The great attribute of a physician is to be able to deal with a person on a personal basis. That is a very bad quality in a manager because you begin to make excuses for the shortcomings of your subordinates. I feel that we should have installed stronger, non-scientific, professional management. But the activity we were in, with the suggestion of human guinea-pig farms, exploitation of the down-trodden, and profiting from the tragedy of illness — all of that made intelligent managers choose not to work in our industry. The world pharmaceutical industry finds great difficulty in attracting quality managers into the medical research area. We suffered from that in our company. Next time round, one would build the framework of any organisation on professional management. Decisions should be more accountancy based than art based, instinctive, intuitive.

But there are the two roles. You can't take a jet aircraft off the ground simply by wiggling the ailerons. You have to have the power, the thrust — and that's the entrepreneur. But you have to have the hands that direct that power, and you have to listen to the traffic controller and watch the radar. The entrepreneur is an energy-source, but he requires a pilot and a navigator. Today, in particular, he needs to be sensitive also to environmental controls. Letting the aircraft go where it will is a recipe for disaster.

I have completed a measurable portion of my life's journey. People ask me how I view this new milestone in my life.

I have always told my students that they should never have an inflexible attitude about how their life runs. Milestones are either stepping stones or millstones. You have to decide for yourself whether the milestone you have reached will be a stepping stone to something new that may be even greater, or a millstone that pulls you down to the depths. I have recently become Master of the Ballymacads. There are a lot of walls in their country and I have become a great respecter of stones of all shapes and sizes, but still see them as a new challenge — they have to be tackled! This new milestone in my life, I want to be a stepping stone, not a millstone. You see the motto there under the Darragh crest: 'Persevere'.

3

Gerry Dempsey

Isn't it encouraging to know that you can do your entrepreneurial thing without necessarily getting rich?

Gerald Dempsey, a chartered accountant, is actively involved in several companies.

He was born in Dublin on 29 November 1928. His father was Patrick Dempsey, the first Secretary of the ESB. His mother was Nora Murphy, wife and mother. He was the younger of two children, one sister.

He is married to Pat McNally. They have four children: Eugene (30), Kieran (26), Clodagh (25) and Denise (23).

He was educated at Glenstal Abbey, at University College Dublin (B.A.), and is a Fellow of the Institute of Chartered Accountants in Ireland.

He worked in Aer Lingus from 1954 to 1986 in various capacities from internal auditor through chief financial officer and, from 1973, as deputy chief executive and chief executive — ancillary activities.

He has been chairman of:

Omni-Dunfey Hotels Corporation (USA);
London Tara Hotel Limited;
Cara Data Processing Limited;

and a director of:

Guinness Peat Group plc;
The GPA Group plc;
The International Fund for Ireland.

He is now a director of:

Waterford-Wedgwood plc;
Gilbeys of Ireland Group Limited;
Abbey Life Assurance (Ireland) Ltd ;
Atlantic Magnetics Ltd — chairman;
The US Chamber of Commerce in Ireland.

He is a member of the international advisory group of Cement Roadstone Holdings plc.

He has been chairman and member of various committees of the International Air Transport Association, President of the Institute of Chartered Accountants in Ireland (1978–79) and is a Fellow of the Irish Management Institute and of the Institute of Transport.

My father often reminded me that when I was nine or ten in Willow Park School, I told the maths teacher there, a famous teacher, Mr O'Beirne, that I wanted to be an accountant when I grew up. This created great merriment in the Dempsey family because they knew that I knew nothing about what an accountant was. My father was a barrister and had been an administrative person all his life — had joined the civil service as a boy clerk. He did his Leaving Cert. and his various barrister's exams by working in the evening. He became Secretary of the ESB at thirty-five and stayed there until he retired at sixty-five. There had never been an accountant in the Dempsey family, but somehow I stuck to my original intention. I did a B.A. in UCD, did my articles with the chartered accountancy firm of Reynolds McCarron, which, years later, became part of Ernst and Young and, shortly after, applied for a job in Aer Lingus. So, even though I had now become an accountant, my application to Aer Lingus and for some other jobs showed that I did not intend to become a practitioner of that art.

My first job in Aer Lingus was as Internal Auditor and Supervisor of Costs and Statistics. You could hardly imagine anything less entrepreneurial. The late forties and early fifties were a time of rapid growth for Aer Lingus — the Viscount turboprop aircraft were being introduced and passenger numbers growing rapidly. It was important for my name-sake, no relation, Jeremiah F. Dempsey, the general manager and his team, to have a lively crop of young professionals around. I think my sonorous title was really a way of taking me into the company as a financial resource. Garret Fitz-Gerald, on the research and scheduling side in the commercial division, Gerry Giltrap in the technical division, Arthur Walls in both engineering and sales, and myself in the finance division, were, I suppose, the beginning of the Young Turks of the airline at that time. We crossed over divisional barriers in a way that our bosses did not find easy. We did not have much regard for bureaucracy.

I moved up through the finance stream and became Chief Accountant in 1961. I was now the head of the accounting function and reported to the financial controller, James Moran. I stayed in that position until Jerry Dempsey retired in 1967 and Michael Dargan became the chief executive. He appointed four of us as his new senior management team: myself heading the commercial function, which was a complete change for me; Neil Gleeson heading a new group called Planning and Development; Arthur Walls heading the technical division; and Finbar Donovan heading the administration division. That was the beginning of a new stage for me in Aer Lingus.

Michael Dargan was a great man for moving his 'young' team around so that they would get a breadth of experience. After about a year, he moved me from commercial into administration, and quickly thereafter I was back into finance again when the older financial people had retired. I had complained to Michael that the finance function needed to be a separate function, now that we were getting into the jet era with heavy capital expenditure. Michael answered that by giving me the job. So in 1969/70, I became the head of that function with the title Assistant Chief Executive — Finance. Around that time a number of the problems that Aer Lingus has subsequently faced were becoming apparent. There were the beginnings of the violence in Northern Ireland which was going to affect travel and tourism. Then there were the beginnings of a price war with the burgeoning of charter flights and mass travel. This involved travel packaging for the first time — including not only the air fare but the accommodation and ground arrangements as well. This would hit us particularly on the Atlantic, where so many of our passengers were tourists rather than business travellers, and expected to pay the lowest possible fare. Year after year in the sixties we had been in the black, even if the profits were not great. But we now saw that that would be difficult to maintain. We saw that we had to diversify. Expansion of air transport from Ireland's small base was at that time not an option, and retrenchment, with job losses, unthinkable.

Clearly, Michael Dargan must get the credit for the concept of diversification and for the determination to get it approved and launched. We began to spend a lot of time thinking about what kind of industries we would get involved in, how we would finance the acquisitions and how we would sell the idea to our board and to our shareholder, the Government. Neil Gleeson and I worked on this separately and in tandem, and from around 1970 I gave it much attention while remaining head of the finance function. This exciting period in which I became more and more convinced of the need for Aer Lingus to diversify, was, I suppose, the first flicker of an entrepreneurial flame in me.

We decided to diversify, first, into the hotel industry, which was a logical step for us; secondly, to expand the aviation-related services such as maintaining and overhauling other airlines' equipment and the handling at airports of other airlines' aircraft; thirdly, the leisure industry, such as resorts and golfing; next, to develop further our computer services businesses; and finally, the banking sector, so as to assist with funding and to lead us to acquisition opportunities.

The process of discussing all of this at board and government level took a long time. It was difficult for the Government to digest the idea that a state-owned company set up in the thirties for the purpose of flying people and goods into and out of Ireland could get involved in other industries. Was this not in some way a breach of its charter? We argued trenchantly that if we did not diversify, the future of the airline would be seriously at risk. Eventually the Government agreed to allow some diversification, but with the proviso that there was to be no call on the Exchequer, so all the money needed would have to be borrowed. We could not go to our shareholder, as it were, for a rights issue for the purpose of diversification. While they were happy to provide capital to purchase aircraft, they would not finance diversification. It was not a very comfortable decision. One of the options was that we would not go ahead on that basis. We gave that all of two minutes' thought. We knew that if we did not look for profitable enterprises outside the airline business, we would soon be in great difficulty. We knew we were right. It was up to us to make it work.

We started with the London Tara Hotel. How we arrived at the decision to start our hotel aspirations by building, on borrowed money, an 850-room hotel in a foreign city, is a fascinating story all in itself — for another day! It was certainly enterprising. We had been involved for some years as a minority shareholder in the Intercontinental Hotels and in Ryans, but now we were determined to get into ownership and operation. We next acquired a banana plantation as our site for a leisure facility in Tenerife and a 400-acre demesne just outside London for the Foxhills Golf and Country Club. We also took a ten per cent stake in a UK quoted company, the Guinness Peat Group, as our move into the financial services world. Internally, we were expanding our computer business and our catering services, both of which needed new impetus. At the same time we were developing the aircraft maintenance side, encouraging other companies' planes into our hangars, essentially to prevent the outflow of jobs if we had to cut back. Initially that was an employment-substitution, rather than a profit-earning, strategy. It subsequently became highly profitable, so was expanded and has been important ever since to Aer Lingus.

Thus, in the early seventies we had moved fairly rapidly, and invested some £20–25 m. in ancillary activities. But that has to compare with over £60 m. invested in aircraft — the two original jumbo jets are still there. Another stricture that the Government had laid upon us and that we accepted as reasonable was that the ancillary activities should not at any stage form more than one third of the assets of the company.

I joined the Guinness Peat Group board as Aer Lingus's nominee. The company had been formed about 1972 through a merger of Lewis and Peat, a long-established broker and trader, and Guinness Mahon, a small but respectable accepting house and merchant bank in London, which of course owned Guinness and Mahon in Dublin. The Guinness and the Peat brought two Irish-sounding names together, but that was pure accident.

In February 1973, the Tara opened its doors and Foxhills opened a year or so later. The Tenerife development had to be delayed for some years due to the greatly changed economic scene following the Yom Kippur War and the quadrupling of oil prices. So we were under way in that 72/73 period. While organisationally I was heavily involved in it, I was still the chief financial officer, and it soon became clear that the diversified enterprises had to have a leader. At this time too, Michael Dargan decided to retire and invited me to succeed him as the chief executive of the company. For some months, I went through a difficult personal period examining what I believed was the role of the chief executive of Aer Lingus, and what I saw as my strengths and weaknesses. I decided not to accept the offer and opted instead to take charge of the new ancillary activities division. A difficult decision — at the time perhaps questionable — but subsequently justified as the right one, I think, both for Aer Lingus and for me.

One of the reasons I was glad to take on the ancillary businesses job was that I had a fascination with turning the concept of enterprise in the public sector into practical reality. I was determined that the investments we had made should work, and I was convinced that the best way for them to work was for them to operate as private sector businesses, even while their parent remained in the public sector. If any of the subsidiary companies felt that they were in the public sector, then we were not going to get the benefit of the admixture of public and private. It was exciting to be pioneering this fascinating and apparently contradictory notion of entrepreneurship within the state sector. You could say that I was the person who conducted the orchestra of diverse businesses. I was the link between the state body and all those subsidiaries which in time grew to be a large number.

I was the chairman of the boards of the larger subsidiary companies and was the bridge between them and the airline, much the same as the chairman of the airline was the link with the government shareholder. My job, as I saw it, was to ensure that what was driving those companies was entrepreneurship and not just a bureaucracy or faceless committee. It became an interesting diplomatic-type task.

I don't think, Ivor, that I saw myself as an entrepreneur within the state sector — I was not doing it for personal gain — but rather as a kind of intrapreneur. I was a full-time employee of the airline but I was using the drives and motivations of an entrepreneur to ensure that those who managed the subsidiary companies were doing so in a creative and enterprising way.

A good example was the acquisition of the Dunfey Hotel Group in America. It was a complicated deal that took over a year to negotiate with the previous owners, a major US insurance company that had been pretty well instructed by the federal authorities there to divest itself of activities other than insurance. It had bought the chain some years earlier from members of the Dunfey family. There were about twenty hotels and over six thousand employees. I was appointed chairman of its board, with Jack Dunfey as the chief executive. Jack was the senior member of the five brothers who had created the business and had led the company when he was a major shareholder and also when it had become a subsidiary company. In the long period I was chairman, although non-executive, I had the power of representing 100 per cent of the shares, and yet I am sure that none of the executives of that company ever felt they were working for an Irish semi-state company. They were encouraged to develop the business in the way they thought best, but with a benevolent proprietor. I think the Dunfey management found us a better parent than the insurance company. We understood the business and had got into it intentionally, witness the Tara in London. But, more than that, we seemed to get things right, taking a smallish company and bringing it to moderate size, and then growing it to being a larger company, perhaps such that could be floated later to the public, and doing all this in a supportive way.

From the mid-seventies to the mid-eighties, ancillary activities went from a standing start and one company — the London Tara — to twenty or so companies with revenues of about £250 m. and net profits of £25–30 m. As a management we had done this with good support from the board and general acceptance of Government, but without any professional guidance as to the best way to do it. David Kennedy, now chief executive of Aer Lingus, and I discussed this often and decided that we needed a review of all we had done, and we commissioned McKinseys. Their report said that we had done everything the right way: that we had a very small headquarters staff — eight or ten people, so we had no second-guessers; we had what McKinseys called the classic 'loose-tight' method, loose in that you let subsidiaries manage the businesses in their own way and tight in the sense that you kept a very close eye on and control of the financials. We had done this intuitively. I don't know whether this was because it was part of the Aer Lingus management culture or because we had become imbued with the entrepreneurial spirit and that, combined with my basic accounting discipline, it produced the right formula.

The first four years of ancillary activities were difficult and somewhat hair raising. The London Tara Hotel got off to a very sticky start. In its first three years (1973–1975), we had difficulty getting the management right and there was a great failure of American tourists to come to London for two years in succession. In addition, the Arab–Israeli situation quadrupled the price of oil, the whole travel business was in disarray and, as a consequence, the Tenerife acquisition had to be put on ice. Foxhills was just breaking even: the projections we had made about the number of golfers who would use it were beginning to look unduly optimistic. A return on our investment in the Guinness Peat Group seemed a long way off. The Tara had cost over £6 m., of which £1 m.

was equity. McAlpines, who were the building contractors, had taken a minority stake in the venture and had paid £250,000 for their share, and because of losses in the early years, they panicked, and we bought it back from them for a nominal £10,000. The auditors were saying unpleasant things to us like, 'You have lost all your share capital so we had better provide for that in the Aer Lingus accounts.' I said, 'Over my dead body!' I argued strongly that we should not write off our investment, that although we had gone in deep by building such a large hotel, the location was good and the values were still there. It was just going through a cyclical downturn and we would get it right. I won most of those arguments, but the jury was out for quite a while, and of course there were plenty of begrudgers who shook their heads knowingly and said we should have stuck to our last.

You know, Ivor, when you look back over the years at difficult periods in your life, you tend to take a fairly relaxed view. But, truly, I don't think there was any time during that sticky period that I lost confidence. I was certainly perspiring at the length of time it was taking to get things right, but I never told myself that we had done the wrong thing. The Aer Lingus Board was sometimes restive and concerned. The civil servants were questioning and often negative, and I remember in 1975 a Minister for Transport took a very close interest in all we were doing and cross-examined me thoroughly for over an hour at a meeting with the board. He was finding it particularly difficult to understand why we had set up Guinness Peat Aviation jointly with the Guinness Peat Group in London to get into the aircraft leasing business. He thought that since we were already in this business we would now be, as it were, competing with ourselves. I argued that by setting up this joint venture we were introducing private enterprise, fresh capital and the ability to expand greatly our interests in the business of aircraft leasing. Little did he or I then know just how remarkably successful Guinness Peat Aviation was later to become. So there was pressure, but it never got to the point where

anybody said we had better wind it all up. It did not reach
the stage where I had to make dramatic speeches from the
dock, although sometimes I felt I was already in the dock.
About 1976, the Tara turned the corner and made profits
for the first time. Since then it has never looked back, under
the dedicated and brilliant management of Eoin Dillon. At
the end of 1975, we bought the Dunfey chain for a cash investment of $750,000 and, in its first year, it made a profit of
$2 m. GPA was a success from the beginning. The concept
was right, the owners were right and the management superb.
We appointed Tony Ryan chief executive soon after forming
the company and sold him a minority stake while retaining
shared control between ourselves and the Guinness Peat
Group. In year one, for a very small capital investment, it
made a few pounds; in year two, it made a considerable
number of pounds, and the rest, as they say, is history. So,
from about 1977 on, I did not have a case to defend. The
begrudgers were defeated. What I had to do from there was
to build on success.

You said, Ivor, that in a way I had uniquely created a job
for myself and then filled it and I suppose there is some
truth in that. It would be more correct to say that the logic
of the situation demanded that Aer Lingus should dedicate
a senior executive to making diversification work. It was
really a classical piece of entrepreneurial activity. We identified the need, researched the options, obtained approvals,
raised finance, negotiated acquisitions, and now it had to be
managed. As you well know from your experience of the
theory and practice of management, good schemes tend
not to work without a champion. By being part of the conceptual stage and active in early implementation, I became,
in effect, the champion for ancillary activities.

My job gave me plenty of variety, constantly travelling
overseas to our subsidiary and associated companies, moni-
toring and directing their operations and reporting on performance to the parent company back home. While I was a
growth-orientated businessman, I never wandered too far

away from my bedrock discipline of accountancy. I kept in touch with the profession and was honoured, in 1978/79, to be elected President of the Institute of Chartered Accountants in Ireland, the first to do so from industry as opposed to practice. My Willow Park forecast was fulfilled.

There have been other examples of companies in the state sector diversifying, either geographically or into products that were not in their original remit, but none of them, I think, has been as obvious as the Aer Lingus story. I suppose this is mostly because, without it Aer Lingus's financial condition would have been in tatters and the profits from ancillary activities regularly made headline news. The state has not been particularly comfortable with this. In most cases it becomes a shareholder in a commercial venture when there is no private capital available. In the 1930s, it would have been impossible to launch, with private capital, businesses like the ESB or Aer Lingus. In these and other cases the state had to become a kind of embryonic venture capitalist. But its agenda is very different from that of a private venture capitalist. It would say that it had set up a company to be an airline or an electricity supplier and that's what they were going to be. If a management team were to come along some time later and say that it believed that the company should engage in businesses different from those originally envisaged in order to grasp market opportunities or avoid brain-drains or employment cut-backs, then the government of the day has a problem. Why should it own something that it did not set out to own in the first place? The state is always going to have difficulty with companies engaging in diversification, whereas the private capitalist is delighted to venture into anything that would increase earnings per share, provided it is clear that management is capable of managing it.

Anyway, I have severe reservations about the state as an owner of commercial enterprise. The state's needs for finance are not in sync with business needs and the state enterprise may get a no from its shareholders for reasons that have nothing to do with the business, but simply because the timing is not right. In many instances, the state has, in its own view, good reasons why scarce money — and it is always scarce — should be applied elsewhere. The commercial enterprise can then be starved of capital, from its point of view, at the wrong time.

I am reminded of the time I was making the case for the investments in the Dunfey Hotel chain. This was in 1975. It was, as I said earlier, only $750,000 up front, but it was a major commitment further down the road, initially as a lessee of hotels and later as an owner. A senior civil servant said to me, 'I think you're mad.' I said, 'Have I not made a good case?' He said, 'Oh, the case is excellent. I'm sure we'll get it through. But look at all the trouble you're giving yourself.' His instinctive reaction was that I should not add to the number of burdens I had. Had I not set up enough subsidiary companies? Why did I have to add another one? That happened again some years later. The reaction to the purchase of the Berkshire Hotel in New York was entirely positive. It made sense to the officials because we flew in and out of New York, although that was not my reason for buying it at all: it was not going to survive on customers flying in from little Ireland. However, some years later when we were proposing to buy the management contract for the Statler Hilton Hotel in New York and we had to get government approval, the attitude was, 'What do you want another hotel in New York for? Haven't you got one already?' What I think was not fully appreciated was that our commitment had become ruthlessly focused on profit. Every enterprise we began or acquired was directed with the single-minded dedication to profit. While this sounds pretty basic, it created a dilemma which surfaced from time to time. Aer Lingus, as the state-owned airline, was dedicated above all to providing a service to the citizens of Ireland and those who wished to visit or trade with it. Thus, the shareholders and many officials in the Government and in the airline did not see profit as the principal objective. I did, and I got sufficient support at management and board level to ensure that profit was the name of the game.

At times it was difficult to get the message across to the staff in Aer Lingus that the basic reason why we had to generate profits was that the airline part of the company was unprofitable. That could be demotivating for people not involved in ancillary activities. This led to communications problems and misunderstandings but, over time, these became less important.

There were not too many opportunities for cross-fertilisation between the air transport and ancillary businesses' staffs, largely because practically all the ancillary businesses were overseas. This was done by design for three reasons. Firstly, the major opportunities and markets were outside Ireland. Secondly, it meant that our earnings were export earnings. Thirdly, if we were to compete with the private sector on the home market, there was the danger of a 'no win' situation. If we did well and beat the local competition, political pressures could force us to back off. If we did badly, the local begrudgers would have a field-day. All in all it seemed wiser to concentrate our diversification efforts on the wider markets overseas.

Coming back to the subject of entrepreneurship, I am not suggesting that enterprise in the public sector can occur only through diversification. On the contrary, in my opinion enterprise and innovative leadership have flourished in our state-owned companies. Over the years many have out-performed the private sector in this respect. However, even though the dictionary may show me wrong, I make a distinction between being enterprising and being entrepreneurial. I believe that an entrepreneur is essentially one who owns or controls a business and thus drives unrelentingly for profit, both for reward and assurance of continuity. Thus both private ownership and profit come into the picture. This does not sit well in a state-owned company, partly because of ideology and partly because the state companies are usually service or utility suppliers and, up to recent years at any rate, were not wholly committed to profit.

Another vital plus for me was that through association with other businesses and business people, I and a number of colleagues were able to avoid the tunnel-vision that can come from sticking too tightly to one's last. There was an excellent potential for training our younger management, and so it proved.

The years from 1974 to 1986 as head of ancillary activities sped by very quickly. I felt privileged to be doing something worthwhile and among people of stature like David Kennedy and his executive team. I had, during my time, two outstanding deputies in Maurice Foley up to 1982, when he left to join GPA, and Denis Hanrahan, who succeeded me when I retired in 1986 and who is now chief executive of Carrolls. They made what I was doing easier as well as more fun. I regard myself as having been lucky. Luck plays a big part in business and while to an extent you can make your own, outside influences can be vital. It is hard for me to imagine how you could do better than to be part of a successful innovation and to enjoy doing it. There were frustrations, of course, irritations and some set-backs too. One major piece of litigation between our US hotel company and an Italian company comes to mind as a terrible pain in the neck that seemed to go on for ages. But we worked at it, held our nerve and came out unscathed.

I enjoyed immensely doing business for so many years in America and, warts and all, it really is the place in which enterprise flourishes: the business climate is right, the banks are right, everything is right. Of course there were approaches to me, but I was so thoroughly enjoying what I was doing and it was so unique that, perhaps, it prevented me thinking about Gerry Dempsey's own balance-sheet. Perhaps I should have listened to the siren voices that I heard in the early eighties when I was not much beyond fifty. But Aer Lingus was a happy company to work in; I had a great team around me and success was attending our efforts. We had so many different businesses in so many different cultures — it was fascinating and very hard to let go.

In 1983, when I was coming to age fifty-five, I started to make noises to David Kennedy that perhaps it was time I was moving on. In the event, I stayed on for several more years which, I suppose, was evidence of how switched on I was. In my case, one of the missing links was the acquisition of personal wealth, but then isn't it encouraging to know that you can do your entrepreneurial thing without necessarily getting rich?

4

Dermot Desmond

There is a line in the Sail Ireland song about
the narrowest line between the hero and the fool.
I'd prefer to walk that line than be a nonentity.
A nonentity to me is somebody that does not do
his best. I think life is about doing one's best.

Dermot Desmond is Executive Chairman/Chief Executive of National City Brokers.

He was born in Cork on 14 August 1950, the eldest of four children, three boys and one girl.

His father was Andrew Desmond, a Collector of Customs and Excise. His mother was Sheila Twomey.

He was educated at Marino National School and Good Counsel College, New Ross.

He is married to Patricia Brett, a statistician, then an air hostess. They have three sons, one daughter: Brett (12), Zoe (9), Ross (7), Derry (18 months).

He worked in Citibank, all departments. He ended up as credit analyst.
He was an IBI lending executive;
Project Leader for World Bank in Afghanistan;
Coopers & Lybrand consultant.
He started NCB in July 1981.
He is Chairman, Irish Futures and Options Exchange (IFOX);
Chairman of Aer Rianta;
Director of R. & J. Emmet plc;
Director of Classic Thoroughbreds plc;
Board Member of the Michael Smurfit Graduate School of Business;
Chairman of Financial Courseware;
Chairman of Quay Financial Software Systems;
Member of the President's Development Council, UCD;
Board Member of People in Need.

He was captain of the team that won the All-Ireland Schools General Knowledge Competition in 1969.

I suppose the beginning for me is the establishment of NCB. But then everything accumulates in life. We're beginning today. We accumulate more information, more knowledge, greater recognition of our own strengths and weaknesses. But to me, establishing NCB was establishing a company in which I could have my own identity. I wanted to do things my way, not in any autocratic fashion, but simply that I saw opportunities in the market-place that I could not pursue were I working in another organisation. That's not a reflection on any of the organisations I had worked with. I had a narrow focus in setting up NCB.

I was moving into an area that was really controlled by just three UK money-brokers. To me it was just a question of knocking out the competition, and to do that, you had to identify their weaknesses. Were there gaps in the services their clients wanted? We saw that they were operationally inefficient, they did not have good administration or information systems, they had no technology, they were not research-orientated, they were not service-orientated. It was simply, 'Will you do business with us because we are nice people?' To give comfort to the Irish banks, they were relying on the fact that they were subsidiaries of UK firms. We said we would turn that around. We would have a linkage with an international firm to whom we would sell twenty-five per cent of our equity. We would retain our Irishness and look for support from the Irish institutions. We would remind them of Louden Ryan's report of 1968 on the development of the Irish financial markets which he felt should be controlled by Irish firms.

The reality of life in Dublin is that if you are starting something new and you want to do business with people with whom you have worked previously or, indeed, people with whom you have grown up, not only do they not support you, they do the reverse. No matter how professional or efficient your service is, you don't win over their support simply because of the competitiveness of a small market. The only way is to stick with it, show that you're not going to cave in, and grind them down. That's what we did in NCB. We certainly did not have the support from the financial institutions. When we were setting up, we met with them and we received encouragement — the right words — but, in practice, when we started off, we did not get their support. We got that support eventually by developing a lot of skills and by innovations that their dealing rooms did not have. Then they recognised that these skills could be translated into profit for them, so they started to use us. We brought the company up to a fifty per cent share of the Irish money-broking market and two of the UK companies decided, when they saw what we were doing, to sell out to their Irish management. So, I suppose we did a favour for the management of those firms and hopefully improved the level of money-broking service all round.

I did not have the skills myself. I simply put in better people: by taking some from the existing firms, by recruiting some from abroad and by bringing in some graduates. I also put in good systems. I thought I would simply be the manager of all this, counting the cash at the end of the week. But, two weeks after we started, we found we were short of staff in a critical area and the boys told me to get on the lines and start dealing. I had never dealt before in my life. I remember well the first deal I did was a three-month Sterling. I remember when I had done the deal, I jumped from the desk as if I had scored a world cup goal. Our commission was £160 a side, to the borrower and to the lender. A few minutes later we were doing the details. Sterling was two days settlement (spot), Irish pounds were the same day. The fellow on the other end said to me that he wanted that Sterling value today rather than value spot. It would have been normal to give him the spot price. I told him I thought he had been talking about spot and that I had misunderstood that it was value today. The difference was in excess of the commission we were getting. I told him I had made a mistake in my ignorance. Some dealers would have said, 'OK. I'll take it out of spot and I'll cover myself overnight', recognising that it was a genuine mistake. This guy said, 'I want a cheque down in ten minutes.' So, from being elated, I was stuffed. I made a rule that I would never get stuffed again and that I would know as much about this business as anybody else. Then I really applied myself to money-broking, as a person on the desk. I did that for close on five years. We built up the market share and we more or less dominated Irish money-broking. We'd start at the desk at 8 o'clock in the morning and finish at 6 p.m. Any management work was done after that or on a Saturday morning or Sunday night.

During that time I used to go out to lunch every day of the week with bank dealers, and I used to go out with bank directors and chief dealers with my wife about four nights a week. I often did it for six nights a week and I remember one time I had lunch and dinner for twenty-six out of twenty-eight days. I put on weight. I smoked more cigarettes. I drank more alcohol. It took a toll in the sense that, in money-broking, you worked hard and you lived hard.

If you have a good day, you feel elated. You got hold of the market. You want to celebrate and you want to do it with the guys in the office because they are the only ones who can understand how we collectively did the deal. If you had a bad day and you were in the downs, you wanted to talk to people so that you got buzzed up for the next day.

It was a very good training ground. There is a lot of psychology involved in money-broking. It's like a stock-exchange for banks. On one day, a particular bank may have surplus money of £10 m. The bank dealer believes he's going to have the money for one night, or a week, or a month, or three months. He does not generally ring up other banks and ask them if they want to borrow from him. He gets on to a money-broker and asks him, 'What banks have you got paying one week, one month money, etc.?' Most business is up to a year. The money-brokers would give him the rates the banks were paying. Generally money-brokers would have a two-sided price: banks that will offer funds, and banks that will pay for funds for a certain period. You may have banks that will offer to lend funds at 8½ and banks that will pay 8⅜. Your objective is to get one of them to deal down to 8⅜, or pay up to 8½, or deal in the middle at 8⁷⁄₁₆. The same thing happens in the foreign exchange market: the money-broker is the exchange. Another way that banks use it is if rates are going up or down. If rates are going up, banks will take in a lot of money so that when the rates go up, they could have cheap funding. We dealt in all the major currencies: Dollars, Marks, Sterling, Lire and Yen. Currencies other than the principal ones are called 'exotics'. There is some humour in money-broking. For example, when you are dealing in several billion lire, you don't say a billion, you say 'a yard'. Did you ever try to write out a billion?

Having found that we could apply skills to money-broking and be successful, we turned to stock-broking. We were money-brokers for four and a half years before we moved into stock-broking towards the end of 1985. You can get a share of 40 to 50 per cent of the Irish money-broking market and anything above that would be unhealthy. If we were to develop, we had to move into a new area. We saw in stock-broking exactly the same situation we had seen in money-broking. It was a concentrated market controlled by three firms: no major investment in their services, not technologically-driven, not research-driven. They were not service-orientated. All they really did was sell and sell hard. Generally they came in at 9.15, while we believed you should be there at 8 o'clock when the markets open up. There is a correlation between money-market movements and gilt movements, and we had a strength there in our pool of knowledge. I researched the business and developed a plan as to how we could take over a stock-broking firm. We went after a number of them and eventually did a deal with Dillon & Waldron. At that stage there were sixteen stock-broking firms in Dublin, and Dillon & Waldron was the seventeenth! I recruited staff the same way we did with the money-broking, dealing staff and research staff. We decided to start off with gilt trading and we became very successful. Tullett & Tokyo had twenty-five per cent of our company. They are among the biggest money-brokers in the world. I had a call-option that I could buy back their share. I bought it back and now we were able to deal independently with all the money-brokers internationally. We were not perceived to be locked in with one. So we went after the stock-broking companies using our own resources. NCB has never had any outside shareholders. Since then it has never had any capital put into it except the original put in by me and Tullett & Tokyo. It never paid a dividend — it has reinvested all its funds. That's called reinforcing your bet.

It was difficult enough to get a stock-broking licence. The other companies around town and the Stock Exchange didn't want us to get one. They felt we weren't the right sort of people, outsiders. They blocked our application and eventually members of the London Stock Exchange had to come over and interview us and pass us. That opposition did us a favour; it made us more determined. We felt it was very unfair that they would not make their accusations to our faces. We asked them to state their problems with us, but they could not give any. I believe opposition is essential. You have got to have something to measure your own skills and abilities against. Eventually, we got the licence through and started off in January 1985. From the first month we were profitable. That was not instant success — I had taken on very high-quality staff seven months beforehand, and we planned everything.

A nice story from that time: naturally the staff we re-cruited were all highly paid. One of them came to me and said, 'Look, with this delay with the licence, we are not earning any money. Don't pay me. Keep the money until we're running'. I said, 'A deal is a deal. I'm paying you.' But something like that makes you feel good. That's commit-ment. That's a value — and it's a value to me until I'm buried. That's real belief. A lot of people make monetary statements: they'll support you if you pay them enough.

We built our customer base on the back of our money-broking and treasury rooms. They already knew the high-quality service we were capable of giving. So far as the other stock-brokers were concerned there was a rumour-a-day put out about us: that we were wrong; that we had bad staff; that we were going to blow up; that we were going to default on a payment — and that has never stopped in Dublin. The best way to silence these people is just to do a better job and take away market share. Every pound we generate is being taken away from somebody. There is satisfaction in that. We also take the view that they should not hold their breath waiting for us to go — it's a long time now. We did on the equity side exactly as we had done on the gilt side. We did not go straight into the equity market — we did everything gradually. We started with money-broking, then on to foreign exchange, then on to new products. We established each one solidly. We had a beach-head in each area before we moved on to the next. We did not try to fight on different fronts at the same time. It was late 1986 when we launched equity services and the first year was very profitable.

In 1987 we started moving into corporate finance. We had been playing around making investments in various companies. We saw there was an opportunity in pure corporate finance services like what they were providing in AIIB or IBI. That's now one of the major divisions in NCB. To penetrate markets we started using technology, developing software programmes, developing arbitrage programmes — a very good guy called Hugh Curran did it. He's now in the UK. Hugh was managing director of NCB starting off. He was both technologically and marketing orientated. He developed the programmes on Spectrum, on Sharp, from zero. Eventually everybody in the market ended up with one of these machines, a Sharp 1500 — very simple, really an enhanced calculator called a computer. We just recognised the power of that technology. I felt we could develop a lot more in the financial services market in software and the integration of information systems, in getting involved in expert systems. I set up an associated company called Deal-formatics. At the same time, we did a lot of repetitive training with new staff.

I came across a company called Computer-Based Training the day before it was going into receivership. I met with the owner, Pat McDonagh. I was convinced of the demand for courseware. Courseware is a way for people to learn through using a computer instead of reading a book. I could see a whole demand in the financial services market for training products. I said I would fund the company's deficit and buy 50 per cent of the company with an option to buy another 25 per cent and then another 25 per cent. I would fund the development of a product for money-markets and foreign exchange. We spent a year and a half with courseware writers and, using our knowledge and expertise, developing a product called Intuition. It's a lovely name. We had a competition for it and a guy came in one morning and said, 'My wife says Intuition', and I said, 'That's the name.' We decided to sell it either through Tele-Rate or Reuters. We set up a little competition between them and decided to move with Tele-Rate. In the first year, the company made nearly a million pounds profit. I bought Pat McDonagh out and he decided to do something in other areas of course-ware. I wanted something in financial services; he wanted a broader base of products. Very amicably, he walked out with a lot of money. A few years later he sold on to Hoskins for £6 m. That's a story I like to tell and I go on to develop it in this way: we went into CD Rom instead of floppy disc. One of these discs has so much power that it can hold the *Encyclopaedia Britannica.* It's a quasi-expert system with which, for example, you can go into swaps or FRAs and it will come up with the answer in a tenth of a second. Over the last few years we have had a major investment programme develop-ing our courseware and technology.

In our accounting policies we write off everything and we have written off about £2.50 m. in investment. If we capit-alised it, we would not have a loss. That company, this year and next year, is entering into major contracts with some leading entities, like the Chartered Institute of Bankers in the UK who are using the product to train people for banking exams. The way I look at it is that, out of Mount Street here, we are in over forty countries world-wide, we have over two hundred international banks, we have thirty of the top hundred banks. If you go from London to New York to Moscow to Tokyo, our product is there. Japanese are being trained indirectly by Irish people.

We set about a very ambitious software programme to establish a number of products. The major product was In-vision, which integrates different information systems. It has taken three and a half years to develop and it's now firmly established. This year, its first year of sales, it will make a substantial profit. The Investment Bank of Ireland, Shield and Irish Life have it here and we are now marketing it to international firms abroad. Something that we're proud of is that we are creating value. Taken that the financial services are, in a sense, parasitical, in here we want to be generators of value. We have been setting up new companies and exporting. We can go back to the banks who first supported us and say that we are creating jobs for Ireland and creating wealth which has got to be good for everybody who provides a service. That, in simple terms, is the history.

What drove me initially was to pay the mortgage, to be wealthy, simply, and to have the power, to feel important. I think that would be the honest assessment that I would give of the first couple of years of NCB. You had this mythical thing of wanting to be a millionaire. You wanted to have a nice house and a nice car — I didn't want to have three yachts and four summer houses and drive a Ferrari or any-thing like that — I wanted to be comfortable so that I did not have to add up my cheque book at the end of the month. I wanted the independence that comes with wealth — that you can walk out and not be dependent on anyone else. You don't have to be nice in a false sense to people.

But the key thing is not really independence. It's happiness. Happiness is enjoying one's life. Enjoying one's life is not playing golf or going on holidays two weeks of the year. Happiness is not just making money and more money. Happiness is how good a father you are, how good a husband you are, the friends you have, how caring you are about the community, your social responsibilities, how caring you are about the development of your country, how caring you are as a global person, what value you are bringing to whatever exercise you are carrying out. All of these form part of happiness.

Five years ago, if somebody was criticising Sail Ireland, I would not have been able to endure the same criticism then as I can now. What happened in between is that I know that the project was motivated by what NCB is about, bringing people together to meet the challenge. We believe that you can bring a group of Irish people together and compete internationally. It has been proved by companies like Smurfit. Sail Ireland was an example of something that you could bring right off the drawing board. Five years ago it could have been an ego-trip. If it's ego-tripping and then you get the criticism, you will fall apart because the criticism defeats your rationale. Now I know that the rationale behind Sail Ireland was not ego-tripping or advertising in the general sense, because we are not a consumer product-based company. It was purely and simply a reflection of the NCB culture.

One of the things that drives me now is the commitment I have got from a lot of the people I work with. You have got to be motivated when you look at the development of their careers. You participate in opportunities for them as well as for yourself. You see new horizons. Another thing that motivates me is asking what have I done that would be in my son's interest in forty years' time. If he is asked what did his father do, hopefully he can say, 'He created some value.' Maybe that value is the establishment of something like IFOX, the Financial Services Centre, or creating a better service in stock-broking. I am not saying that all these can be attributed to me: I participated in them and I got the help and the expert advice of colleagues who worked in here. I get too much credit for what is done by NCB: we are a team. It's just leaving this place a little bit better.

I'm not a bit embarrassed by the word patriotism. I never thought about it until I went abroad. I came across thirty or forty nationalities and I was really proud to be Irish. I recognised how well loved and admired the Irish were and how talented they were abroad. Then you come back here and we're in recession. I said there must be something wrong — we've got to harness our strengths: I have taken people from the civil service, from the Central Bank, from state organisations, from universities — and they are brilliant. And yet people were saying that civil servants were bureaucratic. They are very talented, but they are operating in the wrong environment.

I suppose what I tried to do was to start changing the environment. NCB is changing the environment. My investment is in Ireland — I want to live here; I want my children to grow up here. I want it to be a better place and I'm going to promote the development of Ireland and I'm not going to be ashamed of that. I suppose everybody needs something that they are driven by. It may sound schmaltzy but I enjoy seeing Irish people do well at home and abroad. I don't think I am motivated by looking for some personal gain from what I have just said. There is an intrinsic value in seeing Irish people succeed.

You cannot be patriotic because you want to get applause from the public at large or the politicians. I will never go into politics. I do not have the skills for it and, anyway, the financial rewards are wrong. The only way to go into politics is to be financially independent. It's a hard and complex life, dealing with constituents and cumainn. You've got to be pretty brilliant to be a successful politician in Ireland and I don't think I'm that brilliant. If I were offered a senatorship from the Taoiseach's eleven, I'd take it because I'd like to be called Senator and then could abuse the title in a marketing sense! But, seriously, I wouldn't take it because I wouldn't have the time for it. I would politely refuse, reluctantly refuse.

I now have a reasonable standard of living — there is nothing out there that I'm looking for. My needs are less now than they were five years ago. It's not because needs have been met, it is because I have changed — my need for monetary or physical possessions has been diluted. So far as power is concerned, who has power? What is power? Even in this organisation, I have less power now than when I started out, when it was smaller and you could get more things done yourself. As you get bigger you have less personal power, you are more dependent on other people. Sure, it's collectively more powerful now and there are bigger plays and bigger decisions, but I don't look upon it in those power terms. That's not something that I recognise. I have substantial shares in NCB, but we have never called a vote using those shares. Powerful is a company that is making money, that is solid, that has cash reserves, and that, with it, you can take your place in the community as the captain of an industry, be it small, medium or large. You have an identity.

I have an identity now, whether it is good or bad, and I don't think about it. There is probably a disadvantage in having an identity. A few years ago I could go to a pub and talk with all the staff, have a night out. Now, if I go out, I have people coming up to me asking what do I think about this share going up or going down, or asking me if I have a job for their son. But that doesn't really bug me — in fact I like it in this sense: I like the hustle mentality. But if I want to get away from it, hopefully I am civil to these people and listen to them and thinking that that could be me on the other side. It's hard to get space for yourself — you have no privacy now because you are a public character. Does that mean that the more I participate in business or participate in the development of Ireland, that I am a public figure and that the public have rights over my privacy? Perhaps that's the price that there is to pay. If you get the bouquets you like it, if you get the criticism you don't, but I would really prefer to get neither the bouquets nor the criticism. You say Sail Ireland hit a high profile, but look, we took a decision to go with it, and we were going to run it like a business, and we were going to get the best businessman available for the project, and that was Howard Kilroy. This boat was the new Ireland — it was part of the Golden Age, part of creating confidence. It endeavoured to repeat the pride and the joy of Sean Kelly's and Stephen Roche's efforts and indeed the Irish soccer team's performance. It was also a high-tech type of enterprise. Building the boat in Ballyfermot appealed to us.

I'm a dreamer. I like a good fairy story. I like a happy ending. We had to go through pain barriers. We made lots of mistakes. There were lots of things that we did not succeed at, at first go. We're not afraid of failure. I like the definition: courage is not freedom from fear, it's being afraid and going on. We're afraid and we are going on, and how far we'll go on, I don't know. We don't have a five-year, copper-fastened plan that we are going to have 20 per cent increase a year. We have a corporate plan that we want to improve and learn and give a better service.

Looking back over NCB, I can tell you sequentially and I can try and put order on it, but it was not like that. Somebody could ring me up in the morning with a thought — it just happens. You go off on a wave and you either have the comfort of success or the pain of failure.

My life is condensed. I enjoy life. I am a happy person, but I am no happier today than I was five years ago. I had greater excitement when we bought our first carpet for our living room with no other furniture. That stands out. I can remember the excitement of scoring a goal in a Leinster Colleges match in a quarter-final. People think there is a higher platform of excitement, of happiness, as you go on or as your business is more public. There is not. There is a Sail Ireland song that we commissioned from Shay Healy.

I like it a lot because there is a line in it that talks about the narrowest line between the hero and the fool. I am on this narrow line. But I don't mind walking it. I'd prefer to walk that line between being a hero and a fool than be a nonentity. A nonentity to me is somebody that does not do his best. I think life is about doing one's best. Most people I work with are more talented than me, but I con them by maximising my strengths more so than they do.

5

Oliver Freaney

*I was never afraid of anything — if you can
understand things, you need never be afraid of them.*

Oliver Freaney is chairman and founder of Oliver Freaney & Company.

He was born in Dublin on 16 November 1928, the son of John Freaney, a textile agent, and Maura Hearne, a draper. He was the eldest in a family of four, two boys and two girls.

He was educated at:
Scoil Cholmcille,
Christian Brothers O'Connell Schools,
UCD — B.Comm.,
Fellow of the Institute of Chartered Accountants.

He is married to Kathleen Mullen who was a secretary. They have seven children, five girls, one of whom, Ann, died, and two boys: Patricia (30), John (29), Eamonn (28), Grainne (25), Cathy (22) and Annette (18).

He set out on his own a year after qualifying as a chartered accountant.

He holds seven Railway Cup medals, thirteen Dublin Championship medals, three National League medals, one All-Ireland Minor and one All-Ireland Senior medal — all in Gaelic football.

I was born in Dublin and went to the Christian Brothers where life was uneventful and liberal. I was good at sport. In fact, I became an addict and lost interest in the books. I was constantly being moved back from the A class to the B or C class — at my own request! I played every game. Life was marvellous and the days were not long enough. Like most Dubliners, I am only one generation away from the country — my mother came from the bottom of the Comeragh Mountains. My father was from County Wexford. From the time I was six until I was sixteen, I was dispatched from the city to the green fields during the holidays to live on my mother's family farm. She felt I had to get a feel for the country life. I got to understand the agricultural scene and in later life bought a reasonably substantial farm in North County Dublin, something which amazed my friends, because they thought I was a true Dub who did not know anything about the countryside. I shall always be grateful to the Christian Brothers for the education they gave me in O'Connell Schools. They moulded me as they moulded so many others. They probably accounted for more than fifty per cent of male secondary education in the country at that time. I have since been very happy to advise them professionally with our firm.

After school, I went to UCD — we were comfortable at home and short of nothing. It amused me when I started playing inter-county football to see that the facilities were quite inadequate. I had come from a background where I was not content with cold chicken and ham after a match. I expected the best food and to stay in the best hotels and to have the best transport available to bring me all over the country. I suppose that made me unpopular with a few officials until, here in Dublin, we revolutionised the whole scene. I spent little time studying in UCD, but I went right through without stopping and managed an honours degree. UCD provided me with an excellent and liberal training in addition to teaching me the art of idling gracefully. I would not play club football with UCD — I stayed with our own northside club, St Vincent's.

Having graduated at UCD in the early fifties, I found, to my horror, that with things as they were then, my job prospects were zero. It was a terrible time. The university people were telling us that maybe we could get a job in the civil service, maybe Guinness. October came and the conferring of my degree, and there was nothing available. The choices were the boat or accountancy and it was even difficult to become articled to a firm of chartered accountants. Finally, I got a place with William Crawford who was Secretary of the Institute of Chartered Accountants and of the Institute of Bankers. For probably the only time in my life, I studied seriously as my father had become ill and, as I was the eldest son, it became apparent that I would have to accept responsibility. I even gave up playing football for four months. I got my exams first time and then at least I was in a position to look around for opportunities — but the fifties were grim. I decided that if I started up in practice on my own, things could not get any worse — they could only improve. If I could survive for a year or two, then something might begin to happen.

I had the advantage that from football I was now well known around the country. But I had little capital, I had just got married and I was forced to trade and to take casual night-time work to survive. Then things started to pick up. If I'd known things were going to be that difficult beforehand, I might never have taken the chance. Maybe it's a good thing we don't know what's before us in life. Then, I suppose I was fortunate. The first articled clerk that came to join me was Noel Fox. We have been working together since.

A thing that motivated me greatly in the fifties was the fact that I had deep compassion for all the people who had to go away. It has pleased me greatly that, during my lifetime, I have been able to do something about creating employment. People need not necessarily accept work in their own land, but they have the right of a choice to work there.

In the sixties, the late Sean Lemass set the country rolling again. He gave people confidence in their own abilities. I had by then met the late Ben Dunne, the founder of Dunne's Stores. I spent a lot of time helping him to develop the business. He was by far the most brilliant person I have met. It was a privilege to work with him for over twenty-five years. From the North of Ireland, he had a great love of all the people of the island and a burning ambition to be successful. He taught me that there were a million explanations for failure, but no excuse. He felt that if you worked hard enough, anything could be achieved. Having started in a small way, he built the biggest empire in the retail trade in these islands against all sorts of competition. His mission was to be of service to his country, to give employment, to give good value to the public. He felt keenly the need for Irish manufacturers to be competitive. He was helped very much by all his family: his son, Frank, who first established a grocery in Dunne's Stores. Then all the girls were involved in the business, and young Bernard has become, today, a brilliant facsimile of what his dad was. Ben Dunne was a compassionate and generous person. He helped people all over the place, but nobody ever knew about it.

During the sixties an event occurred which had a deep effect on my life — my eldest daughter died after an illness that lasted some years.

I had spent some fifteen years playing competitive football, and during that time my private life did not exist. In the years before my daughter's death, privacy became essential. Those years taught me the value of compassion. In the middle of a non-compassionate business world, I try to feel concern.

I had a more commercial approach to my profession than was normal. I quickly understood that people were more interested in what was going to happen tomorrow than in what happened yesterday. Commercial firms were changing from a scene where they waited with bated breath to find out from their accountants the previous year's results. That's where some accountants have failed today — they have not learned about commerce, whereas business people have become familiar with figures.

In the late seventies, we expanded our business and opened a number of offices around the country. At one stage we had some 450 people working in the firm. In the early eighties, we concluded that size was not the important factor. Noel Fox and myself decided that levels of expertise and specialisation were what was important. We consolidated our firm and moved principally back to Dublin. We are an Irish firm with large international associates.

In my days at school and college and when playing football, I had developed a sense of Irishness. That was made stronger in subsequent years when I travelled widely and came to see that we Irish are as talented as any other race.

It is important that Irish firms of accountants are free to make a contribution to the national business scene and to say what is right from a national point of view, but we must not work in isolation — close association with international firms is essential.

I detest bigotry or any select sections of society. I do a lot of work in Northern Ireland and, when I cross the border, I feel a sense of outrage when I see young British soldiers, through no fault of their own, standing there with weapons. I hate violence — life is God's gift to mankind and nobody has the right to take it away. But I feel that sense of sadness that Irish people and Ireland are not at peace.

I don't know fear. I live for each day and am confident in my own ability — maybe it was my mother who put that in me. She taught me to reach for the moon saying maybe I would at least catch a star. I was never afraid of anything — if you can understand things, you need never be afraid of them. Fear is born of ignorance. When you don't understand things, you go round in a fog of uncertainty.

Thanks be to God, I have enjoyed good health all my life — not that I take particular care of it. I play a bit of golf and walk a lot. But I think that, at sixty, I'd much prefer to be thirty! I think that the saying that youth is wasted on the young must be true. When I was young, you were expected to be seen and not heard, and had very little right to make any contribution. Now I try to spend a lot of my time with young people. It keeps my mind young. Young people today are much freer to make a contribution than they were in my youth and one of the great things about being sixty is that you can pass on to the young the benefit of your experience.

When I started in business, my godfather who was a very successful businessman used to bring me out once a month for dinner. I asked him how to become successful. He told me that it was very easy to be successful. 'You examine any problem very fully, you understand the whole thing yourself and you get good advice. Then you make a decision and then you act on that decision.' That sounded so simple to me that I spent the next two or three days asking myself why everybody wasn't successful. I went back to him and he told me that my capacity to be successful would depend on my ability to pick the right people to advise me. Later in life, I found that many of the people who were prepared to give advice were not able to solve their own problems. I have always made a point of looking for advice from successful people.

There are not many new things in life, just a lot of old tricks dressed up. I would advise young people that the best way to be successful is to emulate the success of others and not to strike out on totally new and untried paths. I agree with the old entrepreneurial motto, 'Always be second.' Success in life is not just luck. It doesn't just happen. It requires careful planning as well. But you require a certain amount of luck to be in the right place at the right time.

If you have experience, it is not difficult to see opportunities. It would be quite exceptional for a young inexperienced person, without advice, to see an opportunity. I know now what abilities and capacities I have. The Chinese say that when a man knows he's a fool, he's not such a fool.

I feel I'm good at judging people and I'm good in the business scene. What I am very bad at is that I have never had patience, and that it is getting worse as I get older. I find it difficult to suffer fools. I don't become crusty or argumentative. I just don't waste the time. I am prepared to tolerate lazy fools but busy fools upset me. I am a bottom-line man and I find it hard to get into detail. That becomes worse as I get older because I see that I have less time in front of me — I want to get to the bottom line more quickly.

Coming back to this personal freedom thing. When I got married, we had our honeymoon in New York where I was offered quite a substantial position. I didn't take it because I wanted to work in Ireland.

I have talked about contentment which to me meant doing what I liked with people that I liked. In this way I could acquire an inner feeling of contentment. I grew up in a very happy family, all of whom graduated from university. My wife is tremendously loyal to me. I have often said to her that, if I ended up singing in a bus queue, she would be holding out my hat. I hope this will not require to be proved.

In my football days, I knew every little town and village in the country. Things have changed now very much for the better. That has been my greatest single source of satisfaction. We came from the poor fifties into the better sixties and into the beginning of the seventies, when there was a certain amount of euphoria and we were in danger of losing the run of ourselves. The eighties have taught us many lessons which will stand us well. I am confident of the future and believe that Charles Haughey has the dynamism and ability to do for our country in the nineties what Lemass did in the sixties.

In my early days in St Vincent's, the GAA was not important in Dublin. We started an all-Dublin team — people had to be born in Dublin. The first county team I played with when I was sixteen had mainly players who had been discarded by other counties and just lived in Dublin. We decided in St Vincent's that we were not going to play for the county until we had an all-Dublin team. We were unbeaten for about seven years and played championship matches, sometimes before 50,000 people. Everybody turned up to see us winning — well, half to see us winning and half to see us being beaten! We developed a tremendous sense of loyalty to one another: people like Kevin Heffernan, Denis Mahony, Des Ferguson, Jackie Gilroy, Fr Michael Cleary and many more. That fellowship has been there all my life on the northside of Dublin. I'm a northsider and there was always a great sense of comradeship there. Even now, although our offices are on the southside, I feel a sense of freedom when I cross the Liffey going home in the evening.

Friends are very important to me. I suppose you're lucky in life if you have a dozen good friends. I get great pleasure from the success of my friends. I get pleasure from the success of any Irishman, and yet there is still the old Irish thing where success is resented, where people think that if you are successful, it must be because you did something that was almost dishonest. Thankfully that's changing as we become less insular.

Over the years, I have analysed for myself what our strengths are in this country. I think it principally comes down to three: firstly, agriculture, which is our basic industry and has really been very badly developed over the years; secondly, tourism, which we are now beginning to develop; and thirdly, the service industries. These are the areas which governments over the years should have mostly concentrated on. Developing manufacturing industries that are taking the raw materials in from thousands of miles away seems to me an unsound policy. We are just beginning to see the huge future for tourism. Where in Europe can you get a beach like you get in Kerry or Donegal or even in County Dublin? People will at last have the option to stay here and work. It has saddened me over the years to see our young people in New York or London always saying, 'I am going to go home', and knowing that they will never go home. The Italians choose to live in Italy and the French choose to live in France. In the future, people in Ireland will have the opportunity and, I hope, the hunger for success at home. In the knowledge that the hungry fighter fights best, I am excited at that.

6

Billy Hastings

I just love getting up in the morning and going to work. I'm sixty-one but I still feel I am always preparing — always preparing to do something new, something good, the big move. I still feel I'm only laying down foundations.

William Hastings is Chairman and Managing Director of the Hastings Hotels Group Limited.

He was born in Belfast on 17 October 1928. His father was William Hastings, a publican, his mother, Jessie Grace Waters, a schoolteacher. He was the youngest son in a family of five, one brother and three sisters.

He is married to Joy Hastings, who was a teacher. They have four children: Julie (28), Howard (27), Allyson (26) and Aileen (23).

He was educated at the Royal Belfast Academical Institution.

He is chairman of Northern Ireland Venture Capital, a director of Northern Ireland Tourist Board and of Queen's University Business and Industrial Services and is a director of Bank of Ireland Management (NI) Ltd.

He is a Lloyd's Underwriter.

He is a Fellow of the Institute of Directors and of the Hotel and Catering Institutional Management Association, a council member of the Confederation of British Industry (Northern Ireland) and a past-president of the Chamber of Commerce Council.

He is a past-chairman of the Northern Ireland Institute of Directors, of the Ulster Licensed Vintners Association, of Belfast East Rotary Club, of Northern Ireland Hotels and Caterers Association.
He was a city councillor for Belfast from 1970 to 1973.

He is a past-president of Dundela Football Club and a past-captain of Mahee Island Golf Club.

He is a board member of Down Cathedral, chairman of Help the Aged, Northern Ireland Branch, and a trustee of Help the Aged, United Kingdom.

He is chairman of Volunteers NI (an independent charity set up by the Prince's Trust).

He was awarded an OBE, is a Justice of the Peace, was conferred with an honorary doctorate of the University of Ulster and is a Paul Harris Fellow of International Rotary.

I was born into a normal middle-class family and lived in suburbia in Belfast. My father was a fairly successful, hard-working and popular figure in the community. He was a local publican. My mother had been a schoolteacher, but she stayed at home to bring up the family. I went to the local primary school until I was twelve years of age and thence to the local grammar school and did not distinguish myself in anything other than passing my examinations as they came along. I was usually about middle of the class. Seventeen was decision time — would I go on to university or further education or go to work? At that time, a friend of ours, a successful timber merchant, offered me a position. That was 1945 and there were great shortages of timber. I decided to go to work, to have a bit of money to go on holidays and go to dances and do all the things young fellows want to do, rather than go on and be educated and have to wait for my two shillings a week pocket money.

I enjoyed the timber trade enormously — I think those were the most formative times of my life. I did, amongst other things, time and motion study, and learned that everything in business must be measured. I did not call it time and motion study then. It was just getting the most out of every day, getting the biggest load of timber on to the cart and getting your horse away first. It was very basic training but it taught you how to be more efficient, how to turn things round. The timber planks coming in were 2½ in. thick and with what was called a centre cut, you got two planks of 1½ in. We would always try to get planks that were 2¾in. thick, put a centre cut and sell them off as 1½ in. planks which they weren't really. You were ⅛ in. out at each side. You might call that cheating but it was all part and parcel of the timber business. If a customer wanted 10-foot planks, you sold him 'selected lengths' and that got you 15 per cent extra. Of course, we tried to sell everybody 'selected lengths' so that everybody paid the 15 per cent premium. All these little tricks were giving me a basic training in business. I was learning that you've got to take the maximum out of every situation and, working in the docks, you learned pretty fast how to take care of yourself. At seventeen or eighteen I was in charge of dockers and, with timber being so scarce, the different merchants were concerned to get their quota. I was not satisfied until I got a little bit more than the quota.

I was very happy those years. I learned good things and bad things — I learned how to back horses! I never learned how to pick winners. All the dockers were studying horses, so I studied them too. There was a tipster in the *Daily Express* called Riddle-Me-Ree who had a rhyme every day and the last word in the rhyme was the name of the horse. I suppose he was as good a tipster as any of them because none of them was any good. I used to back sixpence a day from my pound a week, but my boss was very generous with bonuses. I got an enormous sum — £100 — twice a year. It took all the money I earned to keep me. I used to go to a dance on a Wednesday and a Saturday night and probably have two Tuborg Gold beers to give me Dutch courage. I was probably smoking ten cigarettes a day — and there were holidays. It wasn't a question of blowing it — you don't blow a pound a week! I didn't have to give up any money at home. I could keep it all, but I had to buy my own clothes and I bought a motor bike, a Royal Enfield 125. It cost me £48.

My father had died in 1940 when I was twelve years of age. He had left four public houses: two for my brother, Roy, and two for me, with an overdraft of £3,000 on each estate. That does not sound too much now but, at that time, it was about half the value of the pubs. He was male chauvinist — he left the pubs to the boys and a couple of private houses to the girls — and my mother lived in the house in which the family was brought up, quite a good one. We were not poor, we were not wealthy.

You can imagine that in 1940 the pub business was not great, so my brother dabbled a bit in property, buying wee streets of houses where the rent for each house would be nine shillings a week. He just tolerated the licence trade, but he did buy other small pubs as they came along. He and I were not close socially because of the age difference between us. He was more the conformist within the family, while I was a bit of a rebel, doing my own thing. When I was eighteen, he took me out to lunch and said, 'Do you know that you own two pubs?' I am not sure that I even knew I did at the time and, in any event, I could not have cared less. He said, 'You have those two and I have those two and I have acquired a couple more. You can come in and work with me or, if you don't want to, that's all right and I will take care of your pubs for you.' I didn't dash in. I had to think about it for a wee while, and then I went to work with him. It was a remarkable relationship — I could not have told you which pubs I owned or which he owned. We both just did our day's work.

My brother was a councillor at twenty-one, the youngest ever in the Corporation. He assumed some of my father's mantles: they may seem unimportant, but he was president of Dundela Football Club, something I did subsequently. Whenever I was president of it, it won the Irish Cup! Small things, but they give you an indication of things you fall into that were created by your father, and then sometimes you create your own.

At twenty-five years of age, Roy was told that he had high blood pressure. He died at age thirty and the years in between were very difficult because he was very active. He died from Bright's disease, a kidney disease causing high blood pressure and the higher the blood pressure the more damage was done to the kidneys — it's something that can be cured now. He did extraordinarily well for his short life but, towards the end, I was taking on more and more. When he died he left me his assets and he left his mother well fixed, something my father had also done. He left money to my sisters. He also left me an overdraft. I took on some of his mantles: I joined the same Masonic Lodge; I took on his position in the football club; I became involved in the Licensed Vintners' Association, though I don't think I was as good at those jobs as he was.

I now had a rag-bag of not very good, working-class pubs, bits and pieces of not very good property and a fair bit of an overdraft. I was also responsible for the management of three pubs owned by the Old Bushmills Distillery, another job inherited from my father. I had started a small wholesale business — really to sell to myself. It was a central buying store. There was no such thing as future planning — these things just evolved. I got married when I was thirty and it took about two years for all these different businesses to settle down, to find out if I was really making money, what way I was with the bank. It never struck me to go near the bank for a discussion about my future — I just lodged the weekly takings and I had a good accountant, Rollo McClure.

I wanted to buy the pubs that we had been managing and I went to Wilson Boyd of Bushmills, thinking that I would get them at a favourable price. After all, we had built up the business in those pubs. Wilson Boyd had never checked on us — not a penny went into the wrong pocket, or ever would. He said he would have to think about it and came back with a valuation of £100,000. I was shocked. This was twice what they were worth. I told him so and that, in any event, I did not have £100,000. He said, 'I'll throw in Mary Craig's of Coleraine.' I told him I did not want Mary Craig's of Coleraine. He said he would throw in Dundela football grounds as well. He was getting no rent for them. He ended up putting in all that, and two shops in Conns-water and £5,000 worth of 'new' whiskey, on which he would make nothing because of his tax situation, but which I could sell for £13,000. He kept on throwing things in, but it was not a good deal in the end.

I just did not like working for him while he owned the pubs. This had nothing to do with him or his personality, I just wanted to work for myself. So, although it was far too much, I paid the £100,000. The funny thing is, I don't ever remember having a problem getting that £100,000 from the bank. I don't even remember asking them — I remember going in and telling them what I was doing. Now, Wilson

Boyd had also told the Bank of Ireland what he was doing and they could not refuse him. So, perhaps, that was why they could not refuse me. I did not go any further than the local manager, a wee man called Mr Napier. I was getting married and I sold the whiskey off very cheaply and sold the football ground to the club for a very favourable price to them, £2,000, and I sold a couple of the wee shops. Anyway, I got back the guts of £20,000. That made things tolerable.

I bought a house when I got married. It cost £6,500 and I got £4,000 from the building society. I remember we had to repay £33 a month and my giving the wife £50. That was only thirty years ago and that was enough to keep her ahead of the race. One of the smartest things I did was getting married to my wife — she was more structured than I was. She was a schoolteacher and a proper lady, while I was a wee bit careless and harum-scarum and doing things off the top of my head. She ran the home and organised me. The new relationship with my wife, whom I was trying to impress in the early days, and, indeed, with her mother who was still alive, did me no harm at all. When you get married you do change to some extent.

I started to sell off the lesser pubs which I did not really like — not for big money, mind you, but to make the bank situation a bit more agreeable. I had a young family coming up and was reasonably prosperous. The pubs were making good money. The wholesale business, which I had started as a sideline, began to develop. I was working very hard — I worked hardest in my life from thirty to forty. I went down to my wholesale business at half-past seven in the morning and got it off the ground, went from that to the pub business at half-ten, late afternoon, back to the wholesale business, went home for my tea and then back to the pubs in the evening, with the few exceptions when I did a bit of gardening. Saturday, I played golf and I did not work at all on Sunday. It was a pretty full calendar.

In 1964, I was not getting that much satisfaction out of the pubs and I bought the Adair Arms Hotel in Ballymena, simply because it did a good bar trade and I could understand that. I had a wee hankering after what the hotel business might be like and I started to spend a bit of money on it. It gave me a taste for the future.

Meanwhile, I became the agent for Carlsberg and for Teachers and I had a little bottling plant in Lord Street. All these blossomed and, along the line, because I had been chairman of the Licenced Vintners, I was appointed to the board of the Ulster Brewery Company Limited which was taken over by an English company, United Brewers, which was subsequently taken over by Bass. I ended up sitting on the local board of Bass Ireland Limited. They had a brewery on the Glen Road in Belfast.

In 1969 the wholesale business began to go particularly well, not least because I had a base to put my beers and spirits into. We had a guaranteed trade and, beyond that, we had five lorries on the road. With a friend, I set up a company which ran the food and drink for Nutts Corner Airport. When it transferred to Aldergrove, we got the concession for there and ran it for six years. With another consortium, we also bought some hotels in the Isle of Man and did some catering contracts. This may sound very impressive, but I was a half-partner in the Aldergrove operation and a third-partner in the Isle of Man operation. I eventually sold out my one third share for £25,000 having paid £10,000 for it — there was no big money in it.

However, the airport company was doing well and out of it we bought a house in east Belfast. You could not get a pub licence in the area but, if you had a 10-bedroom hotel, then you were OK. We bought the house, made it into a hotel, and the hotel itself became more profitable than the bar-trade. My partner, Billy Hamilton, died and I was left with the hotel. I said to Billy's widow, Ruby, 'You get the hotel valued. I don't care what the value comes out at. I'll give you ten per cent on top of that.' Ruby very happily took her money, and I took my other share. Trust House Forte took over the airport franchises and that was the end of that company. I have since spent a lot of money on that hotel and it is now one of my important assets.

All these things were going on at the same time. I bought, for £40,000, Cyril Lord's hotel at Ballygalley. The Culloden Hotel was for sale. I wasn't going to see it — it was a small hotel run by Mr and Mrs White of White's Bakery. They ran it to such high standards that they nearly killed themselves. Don't get me wrong. They are still living and well and I am very friendly with them. I was not really interested because the bottom line was nothing like the effort.

I was lying in bed with one of my very rare illnesses, mumps, of all things. The accountant came through to me and said that the price for the Culloden was £100,000, but the whole thing hinged on the tax losses that could be acquired with it and which would give us a bit of an edge. That seemed to be OK. I gave the go-ahead to buy and went back to sleep — and that was a major step for me. I now had eight pubs, I think, and four hotels, none of which was of any substance. They all needed an enormous amount of money spent on them. The wholesale business was growing apace and demanding more and more money because, with the Carlsberg and Teachers' agencies, the more you sold, the more credit you had to give. The better I did in the wholesale business, the quicker the overdraft went up. Bass offered to buy me out and I did the deal with Sir Robin Kinahan and joined the Bass board at a fee of £2,000 a year — I think to continue to keep an eye on the business. I got £125,000 and that was the start of me in the hotel business because, for the first time, I had real money.

I did not have the money for long because two propositions came on the market. One was Jury's hotel in Dublin and the other was the Ulster Transport Authority Hotels. Jury's was on the market at £1,300,000 and the UTA Hotels were on the market at whatever they could be bought at — subsequently, I bought them for £600,000. This was 1970. There were six hotels and they were in very bad order. I bought them in June while they were still making a profit. With internment in August, they just died completely. I now had ten hotels, four plus six, none making money. The pub business, however, was still profitable and I never put any effort into it.

I started to spend money on the Culloden and to develop the Stormont Hotel. The best UTA hotel was the Midland and it is now an office block where you're sitting. The other UTA hotel left is the Slieve Donard, now doing very well indeed. The City Hotel in Londonderry was blown up two or three times — I did not do well from that, but I got some compensation. The Rostrevor Hotel was a glorious blaze in 1974. I did quite well on the compensation from that and it was very timely. I spent a bit of money on the Northern Counties Hotel and did not fancy spending any more, but was able to sell it to the man next door. I did a Houdini act with the Laharna Hotel — one of those big old touring hotels that had long passed its usefulness and was I glad to get out of it! The whole business was now cleaned up, with the pubs making money and the remaining hotels still requiring a lot of money.

Around 1980, I started to sell off the pubs — or use them in a different way: the Clock Bar is now the Bank of Ireland, for which I get a good rent. Another pub I had on the Ormeau Road is now let out successfully. The others were sold one after the other. That was the best thing because those working-class pubs proved to be a disaster area. I had a hard enough time with them during the seventies, but the real badness came in the eighties. There is now no way I could even trade in those areas — they are really bad.

That ended stage one of the hotels and now I am looking forward to stage two — which is their real development.

Along the way, I got into all sorts of wee business adventures, none of which made a lot of money, but I enjoyed the sociability. I also became a member of the Northern Ireland Tourist Board. I became a Lloyd's underwriter — that's very simple, you just sign a wee form and they keep on posting

me cheques. I have been, amongst others, chairman of the
Hotel and Catering Association. All of those things are very
social — you go and meet people and it's all part of your
business. Now I am President of the Chamber of Commerce.
I was a city councillor from 1970 to 1973, when the Government took over most of its powers. I went up for election
against Paisley's candidate, a man called Gunning.

I was a Unionist because my father and brother were
Unionists. Then this man Paisley muddied the water, didn't
he? I was approached because, in the dark days of 68/69,
they were having difficulty getting candidates for the council. I was fairly popular in East Belfast. There were three
candidates when I went for selection. One was Leonard
Steinberg. Now Leonard Steinberg was Jewish and I was
a local East Belfastman, Protestant and Unionist. You'd
think it would be no contest. We had to present ourselves at
Brookeborough Hall and I was treating it all in a rather
cavalier manner. I asked Leonard what we had to do. He
told me we had to stand on a platform and tell an audience
of forty people what we were going to do for the constituency.
I knew fine well what I was going to do. I was going to go on
the City Council and say things as I saw them and enjoy myself with the sociability of the thing and not worry too much.

That night, in the Brookeborough Hall, when we'd had
our tea and biscuits, Leonard and I were put into a back
room. Leonard was all poshed up with a velvet collar and a
brown bowler, the paragon of the successful businessman. I
think he was quite keen to get in whereas I felt that City
Hall would be a lovely place to be able to park your car.

My turn came and I was quizzed up and down, something
I was a little resentful at. Then they asked me what I thought
about Sunday opening. Being a publican, I said I thought it
was ridiculous that golf clubs and hotels were open and that
pubs were not. I went on at length and there was a hush in
the room. I also said that only lunatics would tie up the swings
in the children's playgrounds. These were the lunatics I
was talking to! One of the men in the room — he's dead

111

now — was Mr Pasmore, the head of the Orange Order. I went for a walk while Leonard was on stage and, of course, he had all his homework done. He didn't fancy any Sunday opening. I came back and had a cup of tea with him and we were both called in to hear who had been nominated. It never occurred to me that there had been a contest. I scraped in, twenty-one to nineteen. I should have won forty-nil! I don't know how Leonard thought he was going to win in the first place but he nearly did. Leonard subsequently went off to Manchester and I was one of the people he tapped to start a new business. He went public and I got ten times my money back. He is now hugely successful.

Paisley's wee man, Gunning, was a decent enough poor soul but I won against him. That was supposed to be a stepping stone into wider politics but I was not interested. I became President of Dundela Football Club and, after that, Captain of Mahee Golf Club. You would think it was a busy life but all these things evolved. They were the social things, but business and social blurred and merged. I could never think of business as a chore. I always enjoyed it and it became a social thing too.

I was very lucky. My children were growing up and my wife was looking after them very well. They're adults now, much cleverer than their father if it goes by degrees. I have a son and daughter in the business with me — my daughter with three degrees, my son with his law degree and his membership of the Institute of Chartered Accountants.

The Culloden Hotel now has ninety-three bedrooms and a separate grill-bar in the grounds called the Cultra Inn. We'll be building on more bedrooms and a leisure complex and, nowadays, you're looking at £80,000 per bedroom — there's a lot of money involved. It's a far cry from the Culloden Hotel with twelve bedrooms that I bought for £100,000. We have two other fairly major hotels, the Stormont and the Slieve Donard. We have three minor hotels, Ballygalley, Fir Trees and the Adair. I have a pub in town called the Drury Lane and one in the suburbs called the Corner House and another pub — so, in all, two grill bars, three pubs and six hotels and a fair bit of property which have been fall-outs from things I had acquired over a period. I am about to embark on a £9 m. development programme over three years for the hotels.

Now, I feel I'd like to buy something new and I'm in the very nice position that I've got cash in the bank. You would think that with high interest rates now, there would be plenty of opportunities but, strangely enough, nothing is going cheap. Or maybe I'm losing my nerve. I might now have to leave the big moves to my son. I've missed one or two things recently because I thought they were not worth the money and they proved to be very good buys. I now feel that my memory and experience and length of time in the business are working against me. Either that or I'm going to lose all reason and pay far too much for something! I would love to move out and I have had a look at Dublin.

I have planned nothing. I would just meet somebody and something would come out of that. I am always buying a few shares in this or that and there are winners and losers, but I always make sure that the fountain, the core business, is pouring from the centre before I interest myself in these wee tadpoles.

In private life, I don't live extravagantly but I'm not miserable with myself. I've got my Rolls Royce and my other car, and my wife has her Mercedes. We live in a very comfortable house and look after it well, Simmy Island, on Strangford Lough, one of the most beautiful places in the world. There's a causeway to it. I own a few acres around it but it is not over-pretentious. We go on good holidays and have a nice apartment in Spain. My wife is very social, too. She has her interest in Combat Cancer and various women's organisations. We're never in.

I'm sixty-one but I still feel I am always preparing — always preparing to do something new, something good, the big move. I still feel I am only laying down foundations.

My father died when I was twelve but I remember him saying, 'Always keep a good overdraft — that'll keep your head down'. I'm a bit unhappy at the moment to have actual cash in the bank because it really is wrong. I've a bit of a careless life-style because I am not responsible to banks or to shareholders. I am really not responsible to anybody but myself. Everybody needs a boss and the banks are as good a boss as you can get. Every time I had an overdraft, I could go out and buy something because it wasn't real money. When you have money in the bank and go out to buy, it's real money you're spending. Whatever I do, I shall finance it myself. I have no intention of going public. No, I have not quite lost my nerve.

I just love getting up in the morning and going to work. I enjoy meeting people and doing things and making conversation. As well as the relaxed times, like making conversation with you here now, Ivor, there is also a lot of routine day-to-day work to be done. There are difficulties and disciplines. There are men who grew up with me and had better chances but have not done so well. I paid attention to the discipline of doing well the ordinary, routine, dull things like, for example, taking stock in the pub and having it done faithfully and having accurate weekly reports, so that you knew exactly where you stood. I insist on knowing exactly how we are doing. It's no use thinking you're doing well and then finding out that you are not. A lot of my colleagues in the trade did not have much discipline. I always believed in paying my accounts monthly, on the nail — that's an old-fashioned sort of thing. Consultants will now tell you to take as much credit as you can, but I don't do that. People who do smart things get away with it for a while but, eventually, nobody wants to do business with them.

When there are difficult things to be done, you have to face them and handle them. If you try to avoid them, they will only multiply. I have never been in the least worried about having to fire somebody who has done me wrong or done a wrong thing. You can't go through a career of forty years trading with people, without having ups and downs and disappointments and betrayals, but they have never preyed on me. I have had far more pleasure than pain out of the people I have worked with. One of the best employees I ever had, Philip Maguire, was shot dead going around with the wages. It was just robbery, just badness — people were gun-happy in the seventies. It was awful sad that.

I am an optimist — I do things and they come right. I'm not all that clever — inflation has been a great friend of people like me who have been optimistic without any real cause. An amount of things came right just because inflation assisted. Some things you did right anyway, and that, of course, was an extra plus! I have an awful lot to be modest about but I seem to have an ability to make people enthusiastic, like when I was chairman of the Institute of Directors or now, as President of the Chamber of Commerce. Anything that was going, I was always happy to assist — like giving lectures to the students in the university on catering. Maybe that's why I got my honorary doctorate! I don't know why else I got it! I don't think I'm all that good at things, but what I do like to do is to go on and on. I don't see any blue lagoon at the end of it all — I have been in a blue lagoon since I was born! When I was riding my motor bike, it was the greatest motor bike anybody ever had. I don't think there is any blue lagoon over the mountain. It' s all great, here, now.

I was born into a Unionist Protestant, not a Catholic Nationalist, family and that is the way you are. Unionist, Protestant and middle-class was a lovely way to be born in Northern Ireland sixty years ago. I was very lucky because I was in the licensed trade and it was ninety per cent Catholic. All my mates in business were Catholics and my friends at home were Protestants. That meant that Catholics were not different from Protestants with me, whereas a lot of my friends have never met Catholics. Isn't that an extraordinary thing? The Vintners' Association was a Catholic organisation and I was chairman of it at twenty-eight when a lot of forty and forty-five-year-old Catholic publicans would have given their eye teeth for the job. Maybe they thought it was the time to let a wee Prod in! My eldest daughter is married to a Catholic and it is not a big thing with me, but I can understand people who cannot move out of the environments in which they were born. I was a Unionist because I was born into it, but then I saw it meant being part of the United Kingdom and I liked that, nothing more, nothing less. I had happy years in the Corporation and then the difficulties arose and I could not get out of it fast enough — I did not want any of the bickering and fighting. The years passed and I heard many Unionists saying things that I did not like, and I did not want to be classed with them. An opportunity arose for me to assist with the Conservative Party in East Belfast and they assured me that they were going to talk pure politics and not to bother with religion and such like. I am now President of the East Belfast Conservative Association. I now feel more comfortable because I have not heard anybody there say things that would be offensive. So I have found a lovely wee niche there but I am not going into the front line, for election or anything like that. I am not a political animal. I wasn't basically uncomfortable being a Unionist, but I was increasingly uncomfortable with the direction in which they were being led in recent years. I was an O'Neill Unionist. That died and I was not happy with Unionism ever since.

I think it would be very hard to get devolution to work here now. I am not going to bother thinking about it. When people are being shot dead all over the place, there is no easy answer. The worst thing about it is that the troubles are being used by evil people for intimidation — and I think drugs and intimidation must be the two greatest evils in society. We're lucky in Northern Ireland that we have the cleanest record in ordinary crime, including drugs.

Unfortunately, the Anglo-Irish Agreement is now being used by the Unionists as an excuse for not participating in talks. The DUP used the Agreement to their own advantage. All reason would say that with things like 1992, and the developments in Eastern Europe, the men of violence would become increasingly isolated, but that presupposes that they fight by the Queensberry rules. At the end of the day, the big fellow, the bully, gets away with an awful lot. Years of development of kindness and of love can get destroyed in a minute by the bully.

There will have to be some third dimension — I am not sure what — to take us out of this situation. It can't be religion — the Protestant churches in the North are all empty. The Catholic Church has lost a lot of grip. The evil people don't care about the Catholic Church but use it when it suits them.

Maybe it's a good sign that the protagonists are getting smaller in number. The extreme-thinking people are shrinking. They can't get a rally together any more. But there is still a latent extremism that can be roused — there's a badness in us. I am going to a rugby match this afternoon and if an Ulster player gives an All-Black a thump, I'll say, 'Good on ye!' If an All-Black does it, I'll say, 'Look at that brute!'

7

Eddie Haughey

The end is never near. If you get to the end,
you've had it.

Edward Haughey is chairman and managing director of Norbrook Holdings.

He was born in County Louth on 5 January 1944. His father was Edward Haughey, a company director. His mother was Rose Traynor, housewife. He was the youngest in a family of three: one boy and two girls.

He was educated at Christian Brothers School, Dundalk.

He is married to Mary Gordon Young, a solicitor. They have three children: Caroline Phillipa (14), Edward Gordon Shannon (11) and James Quinton Stewart (9).

On leaving school, he emigrated to the United States where he became involved in the pharmaceutical industry. He subsequently founded Norbrook.

He is a director of:

Bank of Ireland Management (NI) Ltd,
Norbrook America Inc.,
Acorn Inc. USA,
Bombardier Shorts,
Norbrook BV,
Warrenpoint Harbour Authority,
Southern IteC Limited.

He is a committee member of the Department of Agriculture Strategy Committee for Research, a former chairman of the Institute of Directors, Northern Ireland, a member of the Northern Ireland Partnership and a past member of the Council of the Confederation of British Industry.

He was awarded the OBE and is a JP.

He is included in Debrett's list of distinguished people for 1990 .

W hat did I want to be? From day one, the veterinary profession stuck out in my mind because the vet was a highly respected member of society — at least from my farming background. I asked myself if I was the kind of person who could sit down and study for years. But I got bored with study — not with school. I loved the debate with the teachers. However, I found I could grasp things more quickly than most and then I just sat there, bored. That didn't apply to all subjects — I trailed at maths. I was good at English and science subjects. They didn't have a selective system where you could choose your subjects like you can now. You had to take what was given to you. I think that was the reason why I did not do my Leaving Cert. or go on to university.

I had three uncles living in the US and there was always the encouragement to go out to them. I went to stay only a short time. When I got there I liked it. I got a very low job in the sales office of a pharmaceutical company. I liked it because I was meeting new people. I had, for the first time, to use my own initiative. I decided this was the kind of industry I would like to be in and I set my mind to achieving that.

The world was changing at the time. You had the Common Market. The talk then was like the talk we have now about 1992, except it was a much greater step. American drug manufacture was highly controlled compared with the UK and Europe. In Europe in those days, anybody could make anything. In the US you were subject to rigorous examination on qualifications, on the suitability of the premises, on the efficacy of the drug. The thalidomide thing had just passed. The FDA attitude was that if you say no, you are safe. It was obvious that the rest of the world was five years behind the Americans.

It struck me that the major drugs would just be going out of patent by the time we were joining the European Community. I felt that, when the Common Market came, we would have very tight legislation. I thought I'd better get back home and get something off the ground before those laws came into force. I knew the business, not from a purely technical angle, but from a technical/commercial viewpoint. I felt I knew it better than most of my colleagues in the UK and Europe, the reason being that they were working with one or two products, while the company I was with in the US had a wide range of products. I was sales manager after two and a half years — the Americans measure you on bottom line.

They were surprisingly conscious of the Common Market. They saw a united Europe as a threat. For example, the Italians were big in the pharmaceutical industry — no sooner would a new drug be out but they copied it — something the Americans thought might be protected under European Community law.

I had my Green Card in America and was, if you like, just a step away from citizenship. I got my call-up papers for the Vietnam War. At this time, Vietnam was becoming increasingly unpopular and I did not feel any sense of guilt when I decided to return home. My father had died before I was born and, by that time, my mother had moved from County Louth to Northern Ireland. I was coming home to an environment I did not know all that well.

I made contact with some people in the pharmaceutical industry whom I had known by reputation from the US. I discovered that, for a product to be credible in the UK market, it had to have 'Made in the UK' on it — no indigenous Irish firms had credibility. I had two options — to go to Britain or to stay in Northern Ireland where I could legitimately label 'Made in the UK'.

This was 67/68 and the preliminary thunder of the troubles could just be heard.

I set up my own company, bought some veterinary product from friends in the industry in Holland, put my own label on it and sold it locally. I had also decided to go into the medical field, but then I realised that there was a very substantial turnover in veterinary products. You would, for example, use a hell of a sight more penicillin on animals than you would on humans. I stuck at importing for about two years and, at the same time, I was beginning to get a little production unit off the ground. I expanded it and began to sell in England, where I was challenging the major companies, like Glaxo, ICI and Wellcome. Their attitude was dismissive: 'Who is he? A small Irish company — the product can't be good.' It's easy to put across that kind of propaganda and you must remember that selling to a professional man, a vet, is different from selling to a layman. He has his reputation to protect. It's very easy for a multinational to sow seeds of discontent and that was a major hurdle.

I expanded my manufacturing and learned that it was very difficult and expensive to become both a good manufacturer and a marketer. These were the strengths the multinationals had: they had the money to market and they had the technical know-how. I had built up a lot of know-how — when you are starting from zero-base, you learn all the wrinkles. We now had the Common Market, decimalisation and the Medicines Act. I went around the multinationals and said to them, 'Look. Veterinary is a very small part of your whole operation. Why don't you let me make the products for you?' I got one of the smaller multinationals to come along with me and that gave us greater credibility. Eventually the others fell in and now we control twenty per cent of the world market in the products we make. We control sixty per cent of veterinary antibiotics in the UK market. We make them under our own label or under everybody else's. In Australia we have eighty per cent, and in Canada, thirty per cent. We are beginning to make inroads into the American market.

The time had come to start looking for new products and for spending money on research and development. We took a firm decision to spend ten per cent of our annual turnover on research. We have a very good team and I believe we have one of the largest farms in the business in Europe for target species of animals. We have to produce an enormous amount of data to satisfy EC standards. We now manufacture for all the big names in Europe. Austin Darragh in Dublin did great work in the medical field — we should be doing the same in the veterinary field.

I believe that any project I go into should earn money from day one. When I started from a zero-base I did not have much alternative! Recently I bought three companies in the US: one was in medical — ophthalmic; one was in veterinary ; and the other was in research. They were all in the same group and had lost $20 m. in three years. I got involved with them because they had a number of licences I was using to sell my products in the United States. It's enormously difficult to get FDA licences. If you are going to generate them yourself, you are talking anything from one to ten million dollars and two to ten years. It takes that much time and money to generate the scientific data. I found an easier way, a company with a number of licences they were not using. I got an exclusive lease on them for ten years. While I was using these licences, the company went into receivership. I had no alternative but to buy the companies — otherwise I would have lost the licences. Companies in Chapter 11 in the United States are watched very closely by the courts. Practically every cheque has to be authorised by them. In the State of California, that's not a cheap thing to do. I was able to turn those companies around into profit in the second month. We went in, stripped them down, and started again from zero-base. I spent three months there myself and took with me one of my scientists and one figures man. There were 300 workers — I got rid of 100. Not only were they the fat of the company but they were also incompetent. When you're in the business, you know all about the other companies, and I was able to pick up a good manager from another pharmaceutical company. We were able to sell two of those companies — the medical and the research — to a company called Akorn. It's a public company in the US and we now own sixteen per cent of it. I tell you that story to show that money can be made from day one if you are aggressive enough about it. You might say it's ruthless to slice 100 people off just like that, but it's a fact of life. If I had not done that, I would be doing a disservice to the other 200 people.

We are now at the point where we have to decide whether or not to diversify and to expand into a much greater market. When you are on the upward spiral you are caught on a hook. We also have to come up with new products. We have some very novel products in the pipeline — they will be at the forefront of research. We are turning over £30 m. at the moment — I want to be at £100 m. in four years. I will achieve that and I can't do it unless I go public. You have heard it said, 'He grew too fast.' We are at the stage that unless we share, go public, we cannot continue to grow.

My market is now the world, including the huge pharmaceutical companies. It's about fifty per cent big pharmaceuticals, fifty per cent our own label. Things are changing dramatically around the world. Glaxo and ICI and Wellcome have sold off their veterinary businesses. Now you have one large American company owning at least two-thirds of the world's turnover. That has very little effect on me because they still have to come to me to have the product manufactured. I always insisted on a ten-year contract. You can appreciate that, if a fellow is out of the business for ten years, it's very difficult to get back — so we feel pretty secure.

The future strategy would be to go back further in the chain of production. Pharmaceuticals are so expensive to produce and the technology is so expensive to generate that people tend to specialise in certain areas. Now, instead of buying raw material, we are going to produce it. It's more profitable but, more important, it gives you more control when, like us, you have such a large slice of the world market. You say it is not widely known that I am the biggest in the world with my particular products, but that does not really matter so long as we are known in the pharmaceutical industry.

I am looking forward to going public. I shall retain seventy-five per cent control. The cash will enable me to expand and that more than compensates for any small loss of autonomy. Anyway, you have to be philosophical about it — you can't have the best of both worlds. Sure, things will be different:

you have to watch the Stock Exchange, you have to keep the investors happy. If somebody wanted to sue me for $50 m. now, I would not worry because it would not be true. When you are a public company it could be a different matter. It could affect your reputation. You're just much more political.

You have to go back in time to understand what has caused the present situation in Northern Ireland. If it had not been for the two world wars, Northern Ireland would have been a different place, if not politically, certainly commercially. Before 1914, twenty per cent of the people of Northern Ireland were illiterate, you had heavy industries and you had linen, controlled by four per cent of the population. That four per cent were the people with the know-how, the education, the ability and, indeed, the power. When the 1914–18 war came, they were the people who went to fight and many of them did not return. You lost a whole generation of education and ability. Then the Second World War came. Many products were in demand which were not all that difficult to make, and the people were here to make them. When the war was over, you had the fall-off in linen and, to a lesser extent, in heavy engineering. That was substituted by synthetic fibre, controlled by not more than ten of the multinationals. All the marketing, all the design, all the research were done outside Northern Ireland. You had two generations of people just making things. They were just told to do it and they did it reasonably efficiently. That all collapsed and now we are here with not a great deal of experience of, or exposure to, entrepreneurialism, to the real world. The intelligent people exploited the situation. The aristocracy joined the Orange Order to enhance their power.

Stormont suddenly collapsed and the power-map changed. Power went from the aristocracy, who hitherto had held on to it so successfully, to the fellow in the street who, naturally enough, was neither capable of, nor organised for, handling it — power became diffused. That's when the paramilitaries on both sides stepped in and seized it. Suddenly, a fellow who was working in the shipyards or in a bar in Newry or, indeed, unemployed, had a degree of power. The movement was very rapid, quicker than anybody could handle. If Stormont had not been prorogued, if the system had been changed, made democratic and the ordinary fellow in the street could participate . . . but then violence intervened. Something like that happened in the South in 1922, but you didn't have the fundamental cleavage that you have in Northern Ireland. I believe that can be solved only by Dublin and London and, one way or the other, you will have to have winners and losers. The statesmanship will be to mini-mise both the winnings and the losses and try to get people together — but a degree of enforcement has to be there.

I don't see that the Anglo-Irish Agreement makes any real difference other than providing a talking place and I suppose talking is always useful. But the Agreement makes no fundamental difference. In fact, it is seen by one section of the community as a defeat. History would suggest that the Irish don't like defeat regardless of which side of the divide they come from. The Agreement may be seen by one side as an achievement, by the other as an irritation — perhaps it's neither strong enough nor weak enough.

From an industrial point of view, I think Northern Ireland has something going for it. People are loyal — they have this background of making things. Our image abroad is ter-rible and it calls in question our credibility — with contracts and such like. I think if we were not able to brand our goods as made in the UK, we'd be in some difficulty.

I think, inevitably, Ireland would make more sense as one unit. One unit as part of the European Community is the ideal. I would say to people that Northern Ireland can suc-ceed. We have the academic institutions to give people the training — the one thing we lack is the industry to give them the experience. I worry a lot about the continuing violence breeding the wrong kinds of basic attitudes.

Violence will not end until you remove the cause — the trick will be to do that in such a way that neither side feels defeated. There has to be movement on both sides. I don't think that is achievable within the ambit of the Anglo-Irish Agreement. I think it is much more than that. Peace will come when people feel that they can't justify supporting the men of violence any longer. Let me give you an example. If there is trouble in the Republic — somebody tries to rob a bank — it will be put down very quickly because people don't support it. They will not support something which is to the detriment of the whole community. There *is* a level of support in Northern Ireland and you just can't trample all over it. I agree with the statement by the Secretary of State which drew such criticism, that ultimately the terrorists cannot be defeated simply militarily. I believe the future lies in talks between London and Dublin with *everybody* involved. If people are excluded, for whatever good reason at the time, you will build up trouble in the future — and things change.

It's not a popular thing any more to be a politician in Northern Ireland and, therefore, the best people are not getting involved. This was not true in the past. In the Republic, at least some of the best people get involved in politics. In Northern Ireland, people just don't want to get involved because there is nothing credible there to do.

Where is the middle ground? I believe it will be in an administration that shares and accepts. I believe you would have to take security out of it because one faction would use it to beat the other. You could begin with an Assembly that was involved in industry, tourism, the environment, agriculture, housing and local government.

It does not really affect me in my business life — I don't see myself working in a Northern Irish or Irish context, but in a global one. You have to think globally and understand the fellow in South Africa or Kenya as much as you understand the fellow in London or Dublin. I never think politically when I am dealing with people. I think purely commercially. Living here, I have always made it a point not to get involved in politics. If you don't get involved in politics, I don't think the politicians will bother you and the same goes for the paramilitaries. I have been in business here for twenty years and I have never had one problem. I hope the people would respect my views — I believe I act fairly and firmly. My eye is always on the bottom line and I don't care who helps me to get there. I treat everybody on their ability, not on their background or political views.

I think I always knew that if I could see the picture in the round, I would achieve it. When I was buying those factories in the United States, I literally had a vision of a huge factory. I can visualise things in concrete terms. Unless you have the vision in the first place, how can you achieve it?

When I take over a new business, what I bring to it is the philosophy that there is no obstacle that can't be overcome. It's not such a big task to make a product and to sell it. The only bit extra that I'm asking, is to make it efficiently and to make it good. If you do both of those, it's very easy to sell it.

Look at the way the Germans take a pride in their work and in their machines. I was in the Bayer plant in Liverpool recently. The chief executive asked me to come along on Saturday. The workers were there visiting with their families, simply to admire the plant. How can we instil that kind of pride in Ireland? I believe we have to increase the incentives. Louden Ryan, as Governor of the Bank of Ireland, has been very keen for the wives and families of staff to get to know the business and has been the cause of organising occasions for them to do so. Once a year in Norbrook we have a dinner for all the employees with their wives or husbands or boyfriends or girlfriends. You need this to get a degree of understanding and respect and pride. Of these, pride is the most important.

You can't police quality. It is right throughout the process and in the very premises. Quality depends not on inspection but on the pride and the goodwill and participation of everybody. Quality is an attitude.

I think I am emotive, fair and aggressive. People tell me that I have the ability to work with somebody right at the bottom of the line as well as at the top. I don't see that as an ability, I see it as a normal requirement. I think a good manager has to apply himself to the situation as it is. I once did a test in America and one of the questions was, on a scale of one to ten, where would you rate yourself for aggressiveness? My answer was that, today, I might be seven, tomorrow, two. You must be prepared to change as the situation demands it. So really I'm aggressive when it's called for. Let me be clear. By aggressive I mean actively expressing your displeasure at not achieving what was desired. You can express displeasure by simply saying to somebody, 'Come back when you have achieved the results.' You can be aggressive by refusing to see somebody or, alternatively, you can take somebody in and have a lot of volume in your voice. It's just a demonstration of your unhappiness at what has not been achieved. It's energetically going at what you require.

I don't know whether people fear or respect me. I think they would be concerned if they did something wrong and had to face me. I think they would respect my reasons for being unhappy. I don't get annoyed if people disagree with me — I simply try to understand them. I think it's very important that you listen. One of the most important words in any vocabulary is *why*. If you keep asking why, you'll very quickly understand the other person's point of view and, indeed, learn a lot. If, as I said earlier, you can see the whole picture and you keep asking why a person disagrees with you within that context, you may add more flesh to the bones of your knowledge.

Ninety per cent of my problems come from working with people who do not have the ability to achieve — or cannot both see the whole picture and achieve. You can get one person who is very good at solving a little bit of the problem — and you want people like that. But if you need ten people to complete the picture, then you are in danger of a lot of disagreement. Better to have three people who can both focus on the detail and see the larger whole.

I don't take each step at a time in isolation. When I take each step, I see it as a single move towards an achievement. You must see the full picture. That's where most people fail — lack of understanding, lack of thoroughness. They don't see the thing in the round. The best example I can give you is an architect. What distinguishes the old masters from the rest is their ability to see the whole thing in all its detail. Building a business is like that. If you are going to be successful, you have to see through all your decisions in context and in detail. You must deal with the detail as part of the larger context.

I was brought up in a reasonably comfortable home, but my mother was a very thorough woman with very high standards. Every Saturday night you had to have your bath and you had to have your shoes polished for Mass on Sunday morning. Your shoes might not be all that good but they still had to be clean. We didn't want for anything but we did not have an abundance of it. We got our first car in 1956.

I am a stickler for perfection. The difference between perfection and not is very little, but it makes an awful lot of difference to the end product. I get very annoyed if I hear that somebody has not been efficiently dealt with. You can indoctrinate people, you can expose them to the inter-national market place, but if a concern for quality is not inherent in them, they will never have it. I believe it comes primarily from their parents' influence and, if that is not there, no amount of practical or academic training will com-pensate for it.

There is nothing that annoys me more than going into a hotel and finding dirty ashtrays, or a towel in the toilet that has been used by six people before you and has not been changed. In business, however, you just don't have the time to go back to the cradle to teach people. Maybe it's our par-ticular stage of development as a country — though I don't think that's all of it — but there seems to me to be insuffi-cient appreciation of good and beautiful things.

I pick all my senior people myself and a lot of it is intuition. The person must have the proper academic qualifications but I am always suspicious of someone who has spent too long in academia. I worry about their vision being a bit tunnelled. I like somebody with a good technical training and a lot of exposure to the coalface of industry and who understands that technical training is just a means to the end. It is not an end in itself.

The end is never near. If you get to the end, you've had it. It has to be a perpetual end for which you need customer satisfaction, quality, efficiency. The goal, or the end, is a figment of the imagination down the line.

I spend fifty per cent of my time travelling, and a lot of that would be selling. Selling is the important thing. Anybody can make anything — not everybody can sell it. Selling is what the money comes from. The back-up to that is new products, technology, efficiency, quality. One also has to look at the politics involved — you have to have a certain mentality to work in the African countries and a different one to work in the Americas. I have now grown to the stage where most of my time is involved with policy or with looking for acquisitions.

I don't differentiate between Monday and Sunday — I don't have that many outside interests. I have my wife and family and I like, if possible, to get back at the weekends. My children are at boarding school and that leaves my wife at home at the weekends and I am always conscious of that. I have a flat in London and a house at Heathrow Airport within walking distance of Terminal One. If you are coming in early in the morning from a long flight, it's nice to have somewhere you can throw your shoes on the floor and get your head down. I have my diary set out for me three months in advance and I manoeuvre that as necessary. I am a director of twenty-eight companies. If I did not have Norbrook at the moment I would have sufficient income from my directorships to survive. One of the biggest problems I have is reading through the volumes of stuff and trying to decipher what is gloss and what is reality. Anything that is of real importance, I have to see the fellow's face. I manage to attend most of the board meetings but, where that is impossible, I will read all the material and let the chairman have my views in writing. I believe it is very important to support the chairman at a board meeting. I have no qualms about disagreeing where I find it necessary.

I see the chairman and chief executive as a synergistic duo. They have to work very closely together. The minute there is a crack in that relationship, it's gone. I see the role of the board as falling in behind the chairman. The chairman has to be the link between the chief executive and the board. There is no way around that — if it works any other way, it is inefficient. All boards are different and you have to understand the politics of the situation but, ninety-nine times out of a hundred, if I had a difficult point to make, I would warn the chairman in advance. It's important that the chairman goes into a meeting understanding what his board members are thinking.

I have no qualms about being unreasonable if a situation requires it. Is it fair to ask someone to travel back and forth across the Atlantic twice in one week? The answer must be no. But, if it meant getting a very large contract that was necessary for the survival of the company and the fellow refused to do it, then I would dismiss him. But it would be unreasonable to ask him to do it just for the sake of asking him to do it.

I am a great believer in paying well and giving good conditions, but it has to be a two-way thing. Everybody must have their pride and their status — they are great motivations.

I have no regrets about not having gone to university. I have thirty Ph.D.s working for me and over a hundred and fifty graduates. To my mind, a Ph.D. is somebody who knows more and more about less and less. That is very good as a means to an end, as a segment of the whole we were talking about earlier. But I think you also need the fellow with the clear uncontaminated mind who can put all the segments together to make up the whole picture. If I had had a university education, I fear it might have channelled me in one direction and perhaps I would have been able to examine my actions more carefully and not take the risks I did. I think an academic may know the theory but not the nuts and bolts. The practical man may know the nuts and bolts but not understand the theory behind them — you need both.

I am blessed with a photographic memory except for names. Maybe that's a mental deformity! But, put me under pressure, and I can recall all details and facts and figures.

I like beautiful things and good quality things — you can appreciate in a quality thing the effort that somebody has put into it. I enjoy my house and the things around me. It provides a marker on my way. The only thing is that, when I achieve something and look back on it, it appears very small — I want something, and when I get it I consider it small.

I am not insecure but I am not content because I am ambitious to achieve more. Is that ambition? I don't know. Is that ambition stimulated by a degree of insecurity or by something else? I don't have an answer to that. Perhaps security is not the right word. I feel I can cope with any situation I choose or even that I am thrown into. If I am thrown in to manage a company that is outside the ambit of my previous experience, I still feel I can sort things out. I feel confident and competent enough to debate with any expert in his own field, because I feel confident enough to learn from him. My desire to understand is probably what gives me that confidence. I can see gaps in my own knowledge but I am always willing to learn. Am I bright? Do I have a degree of intelligence? I think there may be three kinds of people: there is the fellow who hears something and can regurgitate it; there's the fellow who can hear something and understand it; and then there's the fellow who can hear something, understand it, and add to it. I believe I can see the whole. I think I can distinguish the various parts and understand what is relevant and not relevant, what has to be integrated, what has to be discarded.

I started off with £1,200 I brought back from America. I had my stock bought in, but the cash was not flowing and the bank manager was on, and it was during those early and difficult days that I learned one lesson that has stood by me since: never promise to do something that you cannot do. You can be as clever as you like. You can manipulate as much as you like. But you can never cheat. The day you cheat, that's the day you're on the road down.

There will always be dark clouds on the horizon. Disaster strikes only when you run away from them. You just get in there and manage your way through.

8

Mark Kavanagh

*The world assumes that to be successful today
in business or management you have to be
single minded to the point of being blinkered.
I believe there is room for a much wider range —
for a mind that can play many different parts.*

Mark Kavanagh is joint managing director of Hardwicke, chairman of the Custom House Dock Development Company, chairman of Mount Salus Press and chairman of Catering Ireland Limited.

He was born in Dublin on 16 March 1945. His father was Montague Kavanagh, managing director of Hardwicke. His mother is Penelope Woosnam, housewife. He has one brother and three sisters, all younger.

He was educated at St Gerard's, Bray, Co. Wicklow and at Downside School, Somerset.

He was married to Lynda Hitzeman (who died in May 1988).
There are three children: Keelin (18), Michael (11) and Serena (7).
On 1 December 1990 he married Kathleen Shugrue.

He worked in England particularly with Jones Lang Wootton in London. In 1969 he was general manager of Screenprint Limited. Later, sales director of Mount Salus Press, in 1975 he became executive chairman of that company. In 1971 he formed Catering Ireland Limited and opened Captain America's Restaurant. In 1978 he took over the position of joint managing director of Hardwicke Limited and became chief executive of Hardwicke American Properties Inc. In 1982 he joined the board of American Exploration Company. In 1985 he became a director of Phoenix Park Racecourse Ltd. In 1986 he joined the board of Imry International plc, which later became Imry Merchant Developers plc. In 1987 he became chairman of the Custom House Docks Development Company Limited, a consortium of Hardwicke Limited, McInerney Properties plc and the British Land Company plc.

He is a council member of the British Irish Industry Circle and a governor of Aravon School.

Where to start? I have very few memories of school. I am always impressed with people who seem to remember in great detail their first day in kindergarten. My memories are none of them very bad, none of them wonderful. I was not a terribly good student nor was I a notoriously bad one. Funnily enough, I now have some close friends with whom I was at a convent school in Chapelizod, while I have very few close friends from my days at Downside. I also have some very good friends from St Gerard's in Bray, my prep. school. It's a big school now, but when I was there, there were only sixty or seventy boys — great! Before going to Downside I had to go to England for a year to a crammer, a little school near Malvern in Worcestershire. Downside — a big English public school, Catholic, a big abbey, not a school I enjoyed terribly. I didn't not enjoy it but I was in that difficult position of an Irish boy going to school in England. Your schoolfriends were with you during term and then you came home to Ireland and left them in England and found that your Irish friends had built their own relationships. There are some advantages in an English public school education, but I don't really think they outweigh the disadvantages. On the whole, an education in Ireland makes a lot more sense today. I think the only reason Irish people might send their children to English public schools today is a snob one. On the other hand, you become more outward looking from an early age if you are educated in one country and live in another. It's a decision I have to make shortly and my current thinking is that my children will be educated here.

The only two things I wanted to be when I was growing up were, one, a barrister and, two, an actor. They are rather close in some ways. I didn't manage to do either.

When I left Downside and came back to Ireland, I did the Trinity Matric. I found that the idea of driving in from the country each day, doing three or four hours' study a week, living on £2 pocket money and sitting around the coffee bars of Dublin did not appeal to me at all. So I got a job as a sort of rep. with a firm of industrial cleaners for three months. I absolutely loathed it. I was tramping the streets of Dublin, cold-calling, trying to persuade people to let us clean their offices. It was good for me in that, perhaps for the first time, I was beginning to see what the real world was like. I was dealing with cleaners who were real Dublin, and me with my accent which, in England, is not completely English and, in Ireland, is not completely Irish.

My father and great-uncle had a business in leather and wool. We were the dominant family in that business in Ireland. My father created Irish Leathers and there was Judd Brothers, whose name is on a plate outside the door here still, but who are now just a trading company. We had a very big wool and hide factory in Hendrick Street. There was an interlude while I spent a year in France immediately after school, both to learn French and to learn something about the leather business — this was before property development played any part in the family's business. Hardwicke was formed in 1934 and was actually based on a company established in 1880, set up by my great-great-grandfather, Michael Judd. In 1934, he split the company in two for his two sons. One half became Hardwicke and the other Raglan. The Judd side of the family now have Raglan, and the Kavanagh side, Hardwicke. In those days, they had 4,000 tenants in Dublin, most of Donnybrook. But they weren't exactly profitable because there was rent-control. The outgoings exceeded the income. So from about 1934 to 1960, Hardwicke was little more than a small, rent-collecting investor. That's the way it was as I left school.

Anyway, I worked in a leather factory in France for a year, lived in the local pub and enjoyed every minute of it. Nobody in the village spoke a single word of English, a tiny little village called Saint Liguaire, between Niort and La Rochelle. After about five months, I went to Paris to meet my father and mother and was told, at a dinner party, that my French — the French of Saint Liguaire — was appalling. It was not socially acceptable — I spoke slang in the local dialect. Eventually I learned to speak proper French. I played for the factory football team, then for the village football team and then for the local town football team. It was one of the coldest winters in history — the river was frozen two feet thick, and the port of La Rochelle was partly frozen. We worked outside with great barrels of raw hides. My grandmother was French and I have always liked the French.

A year later, after the Trinity Matric, I spent five years in England, living in London. My father had expected me to join the business but he was very much one of those people who tell you what is expected of you, and then leave you to make up your own mind. He did not give much encouragement. He would rarely give you a straight opinion if you asked for one. He would give you the pros and cons of something and then tell you to make up your own mind. He took the view that he had brought you up, educated you, and after that it was up to you. He would drive you mental with frustration trying to get an opinion out of him about what you should do: 'It's entirely a matter for yourself, Mark. You've got to realise now that you are old enough to make up your mind about the future.' I'd say, 'But you have a lot more experience than I have, Dad. What would you do in my situation?' 'I'm not in your situation.' He also had been to Downside. During the war he fought with the Lifeguards all over Europe and I am told he was a soldier who 'had a good war'. He never discussed it except, very occasionally, late at night over the second half of a bottle of brandy. I think he would have stayed in the army if he had not had to come back to sort out the family business. It seems to me the real soldiers never want to talk about it.

I can't say that he came back because the business was in deep trouble though I feel that perhaps it was. But he was a man who did not communicate at all with his children. None of us knew anything about what he did — it was just the way he was. I think he relied on my mother to tell us what he wanted of us and, in particular, what he really felt about us individually. He was too shy or reserved ever to say,

'I love you.' I know we all relied on mother to bind the family together and to help us get his agreement to anything we wanted to do.

We did not live a life of enormous luxury but we certainly were not poor. I expect our life-style exceeded my father's income. His life-style was the 'best' but without being conspicuously extravagant. My parents entertained a lot, something my mother is particularly good at and still enjoys an enviable reputation for.

The leather factory in Hendrick Street/Benburb Street burnt down. There was an amount owing from the insurance company and my father decided that the property business was rather more promising than the leather trade. He asked me, 'Do you like the leather and wool business?' I said, 'No. They smell.' He said, 'Fine. That's all I wanted to know because I'm making a decision about whether we rebuild the factory or do something else with the money.' So Hardwicke in its present form really began in 1959/60.

They had an opportunity to buy the old Harcourt Street railway station. That railway station is what the company that I run today with Paul Byrne is based on.

I think I had something like eleven jobs in five years in London. They ranged from driving a laundry van to washing taxis to being sales manager for a company that dealt in fire equipment to working in a racing car garage to working with Jones Lang Wootton. I did that last one because that's what my father wanted me to do. He had decided that I must come into Hardwicke eventually. He felt I should have a professional qualification to do that, that I should become a chartered surveyor. I worked with Jones Lang for a year and a half in management, which was awful; I worked in rating and valuation, which was extremely dull; and I worked in the Croydon office on the leasing and marketing side, which I enjoyed enormously. The partner in charge of the office was hospitalised and a junior and I ran it and did everything — it was a period when Croydon was going through a boom. We used to report to the partner first thing in the morning in hospital and then report back at the end of the day.

I did not want to be a chartered surveyor. I left Jones Lang Wootton and after a discussion with my father — for discussion read deep disagreement — he said, 'Mark, you can't make up your mind about what you want to do. You don't stick at anything.' I told him I would tell him when I knew my mind. At that stage, it had not occurred to me that earning a living was any more than paying the rent and providing for whatever other needs you might have. Hence, I was probably doing what everybody else did who went to UCD or Trinity — having my four or five years to make up my mind, only I was being paid. I loved the period in London and, despite my limited means, managed to live quite well.

Back in the early fifties, Norman Judd had founded Mount Salus Press, a small letter-press printing outfit, and had somehow badgered my father into taking a share and joining the board. My father was not in the least bit interested in it. Mount Salus Press had bought Screenprint with which had come a large factory in Artane. My father and Norman Judd wanted to know what the factory was worth as a property. I spent a week in it, came back and told my father and Norman Judd, who had not asked me, that the factory was viable as a business. Jack Corr, the managing director of Mount Salus Press, agreed with me.

There and then I got the job as general manager of Screenprint Limited for £12 a week and a second-hand Vauxhall Viva. I had been earning about £5,000 a year in London. So there I was, back in Ireland, running a business I knew nothing about, in an industry I knew nothing about, £84 a week worse off and driving a second-hand Vauxhall Viva.

Probably few people have had as much influence on me as Jack Corr. He was tremendously hard working and committed. His poor wife hardly ever saw him. He was, with my mother, the first serious supporter I had in my life.

Whatever it was, Jack saw something in me and he encouraged it. There was nothing we liked better than slipping over to the pub in Ringsend on a cold winter's evening and having a glass of Redbreast.

At Jack's insistence I joined the board of Mount Salus Press, my father agreeing very reluctantly. There was a proposal that we buy 50 per cent of an educational publishing company called School and College Services. The price was £10,000. The board — really my father and Norman Judd — turned it down. An ironic twist to that story is that, sixteen years later, I bought that company for Mount Salus Press, 100 per cent of it for £800,000. It just shows how the wheel turns and how right Jack Corr was. He and I were absolutely certain it was the right thing to do.

Up to the time I joined Mount Salus Press I had achieved nothing. I had no regrets about it but, really, I had not achieved a single thing.

Then I had met Lynda who had come to Ireland with a friend. She was American, with no Irish background. Her family was German/Swedish. However her friend was second-generation Irish and was coming to UCD for a year. Lynda said she would come with her as far as Ireland and then continue on her travels. In fact, she enrolled at Trinity to study psychology and philosophy. We met at a night-club in Dublin and for me, anyway, it was love at first sight.

I decided to leave Mount Salus. There was not much point in continuing in a company in which the board had little interest, and I was not going to become a printing rep.

Lynda, now my wife, was pregnant, and for a delightful year I was totally unemployed. I became a hippy with hair half-way down my back. When Lynda first met me, I looked exactly as I look today except twenty-five years younger. Within a year, with hair down to my shoulder-blades, my whole perspective on life changed and, in a sense, I went to college. I finally dropped out. The California flower-power thing was only coming into Ireland at that time. Lynda and

I were going nowhere — except to music festivals! — and it was great. Some of my friends were doing the same thing. Some were not and thought it very odd and thoroughly disapproved. My father certainly disapproved — I am sure my whole family did. But it didn't occur to me then, nor does it today, that what Lynda and I were doing was in any way wrong.

It was, however, a passing fad. 'Dropping out' — it's funny how dated that phrase has become — was not going to be forever. We were going to drop back in sometime. In a way it was really a sign of the fact that I did not have the faintest idea what I wanted to do with my life. I had no major responsibilities at the time. I had no major ambitions other than to have a good time. I was very laid back. Though, to be truthful, Ivor, it's hard now to know what I felt then. It's easy now to look back and invent emotions and justify them. As a result of falling in love with Lynda, I fell into her student life-style. Even before we married, we shared a house, but we kept on her flat in Ranelagh so that her mother would not be scandalised. Years later, her mother told me she knew all the time. The real reason we did not want to horrify her mother was that we did not want the cheque to stop coming through! Really, it was not a deliberate opting out. It was a life-style I fell into because I fell in love with a Trinity student. You see, from age seventeen, I had been working very hard indeed, mostly in London. I had missed out on the freedom that undergraduates enjoy. I had earned my own money — I hadn't depended on my father since schooldays.

Well, in fact, there is one story about that. He did have to bail me out once, largely because the friends I was sharing a house with did not pay their share of the rent. Years later he was giving Lynda and me a wedding present, a cheque. He told me that the amount would have been X pounds higher had I paid him back what I owed him when he bailed me out! He was a difficult man but I liked him. He quite liked me but he thought I was a terrible waster a lot of the time.

145

I was just as averse to being told what to do with my life as I'm sure he had been.

However, with marriage came the realisation that I had to take life a little more seriously. I decided to open a restaurant. That was the origin of Captain America's and now, nineteen or so years later, it is still there. Captain America's came out of the student life-style I had been leading: I realised that there was nowhere in Dublin catering for that market. I saw a picture in a Sunday supplement, Richard Burton and Elizabeth Taylor sitting in the back of a Rolls Royce eating hamburgers outside a little restaurant called The Great American Disaster. Their chauffeur had gone in to get them a take-away. I scraped together £50, went to London and got a job in The Great American Disaster as a bus-boy. With a second-hand Polaroid camera, I took pictures of everything in sight: chairs, grills, cutlery. After two days, they caught me taking the pictures and fired me. I came back to Dublin. Now I needed money. Through a series of approaches, I found four people to invest in a hamburger restaurant. The first was a perennial student at Trinity, Tom Haran. I persuaded him to put up £1,500 — the key money for an upstairs premises in Grafton Street. That's all the money we had, so we had to find more partners. We found three, two of whom were cousins, who were killed in a car crash in Ethiopia some years later — Randy and Jeremy White. They put up £3,000 and a Ghanaian friend of mine, a student at the Royal College of Surgeons, George Dodoo, put up £1,750. I opened the restaurant with most of that money still in the bank. I persuaded Bank of Ireland Finance, which used to be called Foster Finance, to lease me all the equipment. They were quite convinced from the invoices that it was new. They leased me second-hand kitchen chairs — I don't know if they'll ever forgive me for that.

With the leased equipment and the equity in the bank, we opened what turned out to be the most successful restaurant ever opened in Dublin. It was such a success that I could have, with my head chef, a totally uninterrupted chess game without a single customer coming in. It was full only for about half an hour at lunch time and half an hour in the evening. The thing that the newspapers thought was an instant success was losing money for the first year. Eventually, however, word-of-mouth, which is the only thing in that business, spread. It was good quality, good value, and we had pretty waitresses. Within two years, we could not handle the queues down the stairs.

That was a great period of my life. Lynda had a sandwich bar in the basement of the restaurant building. We lived at a very smart address: 16 Fitzwilliam Square — only we lived in the basement. That basement was also our office and it was where Keelin, my daughter, first came home to. We were flat broke. I was paid £20 a week by my partners to run the restaurant. My assistant, John McCormack, whose grandfather was the singer, Count John McCormack, was paid £15 a week. I had an old scooter — I could not afford even to get the starter-motor fixed. But luckily, Fitzwilliam Square was on a hill and you could push it down in the morning to get it to start. In those days traffic went down Grafton Street, so you could push it that way to get home in the evenings. We worked incredibly hard. I would get there at nine in the morning and leave at three in the morning. That was six days and nights a week, and on Sundays we did the accounts. We built and built and built, and it became an extraordinary success. Over those years, your children and your contemporaries' children would have worked there. Two of my four dishwashers had master's degrees and the other two had ordinary degrees. Captain America's was a fundamental part of my success because, if it was not for it, you and I would probably not be here talking today. Everything else followed from it.

The world assumes that to be successful today in business or management you have to be single minded to the point of being blinkered. I believe there is room for a much wider range — for a mind that can play many different parts. You ask me if I am a property developer, a restaurateur, a publisher, a printer. I answer yes to all those things. I am each one of those things if that's the role I am playing on a particular day. If I am chairman of Mount Salus Press then I am concentrating on that business and being a printer and a publisher. I must understand the business, I must understand the reasons management make proposals to me for investment and so on. To be good at what you do, you must have a genuine understanding — you can't do it from balance sheets or profit forecasts. But you don't need to be limited only to that. The following day I am a restaurateur, deciding whether the future for Captain America's is to expand or to sell. The following day (though, as you well know, all these can happen within one day), I would be acting as chairman of the Custom House Docks board.

Around 1974, Jack Corr died, a young man in his fifties. He taught me to believe in myself. He said to me, 'Mark, you are one of those rare people who can achieve anything if they want to enough. Your problem has always been can you motivate yourself enough, can the project motivate you, can other people motivate you. Once you take a real interest, you are unstoppable.'

When Jack died, Mount Salus Press was totally headless. It had lost its managing director, the board had no interest and there was no organisation structure. I moved in for about nine months at the board's request. The board was for getting somebody in from outside. On my advice, they appointed from within — Gilbert Brosnan — as managing director, which he now still is, and Eugene Tighe as deputy managing director and sales director. They are now heading up a company which turns over six or seven million pounds and makes a substantial profit. That company, when I came in, in 1974, had sales of less than £200,000. It did letterpress only in a converted hay shed in Tritonville Road. Now it is one of the best-equipped printing companies in Ireland in purpose-built premises. Its future will be one of steady growth, well managed.

The next piece of the jig-saw was the expansion of Captain America's. In 1978, I opened a second restaurant called Solomon Grundy's in Suffolk Street. It was not the enormous success that Captain America's had been, but it made a good, steady living. Then we really went mad. We opened a Captain America's in Dun Laoghaire at a cost of over £500,000. It promptly lost £200,000 in less than two years. I sold it for £60,000. From success to even greater success — a real loss of £650,000. That was nasty.

At the same time I had got involved in the Phoenix Park racecourse. We had opened a discothèque, a restaurant, four bars, you name it — a huge complex. We had done a deal with an English company whose parent was an American company through which they got 50 per cent of the action for putting up 75 per cent of the money. The Phoenix Park was a disaster at the same time as the disaster in Dun Laoghaire.

How the Phoenix Park thing happened was this. In December 1984 Vincent O'Brien rang me. The Patrick Gallagher empire had collapsed — he it was who was developing the racecourse. I met Vincent and within an hour he had persuaded me that not only were we going to do the disco and restaurant and so on, but that we were going to spend £4 m. in twelve weeks rebuilding his race-course and stands and everything else, so that it could be open for racing on 2 April. If it wasn't opened, Vincent explained, they would lose all their Racing Board dates. They would never get the Park reopened. In a moment of complete lunacy I said we could do it. There followed the most challenging three months' period I have ever known. For a relatively small fee, I managed to commit the entire top management of Hardwicke — Paul Byrne, my brother Morrough and myself. That is the sort of man that Vincent O'Brien is — he can persuade people. He is a delightful man, a genius, and has a way of asking you to do things that you can't refuse. 'Mark, I don't know anything about building. I don't know anything about catering. I just know about horses. Everybody tells me you are the expert on building and catering — so I go to the expert.' At four o'clock on the morning before it opened, my brother had gone off to get hamburgers. There were still 250 men of Sisks working there. I was standing half-way up a ladder shining a torch on a piece of timber that a painter was painting. We got the place open with a few cleaning bills from people who sat on wet paint.

The Phoenix Park and Dun Laoghaire were not the first things I had lost money on. In 1975, three of us bought a pub. Terry MacInnes, now sadly dead, and David Coyle, very much alive and a great friend of mine, and I bought The Auld Dubliner on the corner of Fleet Street and Anglesea Street, just down from the Stock Exchange. We paid £34,000 for the leasehold interest on the basis that we could buy the freehold for £60,000. Talk about three innocents. We never got to buying the freehold; it was never for sale. We bought the pub because it did a nice luncheon trade. People came from the Stock Exchange and from the Dublin School of English which was around the corner in Westmoreland Street — we used to take their luncheon vouchers — all very polite and well mannered. None of us had thought of checking what the night-time trade was like.

Now, I'm meant to be the guy with the experience — I'm the restaurateur — Terry was a photographer and David is a chartered accountant. I went into Pearse Street Garda Station to get what is known as the *ad interim* transfer of the publican's seven-day licence. I knew the sergeant behind the counter. He said, 'Fair enough. Which pub is it?' I told him it was the Auld Dubliner. He didn't say a word. He turned round, opened the door behind him which was marked 'Inspector', and said, 'Come out here a minute.' The inspector came out. We were introduced and the sergeant said, 'You'll never guess what's he's fuckin' done. He's bought the fuckin' War Department.' They would not allow any garda from Pearse Street to go in there alone — they had to go in in pairs. We had just bought the second most dangerous pub in Dublin.

It had four sets of doors. We had to close them all down except one, so that we could screen the people coming in and going out at night. We put on a couple of bouncers but they did not last long. They were like the new sheriff in town — somebody had to have a go at them. Eventually nobody would work for us. David and I decided we would do the door ourselves. I was still running Captain America's. Run is the right word. I used to have to run down Grafton Street to take over for the tea-breaks at the pub — to let the head barman off. David and I also worked weekends. Our wives were so concerned about us that, as soon as we got rid of the last customer at night, we'd have to call home to assure them that we were not in Jervis Street Hospital. All sorts of things happened in that pub. I was knifed and had a hypodermic syringe stuck in my side. The fighting in the pub had to be seen to be believed. The crowd used to come from Ballymun, Walkinstown, Artane and locally, and particularly for Wednesday and Saturday and Sunday evenings when we had singsongs in the back room. The locals liked us to know who actually owned the pub. There was a lot of struggling, of imposing of wills, on both sides.

In a pub that has a large local trade, the best weapon you have is to bar them. They hate that. It was the ultimate, and indeed the only, sanction we had. One or other of us was in the District Court every Monday morning prosecuting somebody. Still, somehow we managed to earn their respect. We even managed to redecorate the pub despite the locals' objections: 'What the fuck do you want to be doin' the place up for?'

We cleaned the place up, over time. There were some fabulous regulars — let me tell you about 'Muscles'.

I was hobbling around the bar on a stick one Saturday night. I had sprained my ankle in heroic fashion — jumping into a bunker on the golf course. Two junkies (male) came into the pub and locked themselves in the female toilet.

They could not lock themselves in the male toilet because there weren't any locks. I hammered on the door to get them out. The door burst open. One of them stuck a syringe in me and knocked me to the ground. The other came at me with either a bottle or a knife, I can't remember. Muscles was sitting at the corner of the bar, five feet nothing but all of those five feet solid muscle. He charged the two junkies and knocked them flying with backhanders. I shouted to David who leapt over the counter — this was real Wild West stuff — and blocked the door. David was a front-row forward for Lansdowne. He caught the two junkies, slammed their heads together like egg-shells, threw them out in the gutter and called the guards.

That may sound amusing and, in a way, it was. But there was a nasty side to it. Physical violence in a confined space, with people who respect nothing but physical violence, is an unnerving experience.

I promised my regulars that if Dublin won the All-Ireland, I'd fill the Sam Maguire cup with champagne and Guinness. You remember when the Sam Maguire went missing? It was in the Auld Dubliner for a few hours.

That pub was another part of life's experience. I learnt an awful lot about Dublin and a lot about myself. I learnt a lot about my friends, some of whom came into the place, took one drink and never came back. You could not blame them.

It took me about a year and a half to decide to get a headstone for Lynda's grave. Part of the reason was that I wanted to put something on it that described the person I had known and lived with and loved. What I put on it was, 'A free spirit'. That's what she was: free, pretty, amusing — people adored her. Everyone she met, somehow she touched their lives. I think in many ways Lynda was the acceptable face of me when I was struggling hard with the restaurant business or to re-establish Hardwicke. She maintained many of our friendships that I am sure, but for her, would have been lost, partly through not having the time and partly through not having the inclination. She was an only child and it broke her mother's heart to have her only daughter and her grandchildren 5,000 miles from Chicago. This wild will-o'-the-wisp person came into my life, swept me off my feet, and changed my outlook on so many things. We were partners; we were equals; we were great friends; we were fantastic lovers. We were all of those things. Over the past few years, friends have come to me and said how awful it must be, but my abiding feeling is how lucky I was to have known her. I'd say, 'Look, I've had twenty years with her. I could have had only two years and then this would have happened.' We did more living in those twenty years to-gether than any six other people I've ever met. We had a good life, great children, friends all over the world.

It was 3 May 1988. It had been raining very heavily for four or five days — most unseasonal. Lynda loved to go out riding every day with our nanny, Priscilla. Priscilla Clarke was a lovely girl who had been with us for five years. She was part of the family — she was like my eldest daughter. She was a great friend to Lynda and the children all adored her.

Lynda rang me about 4 p.m. I very nearly did not take the call — I was in the middle of a meeting. She told me that she and Priscilla were going stir-crazy, that they had not been able to get out of the house for four days. Now the sun was not exactly shining, but it had, at last, stopped raining. She said that she and Priscilla were going to go riding, but that they could not go for more than an hour because she had to pick up the children before six. I said fine, that I would give her a ring later on to let her know what time I would be home, probably around eight. It was one of the few, perhaps the only, conversation I had with Lynda that I did not finish by saying, 'I love you.' They are the sort of silly things you think about when something like this happens.

We had our meeting here, Paul Byrne and I, and, from about six, I started to telephone. There was no reply. I did not worry. I thought she had probably taken the kids to

McDonalds for their supper. When I could not get a reply at seven-thirty I thought it was very odd. Paul and I and Jody Carr, a very good friend, were sitting here when the phone rang about eight o'clock. It was my son, Michael, aged nine. He said, 'Dad, where's Mum?' He told me that he had just got dropped home by friends, that the house was empty, the doors open and no sign of Mum. I asked him if her car was there and he went around the side and came back and said that, yes, the car was there. I told him to run up to the stables to see if the horses were back. It was pouring rain again by now and he told me that the stable doors were open and there were no horses. I said, 'All right. I'll be home in twenty minutes, darling.' I turned to Jody and told him what had happened and he asked me if I would like him to come with me. I said yes. He followed me in his car. We had only been in the house in Enniskerry for six months. Before I got there, I knew what had happened. I just knew. I knew she was dead. I had the most extraordinary feeling driving over the little bridge near Powerscourt, and subsequently, of course, we found that Lynda had gone under that bridge.

I got home and there was Michael standing, wet through, outside the house, too frightened to go inside. Pulling up at the same time, was my neighbour, Margaret Doyle, who had been looking after our five-year-old, saying, 'Where's Mrs Kavanagh?' At that moment, Brenda Rohan, Ken's wife, from Charleville, one of our next-door neighbours, arrived. Ann Kavanagh, who lives next door was with her. They told us that the two horses had just been found on the road, saddled and soaking wet and that they had been taken into Ann's brother's stables next door to us — Larry Dunne, the local vet. I said, 'Bren, will you take care of the kids?' She said, 'What do you think has happened?' I said I didn't know but that Lynda was not there. Brenda took the children over to her house.

I can't really tell you the thoughts that went through my head. I did think that perhaps they had been kidnapped, but I thought really of an accident. I called the guards and they came. Then I called my daughter at St Columba's, Keelin, and luckily got her. No, I did not call her. She happened to call me — she was calling to speak to her mother. I said, 'Look, darling, I think you had better come home.' At that moment, Larry Dunne arrived. I didn't even know Larry at the time since we had been there so short a while. He said, 'Mark, would you like me to round up a few people to start a search?' Within twenty minutes he had fifty local farmers scouring the countryside. He knew exactly what to do. He had the whole search mapped out in his head. He just took over, and thank God he did. And we had to search the river.

People were fantastic. People we did not know at all came and searched for days.

The search got under way at about 10.15 p.m. that Tuesday night and we searched the river up and down. It was a foul night, driving wind and rain and you couldn't see your hand in front of your face. This little tiny stream, a tributary of the Dargle, was in full spate. It was a swollen, angry thing flooding down the mountain. We searched and searched and were getting desperate — the whole thing was so unreal. Keelin had arrived from school and joined the search. At about half past three, I said to Larry Dunne, 'We can't see any more. Let's call it off until it gets light.' By this time some more guards had arrived and Civil Defence, but nobody was co-ordinating anything except Larry. I should say that the local guards, Pat, Jim, Brendan and John, couldn't have done more for us during the next few days.

I went home and lay on the bed for about an hour. At about six, the first light appeared.

During the three days of the search I just did not know where to be. Should I be out searching? Should I wait in the house in case there was a call if she had been kidnapped? The guards were convinced it was a kidnapping. The Special Branch were convinced. Everybody was convinced except me. Charlie Haughey rang and asked me if there was anything he could do. I told him we needed some divers and possibly a helicopter — you've no idea how difficult the country is around Enniskerry, however scenic it may look from the roads. He was tremendously helpful and supportive. I presume that, at this stage, the government had been advised that it was a probable kidnapping.

I had called my mother-in-law's neighbour in Chicago and asked her to be with my mother-in-law in her house, to support her when the telephone rang.

By the afternoon of the second day, Wednesday, there were about a hundred journalists around the house. It had become a media circus, TV and everything. People had broken into the house. Another good friend, Sidney Minch, who now looks after security for us in the docks, told me I needed some men. The guards said it was not part of their remit to deal with the press. Frank Dunlop arrived and asked me if there was anything he could do. I said, 'Frank, your business is dealing with the press. Please deal with them.' He stayed out there five days, never went near his office, and handled it all for me. Ken Rohan, who was in London, came back immediately, and he and Brenda were there, and Brian O'Halloran and Catherine. All my close friends were just fantastic. And my family were so supportive, my mother and my sisters and my brother and his wife.

David Davies, along with Jody Carr and David Coyle, is one of my closest friends. David, at that time, was in London, chairman of Hill Samuel, the merchant bank, and a former managing director of Hong Kong Land. Pauline Canty, my secretary, had come out to the house and stayed there for the five days. I asked her to get David for me at half past eight on the Wednesday morning. When I told him what had happened, he just burst into tears and so did I and he hung up. At midday he walked into my house. He had literally walked straight out of his office in London, got into a plane and was with me by twelve. He did not leave my side for a week. He just walked away from everything he was doing. He helped me through the most awful things, making the funeral arrangements, identifying Lynda, things like that.

Those forty-eight hours were awful. We kept finding clues that might suggest she was kidnapped. By Thursday morning the police and David and everybody in the house were certain she had been kidnapped and, of course, I was praying that she had been. And then they found her, around lunch-time on the Thursday. I had to go and identify her, and that was the worst moment in my life. She had been in the river for two days — there are a lot of rocks in that river.

The public nature of the whole thing was so disturbing. It was on the front page of every paper, on every television screen — it was on television in the States — on every radio bulletin. It was almost impossible to keep the children insulated from it.

There were telephone calls from all over the world. People coming to the house I could deal with, but every time I went to the telephone I broke down. Somehow seeing and touching people was better.

We were still looking for Priscilla — her family were with me. It was terribly difficult for them. Eamonn Doherty, the Police Commissioner, was very good about things. Once Lynda had been found he redoubled the effort to find Priscilla. And Priscilla has never been found.

We sat down to plan the funeral — and we did plan it, because we knew it was going to be a very big affair. Lynda had been a Trinity Lutheran. The nearest thing to it would have been Church of Ireland and, in fact, the local vicar, Raymond Smith, had been most kind to us since we arrived in Enniskerry. The church in Enniskerry only holds about three hundred people. Fourteen hundred came to the funeral, many from the US and England, and, luckily, it was a lovely day. We had a very simple service and I asked everybody who was there back to the house afterwards. David Davies read one of the lessons and my daughter Keelin, another. I don't know how they managed it, but they did. Dan McInerney said to me afterwards that Keelin even had the presence of mind to switch off the reading lamp before she got down from the pulpit. About seven or eight hundred people came back to the house and we had a party, and that's what Lynda would have wanted.

During that evening, a strange thing happened. I had given Chris de Burgh his first job in Captain America's while he was a student at Trinity. I had told him that he would never make a singer or a song-writer and to stick to business studies — so don't trust my judgment when it comes to singers! Chris used to sit on a stool in Captain America's. I gave him £2 a night, a free hamburger and as much wine as he could drink. That was his first ever commercial singing engagement. We are close friends today. Anyway, people kept coming to me at the party and saying that Chris wanted to sing a song. I told them that I thought that would be in rather bad taste. I was a bit confused. I really let the party go on out there while I stayed in my office in the house. They kept badgering me and at eleven o'clock that night he sang, and then I understood the reason. He had written this beautiful song in honour of Lynda. He sang it to what was then about a hundred and fifty people in the hall and everybody cried except me. About an hour and a half later, he sang it to forty people and again there wasn't a dry eye. Except me — I could not cry that day. I just could not let myself do it that day in front of other people.

Chris put the song on his last album, something I was not sure about at first. But the kids were and said what a lovely thing it would be for Mum. Her mother said the same thing. So it is there with a dedication to Mark and Lynda.

When you lose someone unexpectedly, when you lose them through violence, when you don't know for several days whether or not you have actually lost them, and when all this happens in the glare of the media, you just cannot trust your emotions. It's a combination of numbness and different emotions sparked by different stimuli at the time. It's only later that you try and gather yourself together and figure out what you really felt. I have lost somebody with whom I intended to spend the rest of my life. I've lost the mother of my children. I get enormous moments of insecurity — not just from living without my partner and friend — but about the children. I can now cope with the first part, with myself, but how am I to know if I am making the right choices for the children? I don't know how to put into their lives something they've lost. How do you make sure that they come out the same person at eighteen as they would have done had their mother been alive? They've lost and I've lost the single most important person in all our lives. The children have taken a place of far greater import-ance in my life. Two or three years ago, other things were more important to me. My career, my ambitions, money — I don't know. Money has not mattered all that much to me. I have spent it when I haven't had it and I've spent it when I have. Money by itself is not a major motivation.

When I worked in Croydon I was going in the mornings in the opposite direction to everybody else. All the trains would be coming into London full of penguins and sardines. I and about five others had the train to Croydon all to ourselves. When I looked at all those grey faces crammed into the railway compartments, I decided that I was never going to live like that, that I was never going to work for anybody else. If I ever made a conscious decision about my life, that was probably it. While I will never work for anybody else, funnily enough, I don't find working in partnerships any way difficult. There are strains, but Hardwicke has always done joint ventures, usually with us as the managing part-ner or, occasionally, where we have a lot of respect for the other partner, we'll do it on a fifty-fifty basis. That is when people bring more to the table than just money. Money by itself means nothing. If you have a good enough idea and a good enough structure to put it into practice, you will always find the money. Money is a much over-rated ingredient in nearly everything it goes into. You remember I started Cap-tain America's without any money. When, eventually, my partners disagreed, I bought them out. Money is almost the least important ingredient in any deal.

People who are genuine entrepreneurs — and I suppose I am one — are unemployable. We're very rarely good managers. I suppose I can manage but it just doesn't hold my attention long enough for me to call myself a good manager. I can manage something for a year — for two years — and I can manage it very well indeed. It will eventually lose my attention and, as soon as it loses my attention, I am no longer a good manager. People have skills of that kind that I simply don't have. What I am a good manager of is people: I think I know how to motivate people, to enthuse them.

The Custom House was the greatest example of that in one way. The competition for it set us up against some of the most powerful development and construction companies in the UK, like Tarmac, Trafalgar House, Wimpy and Taylor Woodrow, to name just four. We won that competition through sheer determination to be better than anyone else. I started that process by sitting down and thinking for a month about who I wanted on my team. Who was number one in their discipline? Every single one of my first choices agreed to join us, not anyone else. I think that meant they thought that we could win and that I was somebody they wanted to work with. I told them the only condition under which we would enter the race was to be first, that we were not interested in coming in any other place. We had to be so much better than everyone else that, no matter how badly they wanted to give it to anyone else, they would *have* to give it to us. We couldn't compete on size with many of those companies; we hadn't any particular political clout; we had no large-scale track record. We had to be so much better that it could only be awarded to us on merit. I say that because there has been a long tradition in Ireland of all political parties rewarding their supporters. The seventies in Ireland was a time when it would be hard to say that morality was the first word on every politician's lips. Integrity was something that people had forgotten how to spell.

Really it was Charlie Haughey who caused us to enter the competition. He was making a video. The people heard that our offices were suitable and he asked if he could use them. I was having a cup of tea with him here and he asked me if I was entering the competition. I told him I was not, that it was unlikely that such an unprecedented plum would go to anybody who did not have strong party connections. He told me straight that the competition had been so structured, with independent committees and judges and so forth, that that just could not happen. Justice would not only be done but would be seen to be done. And he was keen for Irish companies to compete. With that assurance, we entered the competition.

We are a partnership of three quite separate and different companies. We in Hardwicke are also the developer, we are the project manager and we put the consortium together, invited each particular member, whether they were partners financially or professionally, to join us. Within the development, I have to range from being a finance man to being a leasing person to having some legal expertise to having a clear understanding of design — all of these facets go into being, supposedly, a successful developer. The Custom House is different from anything ever done before in Ireland because of its sheer scale and complexity. There are six tower cranes on that project and there have never been six tower cranes on a single project in Ireland before — it's bigger than Aughinish Alumina. I've got twenty-seven acres there. You see that spread out in the countryside and it looks like nothing at all. It's rather different in the middle of the city. We had to put piles sixty feet down. It cost us £1.50 m. extra, simply to remove methane gas silt. We have to have a management team down there capable of managing seven separate, sizeable, fast-track projects. To achieve that, we have taken from the contractors several of their normal functions and centralised them in ourselves. We take a day a week on the ESB's mainframe computer. We have a very large team down there simply to plan, design and manage. We had to produce that from a standing start, zero. The Custom House company was simply three people getting together, Hardwicke, McInerney and British Land. When we won the competition, the consortium did not have a staff, yet we were expected to be on-site within fifteen days of signing the contract, with excavation under way. We were. But I tell you that first year was very tough indeed. Everybody on my team was doing the work of three or four people, working twenty-four hours a day.

We were working from these offices to Boston. I had chosen the man I thought was the best waterfront architect in the world and he worked in Boston. We could not have won the competition without fax machines. Ben Thompson is the former Professor of Architecture at Harvard. He worked with Gropius. He is one of the great geniuses. I was warned that it would stand against us that we were not using only Irish professionals but I said I wanted the best. Of course, Burke-Kennedy and Doyle, our Irish architects, are excellent but neither they, nor anyone else involved, had worked on such a large scale before. Ben Thompson had.

I remember I was in here at eight one Friday morning for a meeting and I left at eleven on Monday night. All of us worked straight through the weekend. I felt that if I did not work half an hour longer than everybody else, where were they going to get their motivation from? It cost the company over half a million to run in the competition and if we lost we would get nothing — all the professionals would get nothing. There was no compensation for coming second, fifth or seventh.

The submissions went in on 1 September 1987 and in October the announcement was made that we had won it. There had been tremendous lobbying — it was unbelievable, but Charlie Haughey stuck to his word. We had been judged over thirty categories by independent judges. If you reduced those categories to ten, I learned subsequently that we scored nine and a half, and the next best had scored five and a half. That was the only way to win it. We designed a twenty-seven acre scheme, financed it and did everything else in two and a half months. It's two and a half million square feet. It's now taking us eight months to design an individual building — we didn't get everything right in that two and a half months. It was one thing to win the competition but, after it, I said that we would review every decision we took for the competition to see if we'd made the right one. Too many of them were made under pressure.

The day we won that, I was so proud. Bluntly, I was proud of myself and I was really proud of our team. My motivation had not been only the profit opportunity, though that was a large part of it. No, and even though it may sound pompous to say it, if an Irish company had not won that competition, it would make a mockery of the idea that the country had come of age in the commercial world. The motivation was that an Irish team would win. Now the real acid test is building it and making money out of it.

Lynda's death has changed my values. Before her death, I did not value my wife or my children as much as I do today. That's the basic change. I took them for granted. They were part of my life to fit in when it suited me. It was not always for me to be there for their needs but more for them to be there for mine. Now that's rather reversed: I want to be there for the children's needs.

Could I have got more out of my life before Lynda died if I had had those values? I have no idea. I have speculated about that but what's the point? The lessons I've learned are twofold: one, I now know the time the children need from me and, two, I know my need for them. The children *are* my life now, in a way. My businesses are all very important but I think I see them in a more balanced perspective. I tended to be consumed by them — I tended to devote myself far more to my work than to my family. If my life in the past was devoted to three segments in descending order, the largest segment was work. The second segment was friends and the third and smallest segment was probably my family. I am not saying that work has now become the smallest segment — it hasn't. I could not do what I do and say that honestly. But when you experience for the first time a tremendous loss, you reorder your priorities.

Another change following Lynda's death is that I now have more time for myself, more time to think about what I want out of business. I never really gave it very much thought before. I simply did what I was doing as well as I could do it — there was never any single driving force. Maybe it's just age and maturity or maybe it is that, when somebody very close to you dies, you feel mortal for the first time. Lynda's death did not bring me closer to God. It did not bring me closer to a lot of things, but it certainly brought me closer to reality. I am always surprised at people who say that they would be happy to die — I never want to die! If somebody were to tell me that I could live for another hundred years, I would be happy as Larry. But the real thing is that I want to live long enough for my children to be brought up the way Lynda and I planned. And, for example, I am now much more concerned that my financial affairs are in order than I would have been when I felt immortal. Now I carry decent life insurance and I make bloody sure before I travel that it's doubled up. Any liabilities I take on are matched by an equivalent insurance policy. If anything were to happen to me, then any liabilities would be totally cleared out of the way and my children would not have to be concerned with anything like that. My father died over twelve years ago and we still have not settled his estate.

I do want more time for myself. I do want more time to think. I don't want to reach the age of sixty feeling that I have wasted the time between now and then. I don't feel I've wasted any part of my life up to now.

9

Sir Desmond Lorimer

All my life I have really got fun out of working and creating something: building something up, seeing it develop, seeing people enjoy working and seeing the end result. Success in itself is the driving force.

Sir Desmond Lorimer is chairman and chief executive of Lamont Holdings plc and chairman of the Northern Bank.

He was born on 20 October 1925 in Belfast. His father was Thomas Berry Lorimer, a civil servant. His mother was Sarah Anne Robinson, a nurse. He was the second of two children, one sister.

He is married to Patricia Samways who was a secretary. They have two daughters: Susan (27) and Katherine (25).

He was educated at Belfast Technical High School.

He is a Fellow of the Institute of Chartered Accountants in Ireland — President of the Institute 1968–1969, a Companion of the British Institute of Management and a Fellow of the Irish Management Institute.

He practised as a chartered accountant from 1952 to 1974.

He was a senior partner in Harmood Banner Smylie & Company, later merged with Deloitte Haskins & Sells.

He was first chairman of the Northern Ireland Housing Executive 1971–1975.

He was appointed a member of the McCrory Commission in 1970 — the review body on local government in Northern Ireland.

He was first chairman of the Industrial Development Board for Northern Ireland 1982–1985.

He is Chairman of Northern Bank Limited since December 1986, director since 1983, deputy chairman since 1985.

His other directorships include Irish Distillers Group plc and The Old Bushmills Distillery Company Limited (chairman).

He was knighted for public service in 1976 and holds an honorary Doctorate of Science from the University of Ulster.

My early days were uneventful. I never regarded myself as being clever at school. Being an asthmatic in my childhood years perhaps impacted on my education a little. My sister was the clever one in the family, but I was gifted with two wonderful parents — they were very supportive. I knew from the age of seventeen what I wanted to do as a career. I not only wanted to be a chartered accountant but I knew where I wanted to be one: on my way home from school I used to look up at the gold lettering on the windows of Hugh Smylie & Sons in Donegall Square North, Belfast, knowing that that was the office I wanted to belong to. I served my articles there.

I went into articles straight from school as was the practice then. I enjoyed those five years and established a good relationship with the partners. When I qualified I left Smylie's and went to Hill, Vellacott & Bailey, as it then was. They were the only office at that time in Northern Ireland to have any connection with an international firm. That attracted me as I wanted wider experience. I stayed there for several years and then decided that I would go out on my own. I had always wanted to work for myself, to be my own boss and take my own decisions. I set up in a small office in Royal Avenue and the practice built up quite rapidly.

My father died just before I decided to go out on my own and we were not a wealthy family. That did not stop me taking the decision. I was reasonably confident — convinced there was business to be got and that I could make a living. Being on my own lasted only for three or four years. One evening, as I was sitting in my office, the door opened and Sidney Smylie, a partner in Hugh Smylie & Sons, stood in front of my desk. He said, 'Come on to hell out of this and have a bit of sense. We'll go for a drink. We've got some serious talking to do.' That conversation led me back into Hugh Smylie & Sons as a partner. Events moved on from there — sad events: both Sidney and Cecil Smylie, the two partners, died within five or six years of my going back. I took over the practice — I suppose I was lucky to be in the right place at the right time.

It was an old Victorian office with high desks. The Northern Bank was building a new office block next door and I had tried without success to get Cecil Smylie, the last of the partners, to agree to move into it. I must admit that immediately he died, I got in contact with the agents and got the last floor. An eminent chartered accountant later drew me aside and asked me if I was wise. He said, 'Desmond, you know you'll be working for the landlord.' The rent was 7s 6d a square foot with a twenty-one year lease and no rent reviews! I was a bit shaken by the advice, but from that moment on, the firm never looked back. We picked up the business of most of the public boards that were being launched at that time and very quickly four new partners were introduced. We were one of the first practices to go international when we became part of the Harmood Banner organisation.

My time as a chartered accountant in practice was a very rewarding period. Starting my own practice, then merging it into Hugh Smylie & Sons, becoming senior partner and taking that firm into an international partnership and all the time expanding to become one of the most vital practices was both exciting and fulfilling.

As accountancy was my first love, I was always actively involved in the Ulster Society of Chartered Accountants and the Institute of Chartered Accountants in Ireland and took great pride in my Chairmanship of the Society in 1960 and being president of the Institute in 1968, as well as contributing in the early years as an examiner and as honorary secretary of both the Society and the Institute.

When I was elected President of the Institute at a relatively early age, I felt I had reached the pinnacle of my career as a chartered accountant. I still take pride in looking back on that period and the friendships established.

Up to 1974 when I withdrew from practice, I had done a few odd things in business on my own account. I started a computer company in 1968. At that time there was no computer bureau in Northern Ireland. Having advertised for a managing director, I was fortunate to get Tom Winter who had been with ICL and IBM. Tom worked out of my office and we took six months to do a feasibility study.

There was an enterprise fund in Northern Ireland worth about half a million pounds and I felt my project fitted it very well. I invited the Secretary of the Department of Commerce to lunch in the old Royal Avenue Hotel. He listened carefully to my proposal and then took out of his pocket a report with a green cover. The Department had recently commissioned one of the universities to do a study on the use of computers. He said, 'Read the conclusion.' He saw the disappointment on my face. The conclusion said that there was no foreseeable future for computer bureaux in Northern Ireland. 'However', he said, 'I can sell you a computer.' Harland and Wolff had ordered an ICL computer and the Government were reluctant to pay for it. It had not been commissioned and I got it — with the government grant that was going with it. He explained to me that I would also have to take over the staff that Harland and Wolff had trained for their purposes, but that Harland's work would give a base load for the computer. The whole transaction was completed in two weeks — computer, staff and all — and my company, ICS, was set up at Queen's Road, where it still is. ICS stands for Independent Computer Services. It expanded into Software Ireland and Computer Maintenance Ireland and the latter now operates in Belfast, Dublin, Limerick, Cork and Galway.

I also set up what is now Lamont Holdings plc, having bought a controlling interest in 1973 in a publicly quoted shell company, in partnership with Hugh O'Neill. Lamont was an old engineering company based in Edinburgh: it had belt-driven machinery, a Victorian factory and looked grim when you walked into it. We started out with the idea that we would use Lamont Holdings to take us into financial services. In concept we were right but we were way ahead of our time, being about ten years too early for financial services. We had a foray into the unit trust management business in London, but the whole timing of acquiring James H. Lamont, as it was called then, was completely wrong. It was the mid-seventies and the recession came up on us. Business activity slowed down, so we just battened down the hatches. We got out of our adventure into financial services and ended up with just this little engineering company in Edinburgh. Almost as a hobby, we decided to revitalise and re-equip it.

In effect, in 1974 I took a change of direction and career. The fact that that little company was in being crystallised in my mind my decision to leave the accountancy partnership and do something different. While I was the senior partner, a decision to merge with Deloittes was taken by Harmood Banner at the international level. The merger was probably right for the long-term future of the practice and for the partners, but it was not for me. The new regime was much too restrictive. My leaving the practice was a key decision point in my life. I was financially independent by then. I could have lived comfortably even if inflation had not arrived. Well, in prospect I would have been able to live, in retrospect, no! I wouldn't have been happy without an involvement, and challenge has been a key feature of my life.

The highlight of my life is my wife and family and it has always been one of my regrets that in the children's early years I missed the pleasure of being with them as much as I would have wished. In Pat, my wife, I have been more than fortunate. The fact that I was away from home so much, satisfying my own business ambitions and leaving her with the daunting task of coping single-handedly with the two girls still weighs on my conscience.

Without Pat's active support, so willingly given, I would certainly not have been able to pursue business and public activities with unfettered dedication.

As I have said, in May 1974 I cut the painter completely with the practice and that was the end of that. I stayed on in the actual office because Harmood Banner moved. I was running my own little businesses and James H. Lamont and, at the same time, I was chairman of the McCleery L'Amie Group Limited, a textile company.

A few years earlier, I had been approached by the Belfast Bank, now part of Northern Bank, to have a look at Belfast Ropeworks. I went in as a nominee director of the Bank either to become receiver to the Ropeworks or to turn it around. I always enjoyed receiverships when in practice and the challenge of bringing companies back to life.

The Belfast Ropeworks comprised ancient buildings, ancient management systems and very little young blood. I had met in my professional career three young men who made a powerful combination in the textile industry: one was a genius with machinery, another was a good marketing man and the third was a production man — Tony McCleery, John L'Amie and Garfield Brown. I saw in these three young men the right sort of medicine for Belfast Ropeworks. I reversed their own small companies into the Ropeworks and they became major shareholders. They made money and turned the company around.

The three young men, however, eventually lost interest in each other and in the Ropeworks Group and were content neither to manage the business nor to let it be managed by others — a familiar phenomenon with entrepreneurs. They departed to other activities.

When I took control of the Ropeworks under the Lamont banner, I decided to cut six acres out of the Connswater site, which was part of the Ropeworks complex, for a shopping centre: it's now Connswater Shopping Centre. We have just agreed to sell the entire complex and the remainder of the property for £13 m. You might well ask why not develop the property ourselves. The answer is that we decided to stick to our core business — textiles. We were not really property developers.

I think my interest in textiles was whetted in my Viyella days when I was involved with Joe Hyman back in 1969/70.

Viyella International was a very forward-thinking company and I learned a lot from Joe. He was an eccentric genius with the ability to read a balance sheet, close it up and discuss it with you for the next hour and quote the figures. He was also a great visionary — he certainly taught me to look forward.

I was in my office at four o'clock one afternoon when I got a telephone call from him. He was in Cyril Lord's house in Donaghadee. I intended to get the five o'clock train to Dublin to a meeting of the Institute of Chartered Accountants. I met him at half past five and left him at half past two in the morning. It meant going to bed for two or three hours and driving to Dublin the next morning to be in time for the Institute meeting, but the upshot of it was that he gave me the job of raising the finance for, and acquiring, the Cyril Lord carpet business for Viyella. That was my first large exercise in enterprise. We raised £4.50 m. and in 1967/68 that was a sizeable sum. All the money was raised in Belfast.

Coming back to Lamont and following the McCleery L'Amie acquisition, we moved on to being a reasonably sized company. We had several take-overs. We bought Moygashel from Courtaulds. I remember exactly the number of shares as we had to do a vendor-placing: 4,444,444. The price at that time was 17p. They are now around the £2.70 mark and were as high as £4, pre-October 1987. After that came the acquisition of B. H. McCleery & Co. Ltd created by Tony McCleery, part of the old Belfast Ropeworks trio. The company has prospered since we acquired it. Then we acquired Shaw Carpets in Yorkshire. It was a public company much larger than ourselves and doubled Lamont's turnover. We bought it for £6 m. and made £3 m. in profit in our first year of operation. It had been making a loss, but we turned it round within two months simply by releasing the second tier of management and giving them their head. It's been a success ever since. If we had not taken it over, it could well have closed down.

The most recent acquisition has been Bonded Fibre Fabrics Ltd, based in Somerset, also acquired from Courtaulds. This is a company producing non-woven fabrics for the clothing, medical and hygiene markets and has great potential for the future.

I have always had reservations about go-go companies that in boom times keep issuing their paper for acquisitions and have little regard to the actual consideration that they are paying. I prefer to do nothing, waiting for the moment when the price is right, rather than pay inflated prices, so compounding the risk factor.

Lamont Holdings is rather unique as a public company having only two directors and indeed we were severely criticised for this in our early days. Of the two directors, one is executive and the other non-executive. The City did not like it much but, as we became successful, the complaints ceased. It's only now, as I am getting on in years, that the question of succession has been raised. We have just recently appointed Dick Milliken as chief executive designate to succeed me and I will remain executive chairman for a little while yet. Our Board now numbers three and is probably still unique.

The whole basis of Lamont's success has been that we have given people their head. There has been a direct line of communication and no bureaucracy — there can be little bureaucracy with a two-man board! You may well say that there is the risk of autocracy, but it has worked. Management enjoy it because they can get their decisions quickly. My role has been to motivate people, not only with shares and cash, but with interest and leadership, and my principle has been to give people the opportunity to prove themselves while giving them as much help as they needed. If they were not able to prove themselves, then they would be moved sideways or out to where they were more comfortable, and others brought in who were prepared to take the baton and run with it. I never cease to be amazed at how well young people respond to being given responsibility.

All my life I've got fun out of working and achieving an objective: building something up, seeing it develop, seeing people enjoy working and getting satisfaction out of the end result. That's what has driven me on. Success in itself is the driving force and, if a business is successful, then you put more effort into it. It is often said that money drives you forward but money is completely irrelevant. Being involved and deriving satisfaction is the driving force.

It's very difficult to describe one's motivations in a succinct way. I think I suffer from the old Northern Ireland work ethic. I wouldn't call myself a workaholic but, particularly in the formative years, I really enjoyed achieving, no matter what it was — even if it was just finalising a set of accounts. My motivation has been the desire to be able to put a marker down and say, 'I've done that.' I have never been concerned about the financial aspects of my progress as I have always believed that achievement of itself will bring financial rewards, not the other way round. Being able to think for myself, I had no desire to take orders, and therefore was prepared to take decisions on my own on the basis of whatever my conscience and my desire dictated, and to stand by those decisions whatever the financial consequences.

I like to think that I have the ability to look forward and see the end result of my actions and also to predict trends in industry, or indeed the profession. Many years ago I foresaw the trend toward the larger multinational practice and, when I predicted, in a paper given to an Institute conference, that within ten years we would be left with only around ten major accountancy firms, I was quite severely criticised — but merger mania persists. I would now predict that within another ten years, the break-up of the profession as we know it today will take place. The consultancy side will hive off and possibly float, driven by the greed of the partners to capitalise on the high income earned by that part of the practice. The auditing side will be left as the poor relation, performing a statutory service to the client which, in his eyes, is of little benefit and is a costly obligation. Pressure on fees in this area of the profession will become more intense. The newly developing financial services activities will also tend to break away from the core activity, possibly driven by increasing legislation and conflict of interests.

In one's business life, timing and luck are very important. I have been fortunate, but perhaps the worst thing that happened was when we got the timing wrong when initially we decided to take Lamont into financial services. The idea was good but, because the move was way before its time, Lamont could have perished. That incident did not shake my confidence in my judgment, but it did make me examine it a little more closely. I might have been guilty up to then of being impetuous. It certainly made me a little more cautious — I can see that now, when I am looking for example at an acquisition. You need in business the blend of experience and of the energy of youth. When you're youthful, even if you're impetuous, your enthusiasm will carry you through — that's what happened to me. When that youthfulness is tempered by the experience of someone older, you have a winning combination. In Lamont now we have a good blend of youthfulness and experience — indeed I am the old man of the team.

I'm chairman of Lamont and of Northern Bank and, when you sit at the top of the table, you just have to know what's going on. I agree with you, Ivor, that, as an ordinary board member, it's difficult to make a contribution from down the table and the chairman has to understand that the non-executive directors probably do not have a deep understanding of the business. This, of course, can be one of their strengths — they can stand back and see things from an uninvolved perspective. They can assess a situation better than someone who is possibly emotionally involved. The strength of the non-executive director should be in his ability to sit and listen, and then put his finger on the weakness. It's foolish for non-executive directors to try to contribute just for the sake of being heard and to feel that otherwise they can't justify their presence. There are times when I go to a board meeting as a non-executive and say nothing because there is nothing to be said. Whatever was being put forward was logical and sensible and I had nothing positive to add to it. It is when something is going adrift, then the non-executive director should speak up and make sure he is heard.

I have reservations on the role of chairman and chief executive of a public company being held by one person. This may seem somewhat ironic as I have held the dual role in Lamont. Perhaps it was successful only because of the uniqueness of Lamont with its two-man board. There is a danger that where the two functions are controlled by one person, a dictatorship can ensue and the board could well become irrelevant — it is in just such a situation that the non-executive director has a real and important role to play. The relationship between the non-executive chairman and the chief executive is extremely important. The chairman should provide the shoulder to cry on, the sounding-board, the catalyst. The chief executive should feel that the chairman's door is open and that he *wants* to go and talk to him. He *wants* to tell him what's going on. There is nothing worse than a situation where the chief executive is playing his cards close to his chest and keeping strategic information to himself. The other bad thing is the chairman having no relationship with the chief executive and going to other executives to find out what's going on. Mutual trust and respect are necessary — they're the important things. If they are not there, then distrust will permeate down through the upper layers of management to the detriment of the business.

Apart from building up businesses where I was directly involved, the three most satisfying achievements of my career, in chronological order, have been my presidency of the Institute of Chartered Accountants in Ireland, my knighthood and my chairmanship of the Northern Bank.

The knighthood was bestowed by Her Majesty in respect of the work of the Northern Ireland Housing Executive — I was surprised to receive such recognition and must say that I enjoy the honour.

There is something very nice, stable and satisfying in being a director of a bank. My chairmanship of Northern Bank, which is the largest clearing bank in the province, has given me satisfaction and it has been a great experience to have an insight into the workings of such a financial institution. When I was appointed it was part of the Midland Bank Group, but some three years ago it was acquired from Midland by the National Australia Bank. The latter have a much more developed policy of devolving responsibility than had Midland.

I can't see an end to our present troubles in Northern Ireland. There are no signs of reconciliation between the factions. The terrorists are still active although I take some hope out of what is happening in Europe. The dictatorship of communism is being replaced by democracy and perhaps this may alter the ideology of the terrorist — the IRA being a terrorist organisation that is Marxist-based. Perhaps they will see that communism is crumbling, that it does not last, and that democracy is what the people want.

The Anglo-Irish Agreement has done nothing at all to help the situation — it's a non-event. While it may have given a foothold in Northern Ireland to the Republic through the Secretariat based in Belfast, I don't think it brings any improvement to the situation. It was so insensitively handled at the beginning that there is no way you could backtrack to put it on the rails again. Everyone is on a hook with the Agreement and no one seems to be able to get off it without considerable loss of face. If the Agreement were dropped, it might at least provide a level playing field for new initiatives. Whilst I despair of the Unionist politicians' stance that they won't talk until the Agreement is removed, I have a sneaking sympathy for it — but it does not really matter. If I were in their position, I would want to get on and talk, recognising that the cultures of the majorities in the two parts of Ireland are completely different, are possibly irreconcilable.

Strangely enough, twenty years ago before all the present trouble started, the people were beginning to live with one another and to understand one another. There was a much better to-ing and fro-ing between the Republic and Northern Ireland. The troubles in 1969/70 polarised the situation and put people back into their tribal camps. If the terrorists were to disappear tomorrow, it would unfortunately take another couple of decades to get back that understanding. But there is no doubt that it is they who are the basic cause of the tribalism. It is they who foment it — they need it for their survival. People adhere to their tribal instincts only because of fear and distrust.

We've gone a long way now in Northern Ireland towards integrated education. It was unfortunate that the Westminster Government baulked at the Londonderry Act in the twenties because of pressure from both Churches. There are now new integrated schools and there are many Catholics in the old schools which would, a few years ago, have been 100 per cent Protestant. I was disappointed when the Catholic Church opposed integrated education recently. There is no reason why people of both faiths should not share the same education but have different religious instruction. If we had integrated education in the 1920s, I think we would have an integrated Ireland today. I have been visiting Dublin all my life — I have relatives there. I have never looked upon the South as an alien place. My instincts however — my instincts of birth and tradition — give me a greater loyalty to Britain than to the Republic. I would have to think long and hard about it, but I don't think my loyalty would be a stumbling block towards, ultimately, an integrated or united Ireland. I would probably find it difficult to adjust for a time and a lot would depend on the freedom one had — my fear would be that we would be exchanging one lot of terrorists for another. We might exchange the IRA for the UVF and we would have solved nothing, simply activating terrorism on the other side. My present view is that, for a long time to come, Northern Ireland is better off integrated into the United Kingdom rather than in a united Ireland.

The first thing that is necessary is a period of peace where people can live together and get to understand each other. I don't think either a united Ireland or integration with Britain are all that important to the ordinary person, provided they have peace and security and a decent economic environment.

I just can't see the people — and the economy — of the South wanting the North at the moment. It would be an expensive luxury.

There was a time when the people of the South looked with awe at the business acumen of the people of the 'Black North'. That situation could well have changed over the past twenty years so that we in the North now look to Dublin with great respect. Your own organisation, the IMI, helped to change that perception and, together with Sean Lemass, was the turning point. The Irish businessman gained the confidence he needed. They are now as good as you'll get anywhere in the world. Ireland, as a member of the European Community, has committed itself to being a genuine European and it has reaped the advantages. The Financial Services Centre in Dublin is a great step forward, and though I viewed it with some scepticism at the beginning, I now feel it will be successful. That was vision and the timing was right. It may never rival London, Tokyo or New York, but there is a service to be provided and Dublin is capable of providing it.

The Northern Irelander is rather dour and hard working. We don't think as emotionally as the southerner. We are inclined to be led by our heads, whereas the southerner is led more by his heart. There is tremendous hospitality in the South — when you are there. When you go away, they are inclined to forget about you. They don't write letters or try to keep in touch, somewhat like Americans. But when you come back, it's picked up again and you would not find a warmer-hearted people — but you have got to be present. In a way, I think the Northern Irelander is more sympathetic — perhaps even more kindly but in a less flamboyant manner — than the southerner. A lot of Northern Irish characteristics go back to the work ethic in its best form, to a somewhat puritan tradition — we like to get on with it. We save, we are thrifty yet we are generous, particularly to those in need. We are not, however, a creative race: for example, some of the new buildings in Dublin are beautiful both inside and outside and with great attention to detail. Some of the new buildings in Belfast are completely utilitarian — just functional and no more — whilst you in the South will spend money just to have appearances right. Perhaps we are too practical to do so.

One of the great benefits of an integrated Ireland would be the mixture of the hard-headed northerner with the creative southerner — it could be a heady mixture!

Something I look back on with pride is my involvement with the public sector, e.g. the work of the Northern Ireland Housing Executive. You just have to travel around Northern Ireland to see its fruits. I agreed with Brian Faulkner, the Prime Minister at that time, that I would take on the chairmanship of the Executive for a period of five years and create the organisation. We had to take housing out of politics, out of the hands of local authorities. That was quite a task — with eighty-one local authorities, a couple of new town commissions, Belfast Corporation, the Housing Trust with their staff of more than 2,500, all to be brought into one housing organisation and integrated quickly. This was 1970 to 1975 and, at the same time, we were building houses at super speed as there was great need in particular areas. They were the tough years of the troubles and there were times when it was not a very straightforward or pleasant task, with considerable sensitive issues and undertones.

For the position of chief executive of the organisation I head-hunted Harry Simpson from Lambeth Council. He was a man of great social conscience and with considerable experience in public authority housing. Without Harry I would have been lost, but between us we set up an organisation which today still carries on the basic policies created at that time, with the result that Northern Ireland has some of the finest public housing in Europe. Harry went back to London to take on the top job in housing in the Greater London Council, but during his time in Northern Ireland he always vowed that before he would leave he would have developed in me a very acute social conscience! He has now sadly passed on and I hope, for his sake and mine, that he achieved his objective.

Before the Housing Trust was set up, the main allegation was that councils discriminated on a religious basis in the allocation of housing. So we ended that and we put in a system that removed any suggestion of discrimination. We also built houses in areas where some councils would never have built them. The last scheme before I left was Poleglass in West Belfast — that would never have got off the ground had the old system remained in place. I often drive through Poleglass and look at it with pride. It was built after my time but it was planned while I was still there and the problem of getting the agreement of all the factions in the community was quite something.

My other main activity in public life was my chairmanship of the Industrial Development Board for Northern Ireland. Again it was a first — being asked to set in motion a new board with the object of revitalising the drive for new industry. This was also a difficult task, not least because of the perception of Northern Ireland as not being the ideal place to start up a new business. Over the years this perception has been broken down and the message that Northern Ireland is not only as peaceful, if not more so, than most places in the world, has gained a greater following. I thoroughly enjoyed my stint of three years with the Board and feel that in some little way in that period I made a contribution.

I always think it wrong to continue too long in a public appointment. When I said I would be chairman for five years in the Housing Executive and three in the Development Board, that was it. The organisation was in place in each case and the opportunity was there for someone else to come in with a different perspective and different talents to take them along to the next stage.

I like to live comfortably but I do not like to live ostentatiously. Pride comes before a fall and, maybe it's my old Presbyterian background, but I don't think you should flaunt your wealth on your sleeve so that everyone can see it. I would be horrified even to think of driving a Rolls Royce or a Bentley. It would be anathema to my nature. There is nothing that I want in life more than I've got at the present moment. I've got my home, I've got my family, we can live comfortably without financial worries. I don't want to have a country estate and a shoot but maybe that's because I don't like shooting! It's barbaric to breed pheasants and then drive the poor things overhead to be slaughtered! In my business life I've travelled a fair bit of the world and, whilst business travel is different from private pleasure travel, airports and aircraft are a great bore. I have no desire to take a month or two off to see any particular places, though perhaps in retirement I might visit India and Egypt, but the thought of going to lie in the sun for two weeks on the Costa del Sol would appal me — I'd rather just loll at home with a good book!

Oh yes, I have a regret or two. There are one or two chances I could have taken with Lamont that would have made it five or six times the size it is today. I baulked at those, probably because I was too conservative. Looking back now, I would like to have taken those chances. One of the reasons that I stepped away was that it would have meant my being away from Northern Ireland even more than I was, and I did not want that. Perhaps it's my fault that I did not put people in place who could have done the job for me. This is where I pay tribute to Michael Smurfit — he did put people in place and they helped him to drive the business forward. I have always looked at his company with some envy. He stuck to his core business and developed, and that's something that people are relearning today.

I think the time has come for me to step back a little now and enjoy my home and family, golf and gardening and the other things that I have never had time for. But I still think I can contribute ideas for the future. I would like someone else to implement the decisions, having examined them much more closely than I would. I would rather put the ideas forward and let others run with them if they felt inclined to. At sixty-five years of age, I'm beginning to be conscious of the fact that time is running out, that there are lots of things that I would like to do. I neglected not only the family but friends. I neglected the companionship of other people and as you get older you reflect on these things. It would be pleasant now to enjoy that fellowship, companionship, camaraderie in a more relaxed and genuine social, rather than a business, atmosphere. I'd also like to feel that I didn't have to, out of conscience, go to work every day — not to have the hassle. I find that, even now, if I take a day off to play golf, I have a guilt complex. I feel I'm not playing fair by the rest of the team.

A little more time, a little more space is what is now required.

10

Alastair McGuckian

I am asked if we are doing things for altruistic or commercial reasons. I see no conflict. It is a false question. You can't be a philanthropist and be a failure.

Alastair McGuckian is chairman and chief executive of Masstock International.

He was born in Cloughmills, County Antrim, on 24 August 1936, the third son in a family of two boys and three girls. His father was Sandy McGuckian, a farmer. His mother was Etta O'Doherty.

He is married to Margery O'Donoghue. They have four children: Mary (27), Ciaran (26), Roisin (25) and Garrett (18).

He was educated at:
St Malachy's College, Belfast,
St McNissi's College, Garrontower,
Greenmount Agricultural College — Certificate of Agriculture.

He started work on the family farm at Massereene Park in 1956.
1966–1969 he developed new systems of beef housing, The Masstock System.
1974 prepared a plan for the economic development of a region in Northern Bulgaria.
1976 started the development of dairy farming in Saudi Arabia.
1977 established a company called Almarai to produce and distribute branded milk products throughout the Arabian Gulf.
1980 started wheat production in Saudi Arabia.
1983 formed Richland Limited to provide laboratory analysis and high-tech supplies for the Third World.
1984 formed a food company, Camella Limited, to supply branded food products from many sources to the Middle East, Pacific Rim, China and Europe. Dairy project and processing plant in mainland China.
1985 founded the Masstock Corporation, USA.
1987 formed Ovamass Limited, a joint venture company with UCD.
1988 formed Masstock Zambia Limited, Masstock Thailand Limited and acquired Cleanacres Limited in the UK and Mathis Dairies Limited in Atlanta, Georgia.

He is a founder member of the Council of the Ulster Grassland Society, of the Northern Ireland Agricultural Trust and of the Livestock Marketing Commission.

He is a director of the International Fund for Ireland and of Irish Fertiliser Industries.

He holds an honorary LL.D from the National University of Ireland and a D.Sc. from the Queen's University of Belfast.

I come from North Antrim, a place called Cloughmills —
I was there until I was eleven and then we moved to
Antrim town. My father was a farmer and quite a visionary.
He had been interned at the setting up of the Northern
state in a boat called the *Argenta*. He was there for three
years and that's where he developed a lot of his ideas about
pig production. With pigs, you can go from a very small to
a very large number of animals more easily than with any
other four-legged creature except perhaps rabbits. He had
a plan to have ten thousand pigs. Together with three
brothers, he developed his ideas — and his farm — in the
late twenties and into the thirties. Then, during the war, his
pig farm was taken over. He started off again after the war
and worked until 1952 when he died. I was sixteen. He also
developed shirt manufacturing. After his death, there were
three brothers — one of them looked after the shirts and the
others, the pigs. In 1945, we moved to Masserene Park — 640
acres of heavy, loamy, wet soil, very difficult to work. There
he took an interest in grassland production.

Following school, I went to agricultural college and then
immediately back to this grassland farm. For a time, the
family interests were all gathered together in the hands of
my uncles who were managing the pig farm and the shirt
factory. The Masserene farm was used principally to graze
cattle.

In 1967 the different members of the family realised that
they had different interests and we thought it would be a
good idea to reorganise things. My brother Paddy joined
me and we decided to make something of this grassland
farm. I was thirty then but, in the previous years, since the
time I had left school, I had been quite active in various
agricultural bodies. The main change in my career came in
applying for and being awarded a Nuffield Scholarship,
which the motor magnate, Lord Nuffield, had set up for
young farmers who might be able to influence the farming
community. Ted Heath was looking to join the Common
Market around that time and was turned down by de

Gaulle. Still it was going to happen some time and I decided to study the marketing of beef in Europe. The Scholarship gave me the chance to be ahead of the posse in understanding what might happen when we joined.

At that time also, I felt confined by the walls of the farm. I felt confined by Northern Ireland — a narrow and parochial community. It was also a narrow market-base.

During my study tour throughout Europe, I got a strong feel for the factors that were going to influence the beef and dairy industries. There were quite considerable shortfalls in supply in the whole of Europe at that time. The CAP — the Community support system — was structured to suit that shortage. We are now living with a system that was set up to handle shortages when we have serious surpluses. It became clear to me too that the structure of European agriculture was all wrong: the units were too small and it was not possible to get economies of scale. It was not possible to apply to agriculture all that was going on in the sixties in industry — you remember things like work study. I learned that many of the ideas we were applying at home were well in advance of what I saw throughout Europe.

It was a good discipline to have to write a report on the Nuffield experience. Being of a practical nature, I made several recommendations and some of them have subsequently changed the nature of agriculture in these islands. Twenty thousand copies of that report — and then there were requests for twenty thousand more — were circulated mainly in the UK.

What I did not see in the hundreds of farms I visited was the farming systems and techniques Paddy and I had at home. That is when the concept of Masstock evolved.

The name Masstock comes from mass production and livestock. The farming industry was divided into small units for historical and social reasons while other industries were applying economies of scale — that's what provoked me to think of Masstock. Masstock was set up to sell our experience in a solid practical way that could easily be taken up by farmers. Our farm gates were always open and people came in to see what we were doing. Ninety per cent of them did not understand why we were doing these things and they went home and didn't do anything about it. There were about ten per cent, however, who were switched on, could get the package together and go home and do it. They might do things differently, but they picked out the half-dozen things that really mattered.

I believed that Ireland certainly and possibly Britain could head for the goal of meeting the shortfall in livestock supplies in Europe and we could package the means through which that need would be supplied.

If you went to a farm which had 30 cattle and asked the farmer why he did not have 200, he would answer: 'How could I have 200 when I spend the day running around looking after 30?' But if you go to him and say you could organise his farming system to keep four cattle per acre, when he's only keeping half a head per acre, it's another thing. These are some of the problems that we wanted to help them solve. We would go to the bank manager and say, 'Here are the figures for our farm — this is how our system would be applied to this farm. This man has 30 cattle, he wants to have 500, and now is the time because of the growing demand for beef.' What we were doing was selling both the software and the hardware. We sold the idea, the system, and then installed our own contractors to put the system in place, literally in concrete. We delivered on to the farm, erected and built and set him off. It was a packaged farmyard system. From 1970 to 1975, we set those up on 650 farms in Northern Ireland and the UK. After 74/75 there were a lot in the Republic — it was a slow market to move. We had tremendous success in Scotland and the east of England. To do all this, we had to have people qualified to advise the farmers, we had to have engineers, and we had to have squads of guys to go out and install the systems. And we did that from the Orkneys down to Cornwall and from Antrim to Cork.

It was essentially a marketing job. In the first two years we had every farmer in these islands using Masstock as an adjective. I picked out two or three organisations that were interested in grass — one of them was ICI. I got them to organise the farmers through their agents and I went on a lecture tour. I gave lectures on agricultural systems around the whole of England, Scotland and Northern Ireland. Once in County Durham, my sales-pitch must have been so good that, at the end of the lecture, I had six fellows up to the stage to sign contracts. I was staying with a fellow called Pickering. I remember going to my bedroom in his house that night and wondering how the hell we were going to shift all that concrete and steel to the east of England! We are now involved in considerable logistics around the world but I was more frightened by that particular prospect than anything that has happened since. It was a long way from driving a few trucks up the road from south Antrim to north Antrim, looking after the farmers in Northern Ireland. The Northern Ireland Protestant farmer was a very good client to serve. He had very high standards — things had to be right. Things had to look right too — you could not defile the countryside with tin sheds. We paid a lot of attention to environmental considerations, to doing things well. They were also very straightforward, honest payers. We were used to getting the cheque half-way through the job — when I moved to certain other parts of the world, cash-flow was another thing!

In this company, we do have a special ethos. We are concerned about the broadening throughout the world of agricultural knowledge and know-how. We were in technology-transfer before the term was invented. And even in those early days when we were selling systems in Antrim and Cork, I was over in Eastern Europe where I thought there was a real opportunity to do our thing inside a national plan for agricultural development. My ambition is to produce more food today than yesterday, rather than to have a big successful company. We want to transfer into the Third World the agricultural experience of the developed world. The successful company is a consequence of doing that well.

The sixties were a heady period for agriculture. Any time you went to a meeting of progressive farmers, you found records being broken. We were getting higher and higher levels of productivity. Early in the seventies I saw that this would become a problem and that support for agriculture would become a terrible burden for the European tax-payer. The production of commodity food is a low-productivity activity. It cannot compete as an income-earner with industry. There are people who are earning a pound a day or $300 a year who can supply that food. We are not focusing sufficiently on the fact that we have a surplus capacity in Europe to produce food. The surplus food is a product of that surplus capacity. We are driving that capacity into embarrassing excess. That capacity is what is required in the Third World. It is the capability to turn under-utilised land into agricultural commodities and it can and must be done. I know that when we started it was a long road to go, but now we can take an area of 20,000 hectares, organise it with irrigation, and inside a year or two have 120,000 tons of wheat, which is exactly the size of the wheat shortfall that is causing food riots in Zambia. That's a very easy thing to do — by us, Masstock. Since the seventies, we have been building an organisation that can go to any part of the world and say, 'We'll put agriculture on the ground for you.'

One of the snags is that the Third World is seen as a technical or physical problem and it is never only that. In Central Africa or South America, you may be confronting civil war. But, in every case, you are putting production into a vacuum unless you also organise the marketing side or the means through which you organise the important conduits of supply and back-up. You have to put all of that together to be able to offer agricultural/rural development in these countries.

In 1974/75 we prepared a complete plan for the economic development of a region called Silistra in Northern Bulgaria.

This was for land-use, livestock development, processing and even recycling — and product distribution, the communist term for marketing. Unfortunately, to get them tied down to let us get at the job was nearly impossible. The interesting thing for me now is to read that plan and compare it with what we did immediately after that in Saudi Arabia. The bureaucracy in Bulgaria was manageable neither by the Bulgarians nor by us. We can see that so much more easily now but, even then, we realised it was appalling. The dogma conflicts with itself all over the place. Where you are supposed to have equality of opportunity or access, you have very strict lines of demarcation. You have sub-plans conflicting with the overall plan. It was total confusion.

I suppose Saudi was the most dramatic of our developments — 'making the desert bloom' — and it has a lot of influence on markets we might approach now. You probably could not pick a more difficult environment. I became interested in Saudi after the first oil hike in 1973. A few people from universities had written reports on their experiments in growing grass there. The University of Bangor in Wales was doing the work that most interested me. They gave me some hope that the thing would work there. Because of my belief that you have to put a whole package together — marketing, production etc. — I approached Saudi Arabia differently from anybody else. Most people were there to do a contract or sell machinery or do a consultancy — just to get some money out of there before the oil days were over. Then they would get out as quickly as possible with as many riyals as they could get. I foresaw a dairy industry there. It had to include the basic forage that the animals would have, the management of dairy herds, the processing and distribution of food and, particularly, the development of the whole marketing. The Saudi Arabian people can write a cheque for as much milk powder to be flown in to them as they want. There was no problem at that time in having anything from the face of the earth. Robert Heller had, on the back cover of one of his books at that time, what one day's income in Saudi Arabia could buy — the whole British stock market. It wasn't good enough to offer something for which they could pay — it had to have a particular market attraction. The uniqueness that we decided to emphasise was freshness. The more distant a product is from the market, the more attractive freshness becomes. That took us into considering vegetables and fresh meat, but milk was particularly susceptible to bad treatment, to the ill effects of travelling and of heat. It became a very attractive proposition. Most of the milk in Saudi at the time was bought in powdered form and mixed with water in the home. People could buy sufficient powder to make a litre of milk for about 1¼ riyals. They would pay over 3 riyals for a recombined product in Jeddah or Riyadh. We had estimated that we must get 4½ riyals for a fresh product. That's about 70p. The risk was that when all the investment was made in farms, factories and transport, that that premium would not apply. There are a lot of people in Saudi Arabia today who prefer to buy the recombined product — that is the taste they are used to. They don't know fresh milk. And, when we did produce milk eventually, we found there was no market for it as such. Milk is called *halib* and it comes straight from the camel. When we produced nicely refrigerated milk and presented it to the Arabs and said, 'This is fresh', they said, 'This is not fresh, this is cold.' Fresh to us is a marketing concept. *Taza* is the Arabic word for freshness and it means immediacy. We could not use the word *taza*. Now, however, the terminology has taken on new meanings and values. It took us a year to find the direction for our marketing policy. We did that by observing the Bedouins: when they took the milk from their camels or sheep or goats, they put it into a goatskin and more or less churned it and produced a thing called *laban*. *Laban* is something like a drinking yoghurt — yoghurt came from that part of the world, the microbe in yoghurt is *bacillus Bulgaricus*. South-eastern Europe and the Middle East are the places where cultured milk originated. The microbe was probably handed down from one generation to another in the Bedouin goatskin. We are now probably the leading company in the world producing cultured milk drinks. *Laban* is different from yoghurt or buttermilk: it's a velvety thirst-quenching drink. Marketing *Laban* was a long way from just putting cattle in a field.

The first thing is to be able to irrigate and to grow crops sufficiently to support the animals. The next thing is to have the right sort of genetics in the animals and the ability to withstand the temperatures. The third is to organise a cold-chain and the processing and then, finally, the marketing and distribution. Nowadays, we supply fifty-five per cent of the fresh milk products in the whole region. With 12,500 cows, we have the biggest dairy herd in the world.

My brother Paddy and I own sixty-five per cent of the agricultural company and the marketing company is fifty-fifty. The other half, and a third of the agricultural company, is owned by H.H. Prince Sultan Bin Mohammed Bin Saud Al Kabeer.

It was a grand design all right but it had to be put together piece by piece. The first thing was to sell the concept to the people in Saudi Arabia. They could put as much tar as they wanted on the roads or build skyscrapers, but there had to be some depth in the economy — a food industry. Then you had to get somebody who had land to put the project on. I went into a number of joint ventures with many people. Then I met Prince Sultan and his father who became great champions of Saudi's indigenous agricultural industry. I also had a lot of discussions with the Minister for Agriculture and with His Majesty the King. We organised a farm for the King which we subsequently bought back from the family. But, apart from these relationships, the biggest contract we had was Haradh with the Ministry for Agriculture. This was a place where the previous King, Faisal, had brought a lot of the tribal people together where there was a sheep station. There was a royal decree that the Government and Masstock get together to develop Haradh in a joint venture. This fitted into the overall scheme to have a dairy industry. We planned to have 4,500 dairy cattle there.

It's probably true to say that I was quite arrogant, claiming that we could build a food industry in Saudi Arabia. Problems started to arise. I don't know whether it was the fact of a private organisation coming up against the bureaucracy or pure xenophobia. Both of those were at least some of the reasons why we had difficulties.

Until you're in a country like that for a long time with your psyche under pressure, you can't really get a feeling for the place and in particular for the meaninglessness of time. Time means something different to the Arabs. The year there is not what it is here — you don't have seasons. You don't have a day like today with blue skies and white clouds and the birds singing and everything sparkling. There is no moving into the short nights of summer and then into the long nights of winter. Here, the four seasons are clearly demarked. There it's either half-five or half-six depending on whether it's winter or summer. The Bedouin did not harvest hay with the seasons. When he ran out of fodder for his camels, he just moved to the next place where there was grass. Everywhere you went, if you kept going, you'd see nothing but more of the same. It's just sand and desert — you keep going until you hit the sea. There is very little change in distance and in time. It's 1,400 years since Mohammed and 2,000 years since Christ and many people live exactly the same as they did then, so you get a completely new perspective of history and of space. Back here we might expect to have a cheque on Tuesday — such critical points in time did not exist out there. There was no way you could relate the two cultures.

That period in Saudi Arabia changed my nature. In many ways I'm ambitious and impatient but now I have an overall wider patience. I believe that what I am doing now will not have its full effect for another fifty or a hundred years. When I read your last book I found that the people in it all belonged to the world they lived in. When I look at what

I'm involved in, bringing a concept out from our farm to try to change world agriculture, I believe I need more tolerance and patience. I had to go to Saudi Arabia to acquire it.

There is very little limit to the ambition we have to influence world agriculture. It will be achieved but in a way entirely different from what I had expected originally. No matter how ponderous it may seem, the process is under way, it grows inexorably like a rolling snowball. Good values outlive roguery. All right, there are a number of rich rogues around — but they will come and they will go. The successful rogue has to stay on the tips of his toes all the time. Having left here with certain values that came from our Christian tradition and having seen not dissimilar values in the teachings of the prophet Mohammed, I believe that, if you stick by your principles, things will come right in the end. Biographies are a good way to test that. Let me throw Lincoln at you. He was an absolute bungler, the Civil War was disastrous, but the basic principle that Lincoln started with lives on.

I often wonder to what extent my father influenced me. I know that I subconsciously reflect on what my father would think of what I am doing. He was a progressive visionary and I am sorry he was not here to see our modern technology — the man on the moon. He missed the great learning curve. I would not be where I am but for the work he did in his lifetime. We, all of us, both my parents and my uncles, had certain views about the development of the local rural community and I suppose I have taken that globally. I feel that primary and rural development has to be addressed first before you move on to industrial sophistication. Third World development depends on rural development because seventy per cent of the population live in the countryside.

Then there is the Ulster Protestant influence that philanthropy is better served by honest-to-God successful commerce than by hand-outs. I believe my philanthropy is genuine even though it is within the formula of business development. You can't be a philanthropist and be a failure. I am asked if we are doing things for altruistic or commercial reasons. I see no conflict. It is a false question.

Earlier in my career, I would probably not have been careful enough to recognise the importance of strict capitalist rules. If I expose to risk the family stakes for philanthropic reasons and am not aware of the possible consequences, then I am going a very dangerous road. I put both at risk — the family and the philanthropy. That was another lesson from Saudi Arabia. When it came to the crunch, it was me and my family and everything we owned that were on the line. You see that with total clarity when you're down to the last penny.

I certainly could not be motivated by greed. I don't want wealth for wealth's sake. I am very lucky with the family I have — they are not at all influenced by wealth. If we had had wealth as a singular ambition, it would probably be all around us now and bringing up our family would have suffered as a result.

When I faced that crisis in Saudi Arabia I was probably more religious than I ever was before or since. Not institutionally religious — it was a very private thing. I was forced back on my own resources with just a few people, like my wife, to support me. The thing I am most aware of in religion — to be aware of and not to recite — is the Lord's Prayer. It marvellously encompasses the total relationship between man and God. I get most satisfaction from the Mass because of its historicity, its continuity, its reaching back through the ages with all its pomp and circumstance. I get more out of it that way than as an exercise in worship.

Yes, I have a long view of things. I very seldom get an opportunity to discuss with others the things that most occupy my mind and that's because I take a long view, a global view. I don't recognise borders, which is a way of expressing the same thing. For instance, I had to impress President Kaunda of Zambia that if we put a development down there it had to relate to the world economy. We would be able to do very little if it was contained and owned and restricted within the Zambian economy. A project like ours would flounder inside that economy.

You must see Africa in a hundred years as the hinterland of Europe. Africa is the place from which to supply Europe's tropical, non-temperate needs. Countries like Zambia are the places to grow cotton and exotic fruits. If we go to grow cotton in Zambia and they say that we have to sell all the cotton to them for kwachas which they will then turn into dollars to keep the International Monetary Fund at bay, it can't work, because we have to supply the capital, even though that may seem an entirely reasonable stance for the Zambian Government. The capital is there because of Masstock — and President Kaunda accepted that. But that would not be enough. From our cotton crop, we can get foreign exchange and service our capital, but for the second half of the year we grow wheat for local needs. That balances things out. We earn kwachas from the wheat and they are used to pay local costs.

We want to be farmers of the world. I might have been more aware of the importance of borders if I were brought up in that entity called the Irish Republic and was conscious of the Anglo-Irish Free Trade Agreement and then the European Community and saw myself sallying forth from my Irish fortress — or if I were a Unionist in Northern Ireland ready to defend myself against the depredations of a Romanish republic. I am a total free trader and probably a heretic in European agricultural terms. Apart from the Japanese rice growers, European agriculture is the most highly protected industry in the world.

I think it is right that in time all subsidies should be abolished and the market take its course. Down in Jeddah you can go into a shop and pick up a tin of milk powder produced in Mallow. That was made from milk collected on a farm, brought into Mallow. They used oil from the Middle East to dry it out — it takes seven tons of oil to make a ton of milk powder. It was shipped out at a cost. They paid their port dues at Jeddah. It was distributed by a distributor. A

198

retailer gets his margin — and, after all that, when you add the water to it, it's about the same price as the farmer got in Cork! That's what we're competing against. In order to keep rural Ireland happy, all that money was paid to all those people. That's how the farmers of Ireland maintained their life-style. I belong to that background — I think it is a lovely way of life. From their point of view it seems fair that you try to protect it but, if you go down into Zambia or anywhere in the Third World, and find products dumped on them at highly supported rates, what chance have they ever to rise?

There must be a new world food order before there is a new world economy. The extent to which world trade would benefit from a new attitude is incalculable. If you were to make available to a farmer in Zambia the profit from growing a ton of wheat, what is the first thing he would buy with it? Food. The chances are that he would purchase another food item that can't be produced locally, thus encouraging further world food trade. The farmer on the Ile de France who grows the wheat will probably instead buy a new Citroën or refrigerator or take a holiday.

If there was free trade, there would be tragedy in rural Ireland in the short term. Taking a long-term view, there would be a new world economy. But you can't just suddenly switch over. There would have to be a gradual adjustment of prices, but enterprises of excellence have to have been placed on the ground in the Third World countries so that they can be extended through a period of thirty to fifty years and take the place of current supplies of food.

When I get up before Friends of the Earth or Oxfam or other groups and tell them how I think Third World development should happen, they totally disagree with me. They believe that the African peasant should be allowed to find his own way to achieve sufficiency. They believe that rural development must be done on a self-help basis where the peasant is fifteen or twenty per cent more effective and is able to feed himself and his family. I don't think that's the only way. I believe that Africa is capable of being a large exporter of food. Growing food is the appropriate economic activity for people who are poor by contrast with people who are rich, as we all are relatively in the developed world. That can happen only when examples of efficient food enterprises are established on the ground — when people can see them as models. You can't wait for the slow evolution of peasant farming.

I am sorry to have to go into the terminology of dogma but 'capitalist exploitation' is the big fear. There is a fear that the big boys will move in and set up their large-scale operations and control the means of production. Well-meaning people, with a middle-class view of things, would see the answer as maintaining the sturdy independence of the peasant by, for example, giving him a well. I think there is good work done by a great many people to improve the lot of underdeveloped nations in that way. But look twenty-five years down the road and we are going to have to have a level of productivity in agriculture and the good management of storing and packaging and handling of food that we have in the developed world. That has to happen because there are four billion people who just don't have enough to eat. The problem of the global shortage of food can't be solved only by these rural development schemes, however well intentioned.

I think the same lessons can be applied here where the structure of farming is largely a product of history. There are a lot of social as well as economic influences, many of them tending towards keeping the small unit of production. But then my father's pig farm in the 1940s stimulated a completely new attitude to pig production in Northern Ireland. Then high-powered pig production started in places like Cavan just across the border — so these influences grow. There is no particular reason why pig production should grow in County Cavan other than the fact that they were close to the example. It was the demonstration effect. Centres of excellence and models of high efficiency can be copied by others.

We did that in America. We went down to the centre of Georgia which we chose because there was no tradition of dairy farming in the area. We picked a place called Montezuma in Macon County. We'll soon be among the biggest dairy farmers across the United States. Within only nine months of being there we were in the top dairy farms in the State of Georgia. Where there were no dairy farmers in the top twenty in Macon County, now there are seven. They are doing it because they saw us do it. Before we started in Saudi Arabia, there were 6,000 tons of wheat being produced. Now there are over three million tons.

If we were to wait for this slow-burn, self-help in the Third World, God help the human race. We must transfer to the Third World the capability and know-how of the Northern hemisphere so that the poorer nations can play their proper role in the world and the best way to do that is by practical demonstration.

By 1986, we felt we had the Saudi Arabian operation on a sound basis and we began to internationalise it. We started a dairy operation in Thailand. It was a fascinating scheme that I particularly liked. We've brought three or four hundred people from the countryside into our operation and then we bring them back to their farms and they get ten or twenty cows each. Zambia is the centre of our African operations. From Saudi Arabia we can stretch out across the whole of the Arab world. We needed to have a strong operation in hard currency areas and we chose dairying in the United States.

We now intend to re-establish Masstock from a base in the UK. We supply agronomy services and give advice to farmers on 650,000 acres in England. We intend to use that as a base from which we shall do the original Masstock. Eastern Europe is very attractive but we are not rushing out there. We get requests from every European country every day but time enough.

I would like to become a great deal less peripatetic. I'd rather spend a bit more time at home. I'd like to get to

know what this country is like to live in! And we have
another generation of McGuckians coming up.

Where we are sitting today is not really group headquarters — it's just the house where Paddy and I have
offices. We are two individuals who own all the companies
around the world separately. We don't see a need to do
anything differently yet. We want to keep it that way for
some time. We have worked our capital policy from the bottom up. We take each project and find means of leveraging
it rather than taking funds in. You can only go a certain
distance like that and it takes a long time.

The most important thing to me is my family. I like music
and I spend a fair bit of time at the piano — that really
relaxes me. I might impulsively go off and ski or windsurf or
something like that but I'm not a steady player — except
the piano! I don't like boundaries. I avoid bureaucracy or
institutionalisation as much as possible. While I like to be
able to express my ambitions freely, I like to try to arrange
that other young people can do the same.

The assets we are trying to put together are two — brands
and people. Brands are the expression of our mission —
including the brand Masstock very specially. It's *the* brand.
Our Almarai brand in Saudi Arabia is part of the culture
there now. It's as important as Pepsi. *Almarai* means green
pastures with the connotations of indigenous, fresh production. The second asset is people as the means by which we
achieve those brands or statements of mission. If you can
put those two things together correctly, then all other assets
you might use are strategic. Waterford Glass is an interesting
example. If the brand and people are matched in a collegiate way you have success. If there is a mismatch between
the brands and the people, it does not matter whether or
not you have any other assets, they will disappear, financial
or physical. What we are doing is matching those two things
within our ambition to develop world agriculture.

11

Gerry McGuinness

*All the people who were in class with me
did conventional things. They became doctors,
airline pilots, bankers. Because I was in
something unconventional — publishing,
magazines, newspapers — I felt I had to
prove myself by working a lot harder.*

Gerry McGuinness is a publisher. He was born in Dublin on 1 May 1938, the eldest of a family of four, three sisters. His father was Eiver John McGuinness, works manager in Urney Chocolates, his mother, Eileen Molloy, a housewife.

He was educated at:
Presentation Convent, Terenure,
Terenure College (Carmelites),
London School of Economics (night classes).

He is married to Deborah Wickins. They have one child, a daughter, Kerri (3). He was first married to Alma Carroll (who is now married to Arthur Ryan) and they had two sons, Gerard (19) and Mark (14).

He was executive assistant to Jack Goodlatte, the managing director of Associated British Cinemas.

Trainee, subsequently assistant manager in the A.B. chain of cinemas and then house manager in the Carlton Cinema, Dublin.

In 1963 he joined Hugh McLaughlin to publish *Woman's Way*, the first weekly women's magazine published in Ireland.

Business Manager of the Creation Group.

Launched *Business and Finance* magazine.

1972, launched *The Sunday World*. Is now a substantial shareholder and chief executive officer.

His present positions are:
Chairman of *Sunday World*,
Deputy Chairman of Atlantic Resources,
Chairman of Newspread and other companies and a director and substantial shareholder in Independent Newspapers plc.

He is Chairman of the Ferrier Trust, raising funds for Stewart's Hospital for the mentally handicapped.

I'm only in business to make money. I don't want to be a senator or a politician or have statues up to myself. Commercial success is necessary to live the life-style I want. I don't want to have a racehorse. I have no ambition to own an aeroplane or a helicopter. I have a nice house and a nice car or two. I used to have two nice houses but I sold my Spanish house which I had owned since 1967. At that time the embryonic golf courses in Spain were wonderful, the weather was beautiful, I loved the sun. And it was a good investment — I have had three houses in succession down there, rolled one into the other. But, with the years, things changed and I don't want my children to grow up with the kind of people who are now living in Spain. It is now the Costa del Crime. Also, my friend, Sean Connery, lived there for half the year and worked half the year so we had time to play a lot of golf. Now that he is in his sixties he seems to be working for ten months of the year and he has more or less left Spain. He is doing films back to back. He did the *Indiana Jones* film. He got the Oscar for *The Untouchables*. Now he is just starting a new John le Carré movie. He also made *Family Business* and *The Hunt for Red October*. James Hunt, the racing driver, was there also, mainly for tax reasons. But he left it too. Spain is awful.

My father died when he was fifty-six. He was a sad man, a rheumatoid arthritic in his adult life. When he was young he was a great sportsman. He played full-back on the senior and junior teams for Castleknock in the same year. I think it was because he was so good at sport as a kid that it savaged him when he became an invalid in later years. He was crippled at forty. I was twenty-eight when he died in 1966. I never really got to know him as a man. One of the tragedies in my life and maybe for everybody of my generation was that we knew our fathers when we were at school and then we went off to college or work or whatever. I went off and by the time I came back, my father was gone. He never saw what happened. He was a very modest man, lacking in ambition. I had asthma as a child and took up swimming because it was good for my lungs and I became reasonably proficient at it. I think he was more proud than anything when I won a cup at some gala in Galway or Tuam. But he would have been very chuffed to see the things I've done since.

My mother is still alive. For the past three years now she has been incarcerated in Highfield, a small nursing home in Drumcondra. That itself is a sad story. She was the only daughter of a successful businessman in the small town of Ballina. She had five brothers. She was the one for push and shove in the family and, when my father died, she took up bridge and became quite competitive at it. She was coming home from bridge one night five years ago. When she put her key in the door she found that it was chained on the inside. There were three guys inside robbing the house. They panicked more than she did. They didn't assault her in any way — nothing that left any mark you could see. The robbers pushed past her to get out of the house and knocked her down. She went into trauma as a result, apparently something that is not uncommon with people of her age, in their seventies, whose privacy has been invaded. She was brought to Sir Patrick Dun's Hospital and the neurologist there, Professor Kirker, called myself and my eldest sister and told me that my mother would not see Christmas — this was July. In fact, she plateaued and has stayed the same since, like someone with an advanced form of Alzheimer's disease. She is physically alive but she may as well be dead — her brain is just frozen in her. It is very sad. She is just another unmarked, yet very marked, victim of all the crimes we continue to read about in the papers.

Of my two parents, my mother was undoubtedly the more influential on me. My father, a gentle, unassuming person, was also a writer. He wrote more or less as a hobby for magazines such as *The National Geographic* and *Colliers*. He was a dreamer but my mother was a very strong, ambitious, aggressive lady, the complete opposite to my father.

My father told me three things shortly before he died. They only came back to me years later at about age fifty. 'If

206

you can buy it or sell it, it's worthless — the only three things that are priceless are your health, your friends, and the love of your children.' That meant nothing at all to me at the time. The penny only dropped when, perhaps, I had a child myself or at some other traumatic period of my life.

A major regret is the failure of my first marriage, not because of anything I did or failed to do but I probably got married as some sort of reaction to my father's death. I was twenty-eight and Alma was only seventeen — impossible. It was a miracle that the marriage survived even for a few years. Her father, Billy, a splendid man, should have given me a box over the ears for running off with his seventeen-year-old daughter. The marriage broke up because of pressures of my business career and Alma's career as a singer and various other things. However, it's funny the way the world swings round and in a perverse sort of way I am now a great friend of Alma's, a much better friend of hers than if I had stayed married to her. We see each other regularly — I speak to her several times a week. When I got married to Deborah she was there. It's like a kind of Dallas scenario. At Christmas time we all get together at home here with my three sisters and their husbands and kids and Arthur Ryan, Alma's husband. He is the Chairman of Penneys, works with Galen Weston. He is now as much a part of the family as anybody and that's important. It's important to the boys who, after the marriage, stayed with me while Alma went to work in America. Then, of course, she came back and, at that time, she felt a little on the outside. But now things have worked out and worked out well.

I hate failure. I hate taking on something — like that marriage — that appears to have failed. The reason I became chief executive of Atlantic Resources in 1988 was that we felt we had to give it one more shot — that company was going down at the time. We have given it that shot and it's going to be successful — a small oil- and gas-producing company, which was what it was meant to be in the first place, and this after nine years and £45 m. of shareholders' money. I was driving down with Tony O'Reilly to his home, Castlemartin, for lunch on 23 December. I said to him that the only thing to do with Atlantic was to take it by the neck and shake it and make a go of it. And Tony looked at me and said, 'I agree completely. You are the man to do it.' And in a fit of Christmas bonhomie or maybe Christmas alcohol, I agreed to take it on for six months. It's back, I suppose, to my dislike of failure and of unfinished business. Atlantic was born in this house. Tony would come in on the Friday night plane and come over here for breakfast at half past eight. 'Macker', that prince of a man, Jim McCarthy, Vincent Ferguson and the rest would all come over. We had this tremendous excitement about Atlantic. A couple of years later Atlantic was worth £130 m. or £140 m. — a bit crazy. So, for a company that was teased to the top of the expectations to be dropped to the bottom of the bucket was disastrous. Now, with a major gas discovery, Atlantic has reached its turning point. And recently I was able to say publicly that the share price represents a substantial discount on the net asset value. Atlantic is now almost like a drug. It's a company we've all sunk money into and none of us had anything out of it. Unless it makes a pound a share — which is a long way off — it won't mean anything to any of us who have invested in it. Yet this very idea of sticking a thing into the ground and pulling up oil would capture anybody's mind. It can distract you and take your mind off other things that might be more productive or more deserving of your time.

My grandfather died when he was young and, as I said, my father died when he was very young, from a heart attack even though he also had rheumatoid arthritis. I am a fanatic about my own health. I eat red meat sparingly, I never eat eggs, I avoid all the high-cholesterol foods. I avoid salt, sugar and dairy products virtually totally. I do fifty lengths of the pool every morning, which is half a mile. When I can't do that, I do something else like riding horses and I'm the same weight now at fifty-two as I was at twenty-one. I adore wine and I drink nothing else, but two days a week I drink nothing but water. Tony gives up drink for January, Mike Smurfit gives up drink for November, Jim Stafford would stop drinking for Lent and so on. January is thirty-one days, November is thirty days — I give up drink for 104 days! But if somebody said to me or you, you can't drink a glass of wine or champagne for three and a half months, you'd cut your throat! Two days a week is much easier and it does your system a lot of good because it's not a question of keeping off it entirely and then heaving it back in. The only legacy I have of the childhood asthma is a tendency to hay fever and of course you can keep that at bay with antihistamines. Sadly all my children have inherited the hay fever.

That other part of my father's adage — friends — I still have many of the friends I grew up with. I lost one of them last year, Joe Cahill, whose father was Tim Cahill, Chairman of the Labour Court. He was here at my fiftieth birthday and we were planning his fiftieth the year after. He was a distinguished surgeon in Cork. He was walking in a street in Killarney. He turned around and made a funny face at one of his sons and dropped dead of a massive haemorrhage. I suppose that, recently, I have come to realise that part of the price of being involved in business is that you tend to have too little time with the people who matter most. I have been very lucky with the people who have touched my life: those I grew up with, and those I met through business and that other passion of mine, golf.

I am especially lucky to count as close friends my sisters, particularly the eldest, Eileen; Alma of course, and my two sons, now men, Gerard and Mark, and, of course, Deborah. We met in 1983 on the beach at Sandy Lane, Barbados, where she was on holiday with her mother Dorothy. We only saw each other a couple of times over the next two years, but in 1985 we got together at Easter and were married in November. A bit rushed? Maybe, but I was not getting any younger — at forty-seven and Deborah was only twenty-four. I thought she might find it difficult to settle in Ireland, having grown up in Ascot and gone to school with the

American nuns at Marymount in Rome. Now? She's more Irish than . . . . She loves Ireland and the Irish, especially those in the west. The age thing still bothers me and I realise that time is now the real enemy. Deborah's a special lady, mature beyond her years. I remember a dinner at the Royal Thames Yacht Club a couple of years ago when we were guests of Deborah's dad, David, a committee member. The dinner was in his honour. The Commodore is Prince Charles and the Vice Commodore, Owen Aicher, who used to be Chairman of Marley. Everyone stood up in turn and paid tribute to David, praising his endeavours and achievements — in business, in sport and so on. Nobody asked me to speak as I was an unknown guest, but I stood up anyway and told a few Irish stories which, with some assistance from Hal Roche's scripts, they appeared to enjoy. I had to say something about David and I said, 'I have heard all you very important people tell about all the great things David Wickins has done. From where I sit the only thing he ever did that's worth a damn was to be Deborah's father.' They loved it.

Tony O'Reilly, I have known forever and became closely involved with him in the seventies when we did the deal with the *Sunday World*. I suppose the *Sunday World*, more than anything, made everything possible. In 1972, everything was funnelled into that. I had two partners: Hugh McLaughlin and Tom Butler. McLaughlin was a major shareholder and was uncomfortable and wished to realise his investment. He was substantially older than I was. Michael Smurfit was terribly helpful to me at this stage. The grand plan we had in 1976 was that Michael Smurfit and Tony O'Reilly would buy out my existing partners, I would reduce my shareholding to a third and then we would own a third each of the *Sunday World*. We met in Michael's office in Santry but the deal fell out over little things. In any event, I was unhappy with it: I wanted to retain 50 per cent with the boys at 25 per cent each. They did not like the smell of that at all, at all. But the flavour of a deal in the air made Hugh McLaughlin a definite seller. Several meetings took place with Bartle Pitcher, then managing director of the *Independent,* and Vincent Ferguson who was a director. The deal was straightforward: the *Independent* bought out Hugh McLaughlin and Tom Butler for £1.20 m.—£1.10 m. to Hugh McLaughlin and the rest to Tom Butler. Hugh got about three-quarters of a million in cash and the rest in *Independent* shares. I stayed in with a put option that would require them to buy me out at a four-and-a-half-times profit multiple. At the time, I had no intention of triggering that option when it matured in 1982 because then there was tapering tax relief — the longer you held on to your shares the less tax you paid until, eventually, you paid no tax at all. As my original investment in the *Sunday World* was very small, the earlier I triggered the put option, the more tax I would pay. However, when 1982 came, the tapering tax relief had disappeared. I was paid £2.80 m. in cash and shares and joined the *Independent* board on my birthday, 1 May 1982. I had agreed to act for five years as chairman of the *Sunday World* newspapers and really felt at the time that, at the end of that period, in 1987, I would be out. I saw that proprietor/executive role ending — I had never been a team player up to this. I was not sure how I would perform as a member of a team, something which is clearly called for in a public corporation of any kind. I was not sure how I would get on particularly with Tony and, indeed, with the other members of the *Independent* board for whom I would be a peculiar animal, an owner-manager, even though *Independent* held half the shares. I was not at all sure how they would deal with me when I ceased to be the owner of the *Sunday World.* As things turned out, nothing changed. Tony O'Reilly said to me, 'You are really something. You've got all my money and you still own the business.'

In fact, when I became a non-proprietorial chairman, I worked twice as hard to make sure that the profits in 1983 would be substantially higher than they were in 1982 when they reached the level that enabled me to trigger the put option. The Carmelites must have beaten some sense of honour into me, plus the fact that I did not want it to be seen that I had hyped the profits in one year in my own interest. I wanted the growth in profits to be seen as a continuing trend and not just as something to maximise my buy-out price. It was a stick I gave to everybody to beat me with. With a one-product company, there comes a point where you just can't go on increasing the profits dramatically every year. I think the *Sunday World* has reached a plateau now, but by any measure — return on investment, profit per employee — it is the most successful company of its kind that I have ever come across. Where we go from here — new product-lines or whatever — I just don't know. However, as you can see from the fax machine here in my study at home, I am still deeply involved.

Let me go back a minute to when I launched the paper in 1972. I went around knocking on doors. I remember going to see Maurice O'Kelly who was then managing director of Guinness Mahon in Dame Street. Maurice was president of the students' union of my old college. I was also on the school's past pupils' union council. Maurice offered me all the money within reason I wanted to back any horse I would pick from that day's *Irish Times* but, as for the Sunday newspaper, he did not think it stood a chance. I went to see Ken Wall, then Managing Director of Lombard & Ulster and he did not want to do business with me at all. I then went to see Victor Chambers whom I did not know from a hole in the wall — he was in charge of all the Ulster Bank operations in the Republic. He gave us all the money we wanted to launch the *Sunday World* just because he thought we told a good story and it was a good idea. When I got a cheque for the cash element of the deal with the *Independent,* I sent photocopies of it to Ken Wall and Maurice O'Kelly. I sent a thank-you note to Victor Chambers who had then become chief executive of the Ulster Bank Group. Victor was a smashing guy who told me that he did not invest only in bricks and mortar, he invested in people — a most unusual stance back then.

Money was not easy to come by in 1972 and we really launched the *Sunday World* on a shoestring. We needed £150,000. The Bank gave us half that. We put up the rest.

Nicholas Leonard and I had been talking about a Sunday newspaper since the mid-sixties. The *Sunday Review,* which *The Irish Times* had launched, had failed. There were some good writers involved in it like Patsy Dyke and Liam McGowan, but it was the wrong product at the wrong time. Nicholas and I came to the conclusion that it was still the wrong time in the mid-sixties. In 1971, Hugh McLaughlin and I felt the time was ripe and the *Sunday World* became a phenomenal success. The worst sale it ever had was 206,000 copies on day one.

I used to go to seminars and functions and things at that time to see what I could learn, and I was invited to be a speaker at a seminar run by the Marketing Institute in Brighton in the mid-seventies — the subject was new product launches. The other speakers were Max Aitken, with a little Pekinese under his arm, and the marketing director from Cadbury's who had just launched the instant potato mix, Smash. I told them I was only a little guy from Ireland and rather than make a speech I would answer questions. The first question I got was, 'What publisher do you style yourself after?' I said, 'Lew Grade.' The questioner said, 'With respect, Lew Grade is an impresario, not a publisher.' I said, 'I know he's an impresario — so am I. I get together, as he does in the London Palladium on a Sunday night, a TV star and a pop star and a bunch of naked women and a good sports section and a television interviewer and we call the whole mixture the *Sunday World.*' I was delivering to the consumer what I felt the consumer wanted to read and this is why the *Sunday World* worked.

The beginning was just pure luck, Ivor. The timing was spot on. Anybody could have done the *Sunday World* with the right mixture as we got it. Had I launched the same product, as *The Irish Times* did in the late fifties, it would have failed as the *Sunday Review* did.

This book is about entrepreneurs and I suppose if I have
to go right back to my origins in business I have to go back
to Terenure College when I needed more money than the
ten shillings a week I got for cutting the grass. I was sixteen
and a keen tennis player and on the junior committee of
Templeogue Tennis Club who ran unprofitable Saturday
night dances. I persuaded them to let me run a special
dance on Friday nights. Coca Cola had just been introduced
into Ireland — I used to buy it at threepence a bottle and
sell it for a shilling, a modest mark-up. I was making forty
pounds a week clear profit — an enormous sum of money
back in 1954. I was the only kid around at the time with a
car, an old Volkswagen. Unfortunately, it became widely
known how successful I was and the committee decided to
take over the business themselves. They instantly failed.
Like the *Sunday World*, I had the mixture right: Paul Russell
used to play the drums for me; Jim Doherty, who went on to
higher things, played the piano; Billy Buckley played the
bass; and John Curran played the clarinet. I had two of my
sisters working for me — one on the door and one in the
mineral bar. I paid them ten shillings a night which was
more than they were getting for their weekly pocket money,
so they thought they were in clover. When they read now
that I was making forty pounds and paying them ten
shillings they'll have my life! When the club took it over,
they had to employ professional staff at proper rates.

I did reasonably well at school: I got six honours in my
Leaving Certificate but failed Irish and that put manners on
me because it meant you had to repeat the whole Leaving
Certificate. I spent that whole summer getting ear damage
from my mother and consoled by my father. In October I
passed Irish for the Matric with the intention of going to
college. I didn't really know what I wanted to do. In the
event, I went to live in Crawley on the Sussex border with
my uncle Vincent and his wife, Hazel Molloy. He was then a
subcontractor at Gatwick Airport. I went to the London
School of Economics at night. I studied a bit of economics

and went to work with ABC just because it seemed a good thing to do at the time and came back here to Dublin with them. ABC were tied up with MGM who gave a monthly award of a small silver lion and a cheque for £100 for the best promotion of a film in the 'British Isles'. Once a year they gave an award of a smashing big lion and a substantial cheque and I was the first and only Irishman to win it. I got stuck into promoting MGM films because there was money in it — money for me and money for them and everybody was happy. At the reception for the silver lion award I met Ronnie Lee who was the director of Worldwide Promotions for MGM. At the time, 1960, he was promoting Ben Hur with Stephen Boyd and Charlton Heston and chariot races. He asked me to join him as his deputy for Worldwide Promotions. If I had joined him, my life would certainly have taken a different course.

The reason I didn't join him was that in my naive Irish country way, at the end of my tunnel vision, was a picture of me owning whatever I was doing. The dance in the Templeogue Tennis Club was *my* dance. When the club took it over, I would not run it for them. And I could never take over MGM! When I was leaving school, my mother said she could get me a nomination for the Munster & Leinster Bank. I told her I could never own the Munster & Leinster Bank and got a clip on the ear.

When I was twenty-one I came into my first asset, a house left to me by my grandfather. His name was John Molloy, a builder, who had built a terrace of houses on the canal in Ballina. The canal was not a canal — it was the Moy river and the houses were not really in a terrace, they were semi-detached. However, this was the first reasonable asset I had in my life. I went and took pictures of *my* house — the fact that there was somebody living in it was irrelevant — it was mine. I had an enormous proprietorial feeling about this house — I almost felt you could eat it.

I sold the house to the ESB for their area manager and made my first investment — in Creation Publications, much to my mother's horror. We had an enormous row about that — how dare I take her father's house and sell it! I was twenty-two at the time. I think I got two or three thousand pounds for it because the ESB wanted a house in a hurry. That gave me the seed capital that enabled me to become an investor rather than an employee in this little publishing organisation, which subsequently went broke because it expanded too fast.

All the people who were in class with me did conventional things. They became doctors, airline pilots, bankers. Because I was in something unconventional — publishing, magazines, newspapers — I felt I had to prove myself by working a lot harder. It was not that I sought publicity — indeed, the opposite. Gay Byrne has asked me to go on his show and I have never done so. I went once on the Mike Murphy show and when it was over I asked myself why I had done that. It had not done me any good. It had not done Independent Newspapers any good. It had not done Atlantic Resources any good. In fact, afterwards, I was telephoned by Joe Davy to say that the Atlantic shares had gone up by 50p after the broadcast. What I had said was that anyone who had Atlantic shares should not sell them and that anyone who had not got Atlantic shares should not buy them. They were shares for the rich or for speculators or gamblers — not for widows and orphans or serious investors. This was interpreted as playing down the shares and that made them all the more attractive. Seven years on, only yesterday, I was lacerated by somebody who accused me of leading him into the shares! So, no, I don't court personal publicity. I regard as vulgar in the extreme people who seek to publicise their wealth, or their version of it.

Hanging on the wall there, is a collage that my eldest son made to celebrate my fiftieth birthday. You will see there are only two pictures from the *Sunday World*: one at the launch of the paper and another at the funeral of Kevin Marron who was killed in an air crash. They are the only two pictures of me that have appeared in a paper that I have effectively controlled for the last eighteen years. Noelle Campbell-Sharpe talked me into doing a piece for *Success* magazine. That was the only one I did. I try to keep my private life private — I have had enough troubles! Being a publisher I have found that you are always in the public eye and you have to make at least a corner of your life private. In the publishing business you never get off the stage. When you go to a restaurant they jump to attention not because you are important — you are not at all important — but because you own a newspaper.

I regard what I have done in the *Sunday World* as unusual, but I am not a rich man. Michael Smurfit and Tony Ryan and Tony O'Reilly — they're rich. I met people in Pennsylvania recently and *they*'re rich, hundreds of millions of dollars. I can't tell you the number of times I've been got at to buy a racehorse. When my first marriage broke up, I bought a Rolls Royce — I felt I owed myself a present and bought myself a toy. I have a Bentley now but I never drive it. I have a Mercedes 500 which I love to drive.

I suppose there are just two people whose good opinion I would value and they are both dead: my father and P. V. (Vincent) Doyle — my father, because he did not live long enough to share in any of my attainments, and Vincent, because he was like a brother to me. With Vincent I had the purest form of friendship — we asked nothing of each other. I could tell things to Vincent that I could tell to nobody else on this earth and I think he had the same relationship with me. I miss him beyond belief. I can still see him in the Berkeley Court. I used to go there a lot. I don't go there much now. I go there to have a haircut — I can't eat in the restaurant any more without missing him.

The Haugheys, C. J. and Maureen, are my next-door neighbours and they were very kind when I came here from Castleknock, which would be regarded as a sort of yuppie area, while this is a very old, somewhat closed community. Charlie Haughey's birthday is on 16 September and we always go over there to the family party. Now it's even better because Deborah's birthday is on the 17th which gives us an excuse to stay on drinking wine after midnight!

The real test of friendship is to have someone there when you are in trouble, and Tom Fehily — now Monsignor Tom — was certainly there when my first marriage broke up. Most importantly, he was there for the boys who were very young then: Gerard was eight, Mark was only four. They were in the local school in Castleknock. My housekeeper was rapidly assuming a maternal role for the children which, while it was terrific and worked, I was getting concerned about. I spoke to Tom about it and he said, 'Gerry, you just get on with running your business — I'll take care of the boys.' He told me he was going to send them to Killashee, a school outside Naas, where he was the first pupil to be ordained. It's a French order of nuns, the Sainte Union, and we went down to meet the Reverend Mother, Sister Jarlath, a special and wonderful west of Ireland woman. They told us there was absolutely no way they could take the children, the school was full up. Tom said, 'Absolute rubbish! — school begins in September and that's the end of that.' 'Yes, father', they said. They had this reverential view of Tom. The boys became weekly boarders and that was the saving of my sanity. My mother nearly disowned me, sending a four-year-old boy to boarding school, but it was a marvellous success. Their Daddy saw them off on a Monday and whether I was going to Pittsburgh or Preston or Paris it did not matter, I was there to welcome them home on the Friday. The whole week revolved around being at home on a Saturday and Sunday. The family unit more or less stayed the same, and without Killashee I could not have done that.

I tell you all this because it's an important story: it was through Killashee that I met Dermot Weld. Our sons were there together. I heard the school was going to be closed. Apparently the nuns weren't getting enough novices or whatever and the powers-that-be in Rome had decided there could be no future for the school. In fact, they had signed a contract for sale to the Department of Justice who were going to open a women's prison there. Dermot and I and a few others got together, formed a company, stopped the sale and bought the property for £0.50 m. The authorities in Rome were not too pleased with us in that we had scuppered their deal. They were not too keen either on having anything to do with a bunch of businessmen who now owned their school. Our concern, of course, was to keep the school open and for that we needed the nuns. Finally, the authorities agreed to leave the nuns there for a further year. We would simply run the property and not interfere in any way with the running of the school. After two years, the authorities in Rome agreed to leave the nuns there in perpetuity. Of course, we had a fall-back situation. We had an interesting property on which we could have built semi-detached houses — £0.50 m. was still a lot of money at the beginning of this decade. But that is not what we wanted. I'm still chairman of that company.

We are now great friends with the nuns. We increased the fees dramatically — not to make a surplus, we never made a surplus — but to improve the school. It's now a smashing school where Mark, my youngest, in particular, met all sorts of people, all kinds of nationalities, that he would not have otherwise met. We have not had a penny from the Department of Education. It's our school and we want to run it our way.

That was one of the important things that happened to me and it happened through Tom Fehily.

I am also close to that saintly man, Fr Brian D'Arcy. Together with P. V. Doyle and with a lot of help from Gay Byrne and many others, we got together with him to stop Mount Argus falling down. We raised in all £4 m. The drive was spearheaded by Brian — and that was another important part of that period of my life — Brian, who has done more to bring God to people, especially the young, than anyone I know.

This proprietorial urge in me, this need to own, to be in charge of my own destiny, probably goes way back to when I was about six years old in Ballina. Gavins was, still is, a fairly up-market shop there. Mrs Gavin reared quite a distinguished family. She had several daughters: Mary married Michael Williams and Margaret married Desmond Downes. Mrs Gavin — she was always known as 'Mrs Gavin' — said to my mother, 'Always have them own something — a little shop or something.' It's funny how that went into my mind and stuck there and I was only six at the time.

I'm in business for money, not medals, but, no, I'm not in the business of making more — and more — money. What my purpose in life will be for the next ten years, I frankly do not know because that chapter has not yet been written. At present, that is precisely what I am assessing. I don't regard myself as rich at all, and yet in some ways I am extremely rich — back to what my father said to me. I am very fit. Thanks be to God, all my children are fit and well. I am fortunate to have a wonderful life, so I consider myself rich beyond belief, far richer than several people whom I won't mention who have much more money than I have. They are paupers by comparison with me because of their health or their personal lives or whatever. I want to dedicate more time now to reading, to listening to more music. I want to spend more time with the children — that little daughter of mine gives me incredible pleasure, I can't even describe it. When that little thing throws her arms around my neck and says, 'Hug, Daddy', I'm gone, everything else fades. When Gerard was two, seventeen years ago, other things would *not* have faded: I would have said, 'Hang on a minute, son', while I dealt with a business matter. Now, I'm very conscious of the fact that time is the only thing on which there is an absolute limit. I'm very conscious of the fact that I am not using my time now as well as I might and I have to get that together.

There is another box in my life that most people know about, that nobody ever talks about but that I never hide from. For several years after the break-up of my marriage with Alma, I had a loving relationship from which my son,

Gary, was born. There was no question of marriage — for a part of that time I was still officially married anyway — and Sandie, his mother, explains to Gary that his father now lives in another house but that he loves him very much. I see them regularly.

I have a number of different business involvements now. I would like to help take Atlantic to the next stage — and I am sure there is a good future there. You know as much as I do about Independent Newspapers. It's a small, good multi-national, with a useful geographic spread and a talented and aggressive management. I have some property invest-ments and my latest interest is in the leisure industry, for which there is going to be a big future. About five years ago, I was going somewhere on a plane and I bought one of those novels you buy to put you to sleep. It was called *Cathedral.* It was about the IRA going to blow up St Patrick's Cathedral on Fifth Avenue. There was the usual mix of IRA characters: the intellectual, the drop-out, the weirdo. The intellectual quoted two lines from a poem:

> I only know that summer sang in me a little while
> that in me sings no more.

I thought those two lines were fantastic. A wonderful lady, Sophie Hunt, a little like Tony O'Reilly's Olive Deasy, has worked with me for many years. I asked her to find out who wrote the lines. Eventually we found that they were lines from a poem written by Edna St Vincent Millay, who died in 1950. We had to get hold of a volume of her collected poems and there is a great story there. I was in New York with Vincent Ferguson. (If Vincent Doyle was a brother to me, Vincent Ferguson was more than a cousin.) We were on our way out to the West Coast to visit the broadcasting station, KJOY, that Independent owned at the time. I told Vincent about the book I was looking for — we were staying in the Helmsley Palace Hotel which is behind St Patrick's Cathedral. Next day we were to have breakfast together at seven-thirty. Vincent was missing. When he showed up I asked him where he had been. He told me he had got to bed late the night before. I was surprised at this because we were both tired after the transatlantic flight and I had gone to bed at ten. Then he produced the *Collected Poems of Edna St Vincent Millay*. He had tramped the streets of New York the night before until he found, in the pouring rain, an all-night bookshop which had a copy of the book, a book which has become something of a bible for me. That book was the first introduction to any proper reading that I had done for twenty years. I've read every single poem in it ten times over, the last five years. I got on to the publishers and, with considerable difficulty, got them to find twenty copies which I have given to people who I know are sensitive, like Brian D'Arcy and Susan O'Reilly. Edna St Vincent Millay's sonnets are simply unbelievable. She wrote of God:

> And see not at last how tall I am. Even at noon I cast
> a shadow like a forest far behind me on the ground.

She was a very sad woman. Her epitaph was:

> Heap not on this mound roses that she loved so well.
> Why bewilder her with flowers that she cannot see
> or smell.

Of course Vincent Ferguson, a Sligo lad, had to say, 'Not a patch on Yeats.' So, I got to start reading again from two lines in a poxy novel. I regard that as another significant chance event in my life — if it had not happened, look what I would have missed.

12

Carol Moffett

Every time I meet adversity, I take stock of the problem. Whatever I meet, it is nothing compared with how I felt in the early days of the business after my father died. Overcoming that has given me a strength to cope with anything that has come along. That was the crucible.

Carol Moffett is the Chairman and Managing Director of Moffett Engineering.

She was born in Monaghan on 20 November 1952, the eldest of three children. She has two brothers, Robert and Maurice.

Her father, who was self-employed at the engineering works, was Cecil Moffett. Her mother Ida, nee McBride, is a housewife.

She was educated at Crieve National School, got a scholarship to Monaghan Collegiate School and then went to Trinity College Dublin where she did not complete her studies.

She is a member of the Executive Committee and Council of the Irish Management Institute and served also on the board of the Tyrone Guthrie Centre, Annamakerrig, on the Irish Goods Council and on the regional board of the Industrial Development Authority.

Irish Times Manager of the Year, 1980;
People of the Year Award, 1983;
Businesswoman of the Year, 1983;
Fellow of the Irish Management Institute.

I was born here in Monaghan and went to the local school. My father was always encouraging me, pushing me forward. Very early on I decided I was going to make a career and go to university. In the late sixties, early seventies, there was not the same pressure to get a job. It was more about getting an education and broadening your horizons. I was fortunate I was able to go to university. In those days there weren't any grants and I'm sure my father had to make sacrifices. The work ethic was highly valued at home. If I wanted to get extra money, I had to sweep the workshop floor or get things for my father — he thought nothing of sending me on my bicycle to Monaghan, eight miles from here. I was brought up in a family business environment: a lot of the discussion took place around the kitchen table — the workshop was attached to our dwelling-house. The customers came and went and I probably learned at an early age how to deal with people and of the importance of keeping the customer happy. Considering the path my life took, I realise now that these were all beneficial influences.

I enjoyed going to school and worked hard at my studies. I was sorry in a way I could not go to a bigger school where there would have been more challenges, but I don't think it stunted my growth. I was always keen to travel but my father said I could not do so until I earned the money myself. As soon as I was seventeen I made my first solo trip — to France.

My parents always had total confidence in me and never fussed the way other parents fussed over their children — even allowing a young Monaghan lass off to France on her own. It was just expected that I could take care of myself. I was probably quite a confident child.

When I went to Trinity, I chose, in a haphazard way, French and Spanish. I had vague ideas of working with a multinational company after a post-graduate course in business. I discovered that the literature content of the language courses was high and I was more interested in language as a means of communication. I was not academic but I was not going to give up. I used my summers going to France and

Spain and was fortunate in meeting up with a lovely Spanish family. Living with them — as a friend, not a servant — was an enriching experience. I don't find the French people as warm and open. The result is that my Spanish is pretty good, my French not so good. However, I planned to major in French as I thought it would be a better degree. For my third year I planned to go to France but my father died very suddenly. My whole world was turned upside-down. That was in October 1972.

The business at that stage was two people. My brother Robert was sixteen and was already working in the business, and Maurice was eleven. I tried to continue going to Trinity every week and coming home at the weekends, but it was plain that the business needed somebody to take control and my brothers were too young. Reluctantly I went to my tutor to explain the situation, that I needed a year off to sort out my domestic problems. My mother was not the kind of person to have any interest in the business. She would, of course, like to see it doing well, but she was shy and did not want to get involved in the nitty-gritty. I came home at Christmas. I was supposed to be writing a Spanish thesis on the role of women in literature in South America. I couldn't concentrate on it at all. It seemed so irrelevant.

My father had worked very hard to build up a business which enjoyed a very good reputation. We made special-purpose machines. For example, a local furniture manufacturer would go to a show abroad, come back with a brochure and say to my father, 'I want a machine like that', and my father would build it. He also had his own line of products. There were two staple ones: a friction saw for cutting steel and a range of steel moulds for manufacturing concrete products. That was unusual for a small Irish engineering company at that time.

I got into the car and went to see the customers and tried to sell friction saws and moulds. It was as simple as that. It was important to keep the continuity of the business because people felt that, when my father died, it was gone. He was perceived as the brains behind things, but after he died we tried to pretend it was business as usual.

The customers were surprised at a young lass arriving into them and I got some sympathy, but I quickly found out that I had to know what I was talking about. It was simple, common-sense stuff, no magic at all. There was no point in trying to bluff people, and if I was able to show that I knew what I was talking about, I always got a hearing.

At the time my father died, he was rebuilding the workshop. This was a big financial drain. We were in the position where we had reasonably good premises, very little debt on the business, two very loyal employees plus myself — so we had a basis to work on. All it needed was hard work, application and trying to win the customers back. Well, it was not as simple as it sounds. For a start, the banks were rather sceptical. The early seventies were really the dark old days of banking. When I went in to see the bank manager he looked to me to be a very old man!

I would not say I was particularly close to my father, but I enjoyed debating with him and I was probably more ambitious for his business than he was. He had lots of opportunities to do more things. The IDA came to him and offered him grant assistance to buy machinery and extend the premises — he was not interested in any of that. His joy was in solving problems — he was not interested in money or the hassle of having a big factory and dealing with lots of people. He was a perfectionist in everything he did — which I am not.

My mother probably tried to hold me back a bit. My father was the stronger influence.

We struggled along, getting through one day at a time. In the summer of the first year that I was at home, I went to Spain for a month to keep up my Spanish, because I was fully intent on going back to university. But business had got a grip on me and I was beginning to enjoy it, beginning to realise that it had a lot of possibilities and was a broadening experience and that I was learning a lot more about

life than I could at university. When October came, I decided
to leave it another year before I would go back. I had created
a job for myself in the business.

I put up the price of the friction saw and that was a very
brave thing to do. I enjoyed selling. I then started to
develop a retail side, primarily because we needed cash. We
were buying in steel to make the products, so why not sell
the steel as well, something my father had been doing in a
limited way. I promoted this side of the business to local
companies, also selling bearings and V-belts and pulleys. I
went to Dublin once a week, and if a company needed a nut
or bolt and it took ten calls to get it, I would get it and bring
the stuff home in the boot of the car. It was all part of
showing that we could give a customer service. There was a
new challenge, a new problem, every day. As soon as you
solved one problem, another one appeared on the horizon
and you wondered how you were going to deal with it. A
number of times, I probably bit off more than I could chew
but I had good family support. We had now taken on a third
person — a major step for us, an increase of fifty per cent in
the workforce! One of the two men who worked with my
father is still with us, Jim Allister. He must be with us now
thirty-five to forty years. He is doing exactly what he was
doing in my father's time. When, eventually, we went into
exporting, we split the business and kept on the original
jobbing-shop where he now works.

Nothing very exciting happened for a number of years. It
was just a hard grind every day. Robert had a natural flair
for design. He is a tremendous asset to the business. My
brother Maurice did engineering in the Regional Tech. in
Dundalk and came home about five years ago. He runs the
separate company which looks after the retail sales and the
engineering service business. The three of us have distinct
areas of expertise. The part that I enjoy is international
marketing. Robert has no interest in international marketing.
Maurice wants to look after his local customers and build
up that side of the business. Since we have different

personalities and different interests — and now have an outside production director, Jim McAdam — there is very little conflict. The four of us constitute the board of the company and I am, I suppose, the chairman and managing director, but I don't think of myself as the boss. We don't go in much for titles — unless it is to impress a customer. I would never make a major decision without consulting Jim, Robert and Maurice. The older we get the more we like to discuss things — we are trying to get rid of doing things on hunches, though we have done so and have been successful. I'll take on the role of chairman and managing director if I'm talking to a banker — but not within the family. We are all very down to earth people. Jim is totally in the confidence of the family — there is no inner-circle, but if there are occasions when I feel really strongly about something, I would say, 'This is the way we're going to go.' I do try to bring the others around to my way of thinking. There is a four-year age gap between Robert and me and nine years with Maurice — perhaps that accounts for some of my authority!

There was a job that had to be done — I happened to be the oldest and the job fell on my shoulders. I had no intention in those early days of growing the business to the size it is now, with eighty-five employees. Then it was simply survival: my motive was to keep the standard of living of the family and to keep the two employees — just keeping the business afloat. We lived modestly — my parents were frugal in their ways. My father had the same car for thirteen years. It was a simple life.

I now have a much higher standard of living than if I continued in university and got a job. I have enjoyed one or two luxuries to which my father would never have treated himself. Perhaps I feel a little guilty about that. He made me appreciate the value of an honest day's work for an honest day's pay. If there were a reduction in my standard of living, I would be sorry to see it go, but I would just start all over again.

I am tough. I did not realise that until I began to employ so-called professional people in the company. Sometimes they were put in positions where they had to take hard decisions and I realised that a lot of people don't have the backbone to do the things that need to be done. A very high percentage of the population just want a simple life, no hassle, drift along from day to day and take their money at the end of the month. There are very few prepared to push ahead and take decisions that make them unpopular. People crave popularity, don't they? They don't want to change, they don't want to do things that cause ripples.

I learned early on that the things that are admired in a man in business — that he is tough, aggressive, assertive — are not admired in a woman. People always have a surprised reaction when they meet me. They expect somebody much older or much tougher — a tough old battleaxe. Even people in senior positions have that reaction. I don't find it a drawback at all. I am clear about my goals and, in my pursuit of them, I will use these things to my advantage. When I arrive into somebody's office and he is obviously surprised, I feel that I have his full and undivided attention for about sixty seconds. If I can make a good impression in those seconds, I have a major advantage over a man coming in to do the same job. Even locally, people think I am an engineer — I never did engineering. I don't con them — but I don't disillusion them either. I find that when you attain a little 'success', people assume that you are more successful than you are.

We are in the expensive end of the capital goods market. Ireland is not renowned as an exporter of capital goods. When a person is dealing with me for the first time, he has to be convinced that I know what I am talking about and that I am in a position to make a decision. If people try to treat me frivolously, I nip it very quickly in the bud. It is usually a very junior person who would try that on. Though on occasion it can happen with a senior person. I was at a dinner for thirty-two people — the only woman present. The man beside me asked, 'Mrs Moffett, are you in your husband's business?' I said, 'No, I don't have a husband.' He said, 'I am very sorry.' People say things to you that they would not say to a man in a pin-stripe suit but, in the end, I think being a woman in business is mostly an advantage. The first thing is you get remembered. When a manager is going through his folder, he's looking at hundreds of business cards from male reps. He will tend to remember mine. When I go to shows, people come up to ask me how I am and I can't remember them from Adam.

The most awful thing that ever happened to me was my father's death. The death of a parent is hard to cope with. He died at a wedding. He was fifty-one. On top of the void he left in our lives, he was the bread-winner and he was gone. There were times then when I looked into a deep black hole, but I always believed in my own ability that somehow I would get around the problems. By nature I am very optim-istic. I don't get depressed about things. I am not moody.

I need nine hours sleep every night, but when at last I have woken up, I am usually in good humour. Then I need to get some food quickly — I always have my breakfast before I get dressed. I also eat a lot, yet every year I lose two or three pounds. I am fortunate in that I don't like butter, I have given up milk since I was nine months, I don't eat sugar and I don't eat junk food. I find it very difficult when I go to the States and I'm brought to McDonalds. I like to exercise at least three or four times a week: I swim and walk. It's difficult when I am travelling. You can't just put on a pair of runners and walk around Atlanta — it wouldn't be very safe.

If there is a crisis while I am away, I think my family believes that Carol will fix it when she gets back. I am ex-pected to know the solution to most problems. Nobody has ever said it but I feel that. I don't feel that that is oppressive. I feel that it is my challenge and that I have got to rise to it even though I may not have a clue how we are going to get out of the mess, but I can't give the impression that I haven't. One of the difficulties in running a small business is that you have continually to be seen to know what you are doing and where you are going. No matter how bad things are, you can't let people see that you are finding it tough. It would be very bad for the morale of the company to let that out.

I am happy and cheerful myself and I can't stand the company of people who are not happy, not cheerful, not can-do — they depress me. Moaners and moody people and people who are groaning about things depress me. I hate to be around them. I like to be with people who are full of action, who would see an opportunity and take it, who are even impetuous — not people who are planning and organising themselves for six months in advance. Quiet people unnerve me — I like outgoing people. Quiet people make me shy and nervous and scare me.

If somebody is in trouble in the company I would give them a sympathetic hearing though I am not very good at dispensing sympathy. I am a self-starter — self-motivated — and sometimes I have to stop and say to myself that not everybody is built in that mode. Sometimes I forget to accommodate that in other people. I'm impatient. As I get older, I am trying to learn to be more patient. There have been occasions where I have felt that people were not per-forming because they were afraid of me. I would sit down with them and explain to them that I myself was under pres-sure, that I might have been a bit offhand with them but that there was nothing personal in it. Niceties have got to be left out if you're under a lot of pressure to get something done.

It would be interesting to have a conversation with my father now about the business. I don't think he would approve of all the hassle I've brought on myself. The quality of one's life has obviously had to suffer. The price I have paid is that I have put ninety-five per cent of my energies into the busi-ness. I seldom get home before nine o'clock at night. There are a lot of other things in life that I would have enjoyed doing but there simply is not time. You plan to do some-thing and you discover you have to go and see a customer. The business eats into one's life — to be successful it has to.

You can't say that you are going to finish at five-thirty. The only thing is to leave the place completely for two or three days. Anyway — I enjoy it. I am not bemoaning the fact that that is the way my life has turned out. I am fortunate that I have found in life a niche I can enjoy and in which I can satisfy my lust for travel, selling our products all around the world.

People do tend to put you down a little about this. They say, 'When you are older, you will have a different perspective and you will realise that there is more to life than business.' But I feel a fulfilled person. I can't say, 'If only I had done this or if only I had done that . . . .' I am fortunate in that I enjoy excellent health, fantastic stamina, plenty of appetite for work and I have surrounded myself with people who are like that as well, and I enjoy interacting with them. I get a great buzz from all of this.

I have friends outside business whom I meet irregularly. They are important to me and I would make a special effort to see them when I am in the country.

I feel very little loneliness. I can happily spend a week on my own. I spent Christmas on my own this year, lying on my back on a beach in Phuket, off Thailand. But I always seem to meet interesting people, helped by the fact that I have two or three languages. Even on a Turkish holiday, I spent four days staying with a Turkish family whom I had met up with. I love this adventure thing of getting on a plane and wondering what I am going to do when I get to my destination. I have travelled loads of times on my own, all over the world, and I enjoy it. I need the time on my own to repair my nerve-endings when I have been working flat out for a number of weeks.

I see the future as more of the same but there are things I want to do. For example, I want to go back to France to perfect my French, particularly my technical French, so that I can talk to customers. I want to do the same in Spanish. There are lots of courses I would like to do and lots of places I would like to see and to understand their cultures. The world is such a big place and we know so little about it. A lot of my trips to places have been superficial.

When I am alone I like to read — mostly biographies, or better, autobiographies of successful people. I like to read business magazines and that kind of stuff.

Business is my consuming interest so I suppose I could describe myself as a businesswoman.

Would I say yes to an invitation to join a big, prestigious board? The answer is probably no. I would not know how to contribute. I am completely self-taught. I only go by what seems like common sense. With my colleagues, we set the goals for this little business and we persist, and if we meet a closed door we just try again. Why do people think there is some magic formula or special knowledge? It's application and a lot of hard work and the stamina to stick with it, to make things happen. A high IQ has nothing to do with it. We all possess strengths within ourselves that we don't realise we have. My experience bears that out. The vast majority of people never realise their full potential. If a nineteen-year old can take a little business in the back of beyond and, with some help, take it to this stage, anybody can do it. I was forced into a situation where I just had to. I had to pull out all the reserves that I could muster to cope with a very bleak situation. I think a lot of people could do the same if they were put in the same situation. The important thing is having the confidence and belief in yourself.

Maybe a lot of it goes back to our educational system. The kids are not encouraged to can-do. They're focused on getting their points in their exams. It's a real rat-race. There is very little room for self-development in the curriculum.

Every time I meet adversity, I take stock of the problem. Whatever I meet it is nothing compared with how I felt in the early days of the business after my father died. Overcoming that has given me a strength to cope with anything that has come along. That was the crucible.

Business is a game and it's a load of fun. It's very bad if you get too serious about it. If the problem you face is only a business one, then you can usually find your way around it. I had to cope with much more than a business problem. I don't feel any resentment now that I had to alter the path on which I had originally set out at university. I was faced with a situation and I made the best of it and I have had a lot of satisfaction from doing that. I will always remember the quote from Jefferson Smurfit: 'Opportunities come to pass and not to pause.'

Chris Park of the IMI was arguing with me recently that our native begrudgery was disappearing. I still think it is there. I think people in Ireland like to see you fail — they are resentful of success. If you make it, they are always trying to find what devious thing you did to make it. It can never be just because you have worked hard. That's still there — it is not completely gone. One thing I like about America is that it is the can-do society — everybody believes in the American dream, every kid believes that he or she will some day realise his or her full potential. Listen to American twelve-year olds being interviewed and they are oozing with confidence. They use a vocabulary our kids would not know — and yet their educational system is not nearly as good as ours. Very few of our schoolkids are confident. Irish parents are not great at lavishing praise on their children. They are afraid that if they praise little Johnny or Mary they will get big heads. There is not enough status given to technological education. They want their children to be solicitors and doctors and dentists and accountants. We need lots more status for technological jobs, the jobs that will be needed in the future. Irish parents are very conscious of what the neighbours think.

They should concentrate on their own destinies and not worry about the neighbours.

Young people should realise that they have lots of potential and should have the courage to go out and grasp opportunities and do what they want to do. They should not be pressured to go to university. They should not feel they are failures if they don't make the university grade. It's as simple as that. Irish people need confidence — they seem to get it once they step on the boat or the plane.

I've helped to create a small business enterprise in a remote part of Ireland and in so doing I have got a lot of personal satisfaction. I have enjoyed being the leader of a small tightly knit team who are accomplishing that task with me. I am enjoying competing with big companies in international markets. I have enjoyed travelling and learning a little bit about the world. I am happy in what I do — I have no regrets.

13

Joe Moran

*People get different talents and the Lord said
that we should deliver on those talents. What have
I done? I have got the personal satisfaction of
achieving a certain amount of success. Success
means to me that you get something small or
in trouble and you build it up.*

Joe Moran is Chairman of Irish Wire Products plc.

He was born in Brosna, Co. Kerry on 27 October 1935.

His father was Frank Moran, a creamery manager, his mother Elizabeth Cotter, a national teacher. He was the youngest boy in a family of six, five boys and one girl.

He was educated at:
National School, Knockaclarig,
Rockwell College,
University College Cork (Dairy Science).

He is married to Marie Hogan, a nurse. They have four children: Jean (21), John (19), Cara (17) and Adrienne (12).

Career:

Castlelyons Creamery, Co. Cork,
Springmount Creamery, Cahir,
General Manager, Ballypatrick Co-op (between Cahir and Carrick-on-Suir),
Took over F. & T. Buckley, fireplace manufacturer, Fitzwilliam Lane, Dublin,
Chairman and Chief Executive, Irish Wire Products plc,
Deputy Chairman, Flogas,

Vice-President of the Contract Bridge Association of Ireland.
Financial adviser in the Parish of Ballyboden.

It all began at home — my father was the local creamery manager back in Mountcollins which is on the Limerick/Kerry/Cork border. He was an amazing businessman. If you look at these people who built up co-ops — Lynch of Mitchelstown, O'Donnell of Castlelyons, Deasy in Kantoher — they were really great entrepreneurs. My father had built up his co-op and I suppose somebody said that I should join him there. My mother — Lord have mercy on her, she minded us all — rang me in Rockwell and told me that there was an entrance exam for UCC and that I should do it. I did and entered UCC as a dairy science student. I often hear people say I wanted to be this or I wanted to be that from the day I was born. That's lovely in theory. It's like a business plan. You read in the papers about some company saying they had a business plan, that they knew in year one where they would be in year five. Of course, they don't tell you about the plan until year six.

My first job was in Castlelyons Creamery as a branch manager. Then, in 1961, I became general manager of Ballypatrick Co-op, a good co-op in south Tipperary, the youngest general manager of a co-op in the country. I was young, a bachelor, with a free house and a free phone — it was the ideal world. My father was then about sixty-eight and my mother, who was a couple of years younger, had retired as a national teacher. My father rang me up one day and gave me one bit of advice: 'You're better off working for yourself than working for anybody else.' I'll always remember that. Now that was back in 1963 and I had £2,000 a year, a very good salary and a lot of independence. I was almost working for myself. I often feel that if we had left some of those small co-ops we might have had more spirit in the parish. I suppose Denis Brosnan would not agree with that and perhaps he's right from the financial and the production point of view. Anyway, I asked my father what he wanted me to do. He said, 'Come up with the idea for a business.' I sat down and thought about it. I was quite happy where I was. I had succeeded an old autocratic manager and here I was young and popular with the people.

I thought hard but I couldn't come up with any businesses to go into. I put an ad in the personal column of the *Irish Independent* — I still have that ad today. The ad said, excuse the arrogance: 'Intelligent young man with capital seeks active interest in business. Dublin area preferred.' Isn't that hard to believe — in nineteen hundred and sixty-three? I put it in the paper I always read myself. I got at least thirty replies. Some of them were total chancers: one of them was from an Austrian who was making perfume up in the back of Drumcondra. 'Mr Moran', he said, 'I will make your name famous all over the women of Europe. We will call it Perfumo Morano!' Maybe I was too conservative or too blind to the opportunities, but I decided that wasn't the way to go.

Eventually Gerry Kelly, who made tile fireplaces in, of all places, Fitzwilliam Lane, replied to the ad. We did a deal. Now I was a country fellow looking at Dublin, but Gerry had come from County Limerick and had a brother a priest and I had a brother a priest and they sort of knew each other. We — my father and I — bought the business for £4,000 and we offered Gerry £2,000 for the stock. I went back to my father, who had put up the money, and said, 'You have a business for £6,000 but I want fifty-one per cent of it.' He told me not to be cheeky. I had this fear — it may have been a country fear and I've lost it now — that you had to have somebody in control and the only way to be in control is to own more than half the business. Then you would not have two or three people arguing about what has to be done. That's very important in small businesses that you're building up. I have seen too many cases where fifty-fifty doesn't work. My father said, 'That's absolutely ridiculous. I'm putting up the money. Are you saying that we wouldn't get on?' I said, 'No, Boss' — we used to call him Boss — 'You could be dead and gone and I'd be arguing with my brothers and sister.' I ended up with fifty-five per cent and he eventually gave the rest to my brothers and sister. The tile fireplace business was called F. & T. Buckley and employed four or five people.

Talk about due diligence. It was not until afterwards that we found that Kelly was only renting the premises from a fellow called Buckley, and Buckley hadn't even a title to be there. We left that premises after some years and, a week before we left, we were served with a summons telling us to get out, that we were unlawful tenants! It just shows that, when you're starting off, you're not too well up in all the precautions to take. You must have a bit of flair and you must take a certain amount of chance when you're very small — things that we couldn't do now in a company like IWP.

We built up that business little by little by sheer hard work. Looking back on it, it was an amazing move for me — even trying to get my bearings in Dublin. Gerry Kelly, the man that I bought it from, stayed on with me and one day the two of us went out to see Park Developments who were building houses at Foxrock. The following day I got a call to take something from their site. When I had gone out with Gerry we went out the Bray Road. The next day, when I went out by myself, I went out the Blackrock Road and got totally lost. It was also a change in the scale of operations. The office was so small that, when Jack Farrelly, the part-time accountant came in, he couldn't get out again until whoever else was in the office moved his chair. We had no truck — we had a fellow who used to hack stuff for us. He was most unreliable. I'd book him for a load for McInerneys for Wednesday and he might not turn up till Thursday or Friday. I got fed up with this. I was in school with Donal Burke of Burke's Garage in Cahir. I rang him and said, 'Donal, have you any old truck down there I could buy off you?' I got the train down to Thurles and my brother, who was in the bank there, drove me to Cahir. I bought an old cattle truck for £275, cleaned it out that night and drove it back myself to Dublin the following day. So as not to come back empty, I loaded it up with fire-clay on the way back. That's the kind of thing you want to build a business — sheer hard work and determination. That and keep the costs down.

The first year I dropped my salary from £2,000 to £1,000.
We made a profit of about £4,000. The second year we
made about £8,000. In the fourth or fifth year we were up to
about £50,000. Every penny went back into the business. We
started to expand into being a small builders' merchant. We
had moved by then over to the back of the Ashling Hotel in
Parkgate Street — Ben Naughton had just started there. I
could always see that we needed room for expansion and
then we made a good move. We bought eight acres of land
on Robinhood Road, just off the Naas Road. We paid
£20,000 for that. We were offered other land that has since
been developed into the Robinhood Industrial Estate, but
we just couldn't afford it. The fellow who financed that was
Gerry Tierney who was in the Northern Bank Finance
Corporation. I went into AIB first — now I have the greatest
respect for AIB, it's a wonderful organisation — but they
were looking for this security and that security and they
would let me know. I went into Gerry Tierney and he asked,
'How much would you need?' I said, '£20,000.' He said,
'Hold on a minute. You'll have to put a building on that.
You can take it that, as of this evening, you have a facility
here of £40,000.' I'll always appreciate that.

In 1969, Jim Stafford approached me and offered me
£250,000 for the business. A condition was that I would have
to stay on for five years, but I did not leave the co-op to
work for Jim Stafford.

In 1973 we had moved to the Robinhood Industrial Estate
and I was approached by Tony O'Reilly, Nicholas Leonard
and Vincent Ferguson, who were starting up Fitzwilton.
They had taken over McCarthy's in Cork and Dockrell's in
Dublin — Jim McCarthy was running it. We went down that
road a long way and agreed a deal of £780,000 for the
business. That was not a bad bit of money back in 1973. I
learned a lot from that deal because it went wrong for personal reasons. It taught me how not to do a deal. They were
so busy that they did not wrap the deal up properly. It was
not handled well on a personal basis — not O'Reilly, Leonard,

Ferguson or McCarthy — they handed it to somebody further down the line who didn't get the personal thing right and I think that's very important. It was a small thing, the way you can switch people off. Part of the deal was that I would have a contract for a number of years there. We finished up in a solicitor's office. Nobody turned up from the Fitzwilton camp. The solicitor started off, 'Now, Mr Moran, we want to go through this contract. What hours are you going to work?' I was working at this stage from eight o'clock in the morning till ten o'clock at night. You had this young solicitor, a fellow who was doing his job, asking me that kind of question. Rory O'Donnell, my solicitor was with me. He said, 'Now, take it easy, Joe.' So I said, 'Nine-thirty to five-thirty.' 'What holidays do you take?' I said, 'Excuse me, I take holidays when I feel like it.' I was getting a bit emotional — which people do when you're selling a business. He said, 'Mr Moran, you are now working for somebody else and we'll get your holidays straightened out.' Then he said, 'What type of car?' At that stage, I said, 'Don't be annoying me — as far as I'm concerned you can put down Morris Minor.' With that I got up and I walked out. That was the start of that deal going wrong but, in fact, we fell out over a number of things.

The lesson I learned from that was that if you are taking over a business from somebody who has run it — and we did that successfully in IWP — be very careful how you handle things. You are dealing with somebody who has built up the business and you can't just walk in and take it over. There's a lot of emotion involved. That deal did not go through.

We developed the business. I met Jim Flavin who was running ACT with Allied Irish Investment Bank. He said, 'We'll take a stake and we'll value it at the same price that Fitzwilton were going to give you.' We got £170,000 — the first money we ever got out of the business after ten years in it. The bank ended up owning 27.5 per cent of the business — the Moran family held the balance. We then formed

the Moran Group. We bought a business in Limerick from
R. & J. O'Dwyers and we bought Meldrums of Sligo and we
bought the Cork Iron and Hardware Company. I can assure
you that I applied to the acquisition of those businesses the
lessons I had learned myself. I remember I was buying, with
an adviser, that last business from Ralph O'Dwyer. They were
looking for a huge price. My adviser was there quoting all
the rules and regulations and multiples of profits and P/Es
etc. Your man couldn't care less about P/Es or ratios — he
wanted a price for his business. My adviser said, 'We could
buy the Bank of Ireland for a cheaper multiple than that.'
Ralph took up his papers and said, 'I suggest that you take
the Moran brothers back to Dublin and buy the bloody Bank
of Ireland!' My adviser was first class, but when you are
buying a business, you have to put yourself in the vendor's
shoes and come up or down to his level as the case may be.
Eventually we did the deal ourselves.

In 1978, we were making a profit of about £600,000 a year.
Jim Flavin had left the bank at this stage and had formed
Development Capital Corporation. Niall Carroll was then on
our board — he's in charge of ACT now. They were always
saying that we should do something with the business, either
go public or do a take-over or something. We were not paying
any dividends — we couldn't see any point in doing that in
a family business. All we wanted to do was to build up the
business — the money was irrelevant really. I don't believe
that money is the driving force at all behind people.

It's unfortunate really that money is the measure of
success. You have to make more money each year otherwise
you're not successful, but it's the desire for success that is
the driving force. Success is to do better, literally to keep
building up, to do a better job this year than you did last
year, for your own personal satisfaction. Essentially, you are
competing against yourself. Applause is not important —
applause from people you hardly know is irrelevant. Applause
from people in a small circle, your friends, is important. It
would have been nice if my father could have seen the

success — it was he who had the foresight to tell me to go and do that business. He himself would have built up a fantastic business had he been working for himself instead of for the co-op.

My one claim to fame is that I was born in the same townland as Denis Guiney. When my father came to Dublin, he and Denis would drink together in the Beachcomber. Denis would not waste too many words on you. He asked me once, in his gruff manner, 'Well, what are you doing?' I told him we were starting up a business and that it was tough times. He said, 'It's always tough times.' I said, 'When you built up Clery's, Mr Guiney, there were more opportunities.' He said, 'There are always opportunities if you have the courage to go out and grasp them. There are always the same problems.' I thought that was very good from Mr Guiney.

I think that your family is very important. My brother, Noel, was very much involved in building up that business, despite the fact that he was a priest in Kerry. He used to attend meetings regularly and you always knew that he would tell you out straight what he thought. When you are building up a business, there is always the danger that your subordinates will not tell you what you don't want to hear. Remember, you are paying those fellows. If you are giving a fellow a rise from, say, £40,000 to £50,000, there is always a danger that that's what he would be thinking about. There is always a danger that people, over whose lives you have control, will tell you a little bit of what you want to hear. They definitely won't tell you everything they should — the bad bits. The danger is that it is you who has the £10,000 to give. You could always trust Noel to come back up and tell you all the unpalatable facts. He had nothing to lose. That is the strength in having your own family involved. Even when they're criticising you, you know that it's going to be constructive criticism. You may not like it but you have to admit it. Jim Flavin — and I have a great admiration for him — in the early days, had a tremendous input into the company. I have not always agreed with him, but he is a man that says out straight what he has to say and can be very constructive. That's what you need.

In 1978, AIIB came along and said, 'What would you like to do with this business? Would you like to sell it?' I said, half jokingly, 'I suppose we'd sell anything if we got the right price.' The bank estimated that £2.25 m. would be a good price for it at that stage. I said no way would we sell it. At that stage also we had got involved in building. We had a small building company, John J. O'Brien, part of the Moran Group. The first main scheme was on the Leopardstown and Stillorgan Roads, near White's Cross. Eventually we were offered £2.50 m. and I sat and thought and asked myself the question why people sell businesses. I said no. The bank came back and said, 'We think we can get these people up to £3 m.' I said, 'If they make a definite offer of £3 m., I'll allow them to come over and look at the place, but I am not making any commitment.' Eventually we agreed a deal at £3.45 m. I often wonder myself since, why we took that money. Why did we sell a business that I had built up? I had put huge hours into it. It had net assets of about £1.50 m. or so. It was a £2 m. premium. What makes you do that? A number of things, looking back on it. I went through days of agony as to whether we'd take the money or not. People don't realise how hard it is to sell a business that you have built up. But you suddenly look at security, believe it or not. You never think about security when you're building a business. I think the first thing is that somebody says to you, 'That money is there now.' Another thing is that you probably look for a different direction in your life — it gives you an opportunity to do something else. They were the two reasons why we accepted the money. At the end of 1978 we sold the business. It was one of the most difficult decisions I ever made.

The first morning I woke up after the sale, I said, 'What are we going to do now? Let's get out and do something.' I immediately started looking for other avenues. With the money, I now had an opportunity to do something else but the security thing was also there at the back of my mind. I am trying to be totally honest about why we took the decision and the security thing must have been there. I have seen it with people from whom IWP has bought businesses. Security may not be the right word — because you have a business that you own and control and that is making £600,000 a year. That is absolute security. I suppose it's really that you have so much cash under your control and you wonder if you can do better with it. It's not security in the sense that you worry about having enough to eat and to live.

My mother was a great woman. She went to this small farmer in hilly country and asked him why he would not let his bright young daughter go on to secondary school and he said to her, 'Mrs Moran, won't she have enough to do, and a place to sleep and enough to eat?' When you look at it, is security so important when you have those three things?

Anyway, I immediately got down to buying other businesses. I met somebody who has been very much involved in my life ever since, Richard Hayes. He worked with the bank and was the ideal man to go around the country scouting out opportunities, without the whole world knowing what I was up to. Richard is almost the direct opposite to me, English-educated, a thorough professional, an accountant out of Coopers & Lybrand in the UK, he worked with Laurence Prust, the stockbrokers, and then came back to Allied.

I got involved with Flogas with Jim Flavin and Eugene Quigley — and Tom Roche was in it at the time. I became chairman of that immediately. Richard produced Arthur Rings, a shutter and door company out in Baldoyle — so we bought that. That got me going, but I still felt that I was under-employed. I still had the building company, John J. O'Brien — I did not sell that as part of the Moran Group. Richard went in as chief executive of Rings and I went in as chairman. I then got involved, believe it or not, in West's of Grafton Street. The bank rang me up one day and asked if I would be interested in a jeweller's shop in Grafton Street. At first I thought not on your life, but I ended up owning fifty-five per cent of it which I still own today. I started trying to sort out the freehold of that property in 1981 and it has taken me until now to do it. It's amazing the number of people who come up to me and say, 'My wife got this ring. Do you think it would be worth so much?' I say, as they say in Kerry, I might as well be looking at a bush in a gap.

I met Jim Flavin one day and he had taken a shareholding in Irish Wire Products, a public company. I became executive chairman and got quite involved, going down to Limerick three times a week, Tuesday, Wednesday and Thursday, trying to straighten it out. Richard Hayes and I saw it as an acquisition vehicle, but the first thing was to stop the rot in Limerick. It was losing money. In 1980 I went to the United States with the IDA and I remember trying to find a nail and screw plant within a hundred miles radius of New York. We could not find one because all the product was being imported from the Far East. Looking back now, I think the mistake we made was that I did not come straight back and close down Irish Wire. But no, I was still young enough to have this arrogance that I could fix anything myself. That's where a lot of people make a mistake: no matter how bad the company is, *I* can go in and put it right. We struggled on but we could not stop the losses. We put up more money ourselves trying to keep it going. In July 1986, we tried to put a rescue plan together and it did not work. Jim Flavin and Irish Base Metals, who were significant shareholders, decided to put no more money in. They were right — it was attracting a lot of adverse publicity and doing nobody any good.

We had a meeting where we decided to close the place. A true story: I left that meeting in DCC on the Friday morning of the August holiday in 1986. Frank Plunkett-Dillon, whose father was chairman before me of IWP, said, 'Joe, don't close it yet.' This was despite the fact that we had had a board meeting and had decided to close it! I drove down to Limerick on my way to Kerry saying to myself that maybe Frank Dillon was right. I met the fellows there and

they were all going on holidays. Eoin Cody was the accountant. He said, 'There's not much point in not telling these
fellows that the factory is closing.' I thought about it and
wished the fellows well for their holidays and never opened
my mouth about closing the place. I thought about it for
the next three weeks and decided that we would give it one
more go.

Something which motivates a lot of people is that they
don't want to be associated with failure. I still believe that if
you try hard enough and work hard enough, success will
come. There is absolutely no doubt about that in my mind.
I remember a teacher in Rockwell saying that the only place
where success comes before work is in the English dictionary.
I tell that to my kids and they say, 'Buzz off, Dad. We know it!'

Foir Teo had been into Irish Wire at this stage and had
written off their money. Richard Hayes and myself got together — Richard had left Rings now and, with me, had
started a company called IFG. That stands for Investment
For Growth. Irish Wire Products was capitalised at 1.1 million shares freely available at 20p at most. In the previous
three years it had lost £700,000–£800,000. I told Richard it
needed an injection of £300,000. AIB gave us enough working capital to keep the company going. We give out about
bankers, but Brian Leany of AIB had the vision to see that
the thing could work. He gave us the commitment provided
we changed our direction completely. The Bank of Ireland,
who had been our bankers all along, took a narrow view —
the sooner the place was closed the better. Banks will just
have to take more risks with people — they'll have to make
judgments about people as well as about balance sheets.
The Americans say that the only advantage of a strong
balance sheet is that it takes you longer to go bust.

I raised £300,000 from a whole lot of relations of my own.
DCC and Irish Base Metals put all their IWP shares on the
table for one solitary pound. They owned about thirty per
cent, we owned twenty-five per cent and the public owned
the balance. We divided up the shares to the people who

had put up the £300,000. Our target was to have the share price at 25p within six months and that, within a year, we would get them to 50p.

Richard and I looked at companies here in Ireland and in England who were seeking a shell. One morning Denis Jones arrived in here. Richard had known him through Laurence Prust. At this stage, we had spoken to about fifty companies and we had narrowed that down to three in Ireland and three in the UK. They never made a decision. You'd meet them, you'd have a very nice lunch, you went through all the questions, then they would go away saying that they would think about it and come back and ask more questions. Denis Jones walked in here and made a decision. He came at twenty-past-nine and at ten-to-ten we did a deal. He took a million shares in IWP at 45p a share — that was within six months of my friends putting up their £300,000.

Now I don't do the same type of work that I did twenty years ago. Now my job is to meet people and to build up a team. It's very important that you get on with the people you work with. Work must be a place where you like people. Otherwise, what's the point of the game?

Building up a business is a bit hard on the family. You have to be committed — my father used to say, 'It's better to wear out than to rust out.' A lot of wives would like their husbands to be home at half-five or six and to help the children with their homework and to go for a drive on Saturday and Sunday. I was home early last night at half-past-eight. The night before, I was at a meeting that finished at 11 o'clock. You have to have a family and a wife who will understand that. I also find that if your executives do not have a stable family life, they don't work out well in business.

People get different talents and the Lord said that we should deliver on those talents. What have I done? I have got the personal satisfaction of achieving a certain amount of success. Success means to me that you get something small or in trouble and you build it up. I am absolutely convinced that the private enterprise system is the best way to go for any economy — I think I have proved that to myself. It works. There is an obligation on all of us to provide jobs here in this country — I think we have done something for that. I don't think we should start off to provide jobs — that's a trap that people fall into. I don't think people should come in saying we are going to provide 300 jobs, but if you come in saying that you want to build up a successful business, I think, in the process, you will employ people. It can't be the primary reason for establishing the business — that's starting at the wrong end. And, if you are in a position to pay taxes, that helps the less fortunate people who, for one reason or another, did not get the education, didn't get the opportunities, didn't get the breaks. Deep down, we all like to be socialists, but the word has been abused — we all like to help people. The best way to do it is by private enterprise.

14

Emmett O'Connell

The one guideline is, whatever you are doing, jump right into the middle of it and don't hold back.

Emmett O'Connell is Chairman of Eglinton Exploration plc, Granuaile Shipping plc and Granuaile Navigation plc.

He was born in New York City on 29 June 1936. His father was Michael J. O'Connell, a trade union organiser and civil servant. His mother was Nellie Taaffe. He was the second son in a family of five, two boys and three girls.

He is married to Mary R. O'Kelly. They have three children: Roisin (27), Robert Emmet (22) and Oisin (17).

Education:
St Jerome's Parochial School,
Cardinal Hayes High School,
Pasadena City College,
University of California at Berkeley,
University of Uppsala.

Career:
Engineering designer, Shell Oil Refinery, California,
Editor, *Development* Magazine,
Director, Pomeroy Press Limited,
Managing Director, Numismatic Metals Limited,
Managing Director, Investors' Portfolio Finance Limited,
Director of Osceola Hydrocarbons plc,
Director of Bryson Oil & Gas plc,
Director of Ovoca Gold Explorations plc,
President of Continental Pacific Resources Inc.,
Managing Director of Resources Development Corporation,
Director of Texas Continental Securities plc,
Chairman, Eglinton Exploration plc,
Chairman of Granuaile Shipping plc,
Chairman of Granuaile Navigation plc.

Honours:
Knight of St Gregory,
Gold Cross of the Holy Land,
Knight of Malta (Hospitaller),
Attaché to the Order of St John in the Seychelles,
Knight of St Patrick (Honorary), New York,
Accademico Corrispondente, Accademia Tiberina, Rome,
Centurion, Archdiocese for the Military Services, USA.

Your early years shape and form you without your knowing it. As soon as you become conscious that they are shaping you, they no longer are. One of the major formative influences in my life would have been being born and raised in New York City and in particular in the South Bronx. There was a unique micro-society there. The older people were almost entirely immigrants — Irish, Polish, German, Jewish or Italian. Though you were an American you were not the same kind of American who was growing up in Iowa or Nebraska or Texas. European ideals and morals and ethos were shaping you. The Irish were very much of the old school — strict disciplinarians — the Church played a big role in their lives. Large families were as common there as they were in Ireland. It was a very tight-knit system. Although in the early years I went to a public school, as soon as your parents could afford it, you would be transferred to a Catholic school. Thanks be to God the Christian Brothers were around at the time — they allowed us to go to Cardinal Hayes High School paying only half-tuition. That was a big concession.

You had to work those years because the competition was so keen in New York City — eight million people with two million in the Bronx, every colour and creed under the sun. Whatever you were doing — sports, literature — you were in against keen competition. It was through athletics that I got, for the first time, out of New York, west of the Hudson. The space, the green fields, the lack of people were a stunning revelation. I couldn't believe that this could be the same world and, boy, when you brought the competitiveness and discipline of the Bronx out there, you went like a hot knife through butter. I was a long-distance runner, a cyclist and a skater. I lost sixteen races in a row and then went on to become state champion, regional champion and two- and five-mile national champion in skating.

There are interesting studies being done now as to why the Irish have come to the fore so much in the last fifteen years. If you take the *Forbes 500*, the Irish chief executives are predominant. Why the sudden surge since immigration had been going on so long? It had been put down to the fact that John F. Kennedy became president and that that somehow unlocked it. That was certainly significant — it brought a seal of respectability that had been lacking before. But the GI Bill of Rights after World War II was, in my opinion, the most significant structural reason. The desire for education was very much a part of the Irish-American upbringing. You had the teaching brothers and nuns and the push coming from the Irish mothers but the economics were wrong because, with large families, the first or second always had to go out to work. After the war, all those Irish GIs were disgorged on to the labour market and the Government would pay forty dollars a week and their tuition. Suddenly the Irish flooded into the universities. What we are seeing now is that whole surge coming to fruition right across America.

It never fails to amaze me, the numbers of them that there are. One of the projects that Texas Continental undertook in the last few years was *Irish America* magazine. It was founded by Brendan MacLua who runs the most successful ethnic newspaper in these islands, *The Irish Post*, in the UK, Neil O'Dowd, who was the editor of *The Irishman* in San Francisco, and myself. The Irish newspapers that hitherto had existed in America were very local — they were New York or Philadelphia or San Francisco newspapers. There was no Irish-American newspaper covering the whole United States. The older papers associated themselves with one family and they had become structured. They did not represent the new Irish demographic mix at all. We found there was a niche market for Irish Americans, who did not relate back to Ireland, but who stood on their own in America. There was a need for something that reflected the progress they had made in the United States. Within a very short time, the *New York Times* referred to our magazine as 'slick and successful', an accolade. The kind of people we concentrated on were, for example, John Phelan, President of the New York Stock Exchange; William Brennan, Justice of the Supreme Court;

McGillicuddy, Chief Executive Officer of Manny Hanny —
Manufacturers Hanover Trust; Dan Tully, President of Merrill
Lynch; Donald Keough, President of Coca-Cola; Denis Long
of Anheuser Busch. These were people of enormous influence and they were getting little recognition within the Irish
community. We started high-lighting their success stories
and the feed-back was fantastic as one became aware of the
other. *Irish America* eventually led to *The Irish Voice,* a weekly
newspaper, now majority owned by Smurfit and which, last
year, produced the largest Irish newspaper ever published
anywhere ever in the world — 168 pages. All that reflects the
success of the Irish Americans in America.

When I was growing up we did not think of ourselves as
being Irish Americans, we just thought of ourselves as being
Irish. That's something that people here in Ireland find
hard to relate to. To be Irish in New York or Boston was to
be king of the world — you strutted. You said you were Irish
and the Jewish fellows, the Polish, the Puerto Ricans all
wanted to be on your team. The Jewish boys often joined
the Irish regiments in the Army Reserve.

We did not relate at all to the WASPS. They were the
bankers, the landlords, the insurance companies. They were
the general establishment — I won't quite say the oppressors.
They were not ours and we did not belong to them.

One of the first inklings I had of the wider world was
when I was about fifteen and when, in history class, I heard
that one of the signatories of the Declaration of Independence was a William Morris. The area I grew up in was called
Morrisania and Morris was buried in St Anne's Church on
141st Street and St Anne's Avenue. We lived on 139th Street.
It was quite something to find that a signatory of the
Declaration of Independence was buried a block and a half
away from where you lived and it was not a high-rent
district. I walked around to the churchyard, an old Protestant
church with a high wrought-iron fence. I looked through
the bars and saw the little obelisk over his grave. My first
thought was, 'My God, he was a good guy and he's buried in

a Protestant church!' That meant he was a WASP and how could a good guy be one of those? Not much longer after that I learned that Robert Emmet's brother, Thomas Addis Emmet, was buried in Trinity Church down on Wall Street. He has a fine tomb and the inscription is written in French, Latin, Gaelic and English on the four sides. That's the church that George Washington used to attend. I had no problems with that because I was brought up to know that Robert Emmet was a Presbyterian and I knew that Thomas Addis Emmet had become the Attorney General of the State of New York. But what really surprised me with Morris was that a revolutionary could be a WASP.

In any event, we would just not have known any WASPS. In our area you had the Corcorans — this is house by house — Kellys, O'Donnells, Flynns, O'Connells, Whites. Denis White was notable because in our whole area he was the only one with an American-born mother. The only people who spoke English as their native language were the Irish and the coloureds — the Germans' parents spoke German, the Poles spoke Polish, the Italians spoke Italian. Being Irish was a badge of distinction.

Money was tight at home. My brother and I bought the first television set when we were in our early twenties. I got my first bicycle when I was sixteen. There was nothing extra. You could not just *go* to university — you could *work* and go to university. I had done well at school. California had a tremendous educational system — open and welcoming universities — and it was beckoning. You could go to school for fifteen dollars a semester. I went first to Pasadena City College, a two-year college. At the same time I was working for an engineering company, C. F. Braun & Co. I soon saw that there were courses other than engineering that I wanted to do. I could not say so because then the engineering company would not pay my fees and give me money for the books and time off for classes. I fudged the issue and went on to do work in Greek archaeology and pre-Christian philosophy! I never got an engineering degree. Liberal arts and history and archaeology completely caught me up. Then, when I was at the University of California at Berkeley, they had an exchange programme for a semester at the University of Uppsala in Sweden. I was married by then, left my wife off in Dublin and went on to Uppsala — and I finally left the States in 1968.

The war in Vietnam was on. I was in subcontracting in the oil business in the Western States at that stage and that's where I made my first little pile of money. I was campaigning real hard for Bobby Kennedy, particularly in Northern California — I was the head of one of the local committees in Concord. When they killed Bobby Kennedy, that really was a bitch . . . I packed it up that summer and came to Ireland.

I had first visited Ireland in 1958, came back in 1959 and stayed till 1962. During that period I met my wife here.

Everything I had done in business up till then, I seemed to get the wrong end of the stick — it never came together. I regard my daughter Roisin as my lucky charm — from the day she came into the world, everything I touched has turned to gold. The day she was born in Dublin I sold my car and with the money bought boat-tickets to America for the three of us. I went to work for a year for the *New York Times*. From there I went to Minnesota, then to Southern California, worked around Oklahoma and Texas — in the oil fields, in engineering, in what was called the superstructure, that is the things above ground, tank farms, pumping arrangements, discharge facilities, loading facilities — that type of work.

So September 1968 was when I really decided to settle in Ireland — that's the marker. My wife wanted to come back. I had a little money. Things were picking up here — but it was not like America. You could not just walk into a job. My background suited fine — if you have one or more parents who were born in Ireland, as soon as you set foot here, you are considered an Irish national. You can apply for your Irish passport and there is no question of having to get a work-permit.

The first job I got was with Wilsons out of Lisburn in Northern Ireland. They used to turn meat offal into chemicals, in what is sometimes referred to as a knacker's yard. Shortly after that Uinseann MacEoin, Finn Gallen, Mary Eaton and I started a publishing company called Pomeroy Press. We published *Development Magazine, Build*, which was planning and architecture, *Stream and Field*, and *Trade Fair*. I was editor of *Development* and started writing and writing and writing. I interviewed a lot of people in Dublin — the financial scene was very elementary. I quickly saw an opening for a company that I called Investors' Portfolio Finance. Money-brokers had not yet started up — people were still leaving large sums of money in their current accounts to earn the goodwill of the bank. There was very little competition in financial circles. I applied for and was granted the first licence outside the four major banks to import and export gold. They did not deal in it so, in effect, I became the only importer and exporter of gold in Ireland.

In investment as in so many other things, the important thing is to get the big play right. You have to find the major current. If you can get on the back of it and ride it, like charity, it can cover up a lot of mistakes. If you are fighting against the major current, it's difficult to come out ahead.

One of the big moves that I managed to get right was the decline of the dollar. In the early writings in *Development*, I was well ahead of that posse. I believed in the inevitability of the break in the link with gold and the consequent rise in its price.

I then left writing and went full-time into the investment company. From the investment company I formed Numismatic Metals. I wanted to call it Precious Metals — but if you said numismatic then you could say that you were dealing in coin, not bullion. Coins of the realm, legal tender, were not subject to VAT. I had a lot of dealings with the Central Bank and they were feeling their way at the time too. In America, in all these regulatory bodies, there is a rule-book which you, as a citizen, are entitled to see. If I can find a way around the rules, then that is perfectly legitimate. You can imagine their bewilderment in the Central Bank when I asked what the rules were for the import and export of gold. I always preferred to write letters because the name Emmett O'Connell would get me by. Face to face, however, after speaking the first two sentences, they would say that this guy wasn't Irish and all their defences would go up. They asked me what I wanted to do. I said, 'I don't really want to tell you what I want to do — I want to know what the rules are.' That's not the way things are done in Ireland. They said, 'You tell us what you want to do and then we'll decide whether you can do it or not.'

In the event, I struck up what was quite a good relationship with the Central Bank. I detailed exactly what I was going to do and showed them how I was going to make money. Well, it was not all that easy — there was the usual stalling. I went over to the Bank one day and the girl at reception handed me a letter. In it were seventeen questions to which they wanted answers before they'd consider letting me get on with my business. I asked her if she had a pad. I sat down in reception at about eleven-thirty and wrote until about two-thirty. I filled most of her pad. At half past two, I handed her back the pad and a letter with seventeen lengthy answers. Then they began to ask themselves, 'How do we get rid of this guy?'

The Wilson Government was in power in the UK at the time and I felt the price of gold would rise, and as a result they would bring in interventions to prevent the market working. This would create a two-tier system for gold: one an internal price and the other a world price. I wanted permission to import gold into Ireland and then export it to the UK where, being inside their market, I would get the higher internal market price. The Central Bank gave me permission to do it but on condition that I wrote them a monthly report on the gold market in Ireland. One of the guys who worked there and later moved to AIIB told me, 'Emmett, we did not know a thing about the gold market, but we did not want to say that!' Anyway, I got the permission and then what happened is interesting.

I brought in a big shipment of Krugerrands. I rang Rothschilds in London and put them on sale in the London market. The following day I rang them to get the completion. The Rothschilds man gave me the external price and I said, no, it's the internal price that is applicable. I told him that I could make delivery into the sterling market of which Ireland was then a part so that he could not treat it as an external investment. It was an internal transfer. He said, 'Oh no. I know what you're doing.' I said, 'And so does the Central Bank here.' He said, 'We're going to report you to the Bank of England.' Next thing I got a letter back asking for the written permission from the Central Bank. Do you know what? They had the neck, Ivor, not to send me back the letter from the Central Bank! Nor would they complete the deal. I went back to the Central Bank and told them that I had the gold, but I could not sell it anywhere else because in London they were hanging on to my letter of permission. To their credit, the Central Bank said they would give me another letter. They said, 'You tell them either they give you back your original, or we'll supply you with a letter every time they swallow one.'

Years later I was at a lunch at IBI. There was a guy there from Rothschilds and, when he heard my name, he said, 'Weren't you in the gold business? You can't imagine the trouble you gave us!' Eventually, of course, the British Government did close down the loop-hole, but for a time it was very remunerative.

If you fail in Ireland, people always like to be able to issue their condolences. If you succeed, they all wonder what funny business you are up to. So, as with that Central Bank permission, I like to put everything up front *ab initio*. Years later, when I was in the oil business, we were faced with a great rigmarole from the Central Bank and I used to tell the fellows to put *everything* into the letter — give them the whole nine yards even if it takes hours of time to explain.

You don't want them unravelling something later on saying, 'You did not tell us you were going to do this.'

That was the gold caper. We repeated it with silver, but then Bunker Hunt went belly-up and the silver market collapsed. There was no way you could describe silver as numismatic — it was bulk and subject to twenty-five per cent VAT. So I took my winnings and bought a farm down in Woodenbridge, Co. Wicklow, something I always wanted to do. I bought an old rectory, the Glebe House. I remember walking with my wife by the river on this broad expanse of green pasture and saying to her, 'What the hell do we do now?'

I hadn't the vaguest idea what to do, where to get a cow or a pig. Once again it was, 'Gimme me the rule book!' The farm was about fifty acres so it was manageable and I didn't do any other business for two or three years. I just worked flat out at it. I learned. I bought a lorry and made a neighbour of mine, a fine strapping young man, a partner. We went down west and bought old cows, fattened them and brought them to the mart — I was a cattle dealer and had a wonderful time. My friends in Dublin and in Texas were saying, 'What is he doing? Get him back into harness!' But for two or three years I totally immersed myself and really enjoyed it. I did very nicely out of it and bought a farm in Roscommon at the same time — a 145-acre place, Cloongowna, outside Carrick-on-Shannon. In that little area, from Carrick-on-Shannon to Sligo, nothing ever happens. It's like a peninsula and it's full of history. You are into a time capsule. I hired another young man — from Ballycoog in County Wicklow, and he went down and lived in the rambling old house in Roscommon. I used to go down and stay there two or three nights a week. We put 180 head of cattle on slatted floors, the latest thing at that time. The Irish think that if you even go outside your parish, you are in distant lands. I always reckoned that if you didn't have to get on an aeroplane, it couldn't be far away.

My wife did not like it. She is a Leinster woman and anything past the Shannon, she expects to see Red Indians.

Eventually I sold out and bought this place where we are today in County Wexford. It was about a hundred and fifty acres — I have since added another two hundred acres. I like to think that the two farms I sold — and a third one I bought in County Leitrim — were left in better order than when I bought them.

John Healy and Douglas Gageby of the *Irish Times* have said that when they were growing up in the fifties, they did not realise that they were hard times. This Irish obsession with recession and hard times is a function of the centralised bureaucracy in Dublin. They are forever dealing with each other and with statistics and they have nothing else to do. If you're a farmer or a cattle dealer or a ditch-digger, you are too busy working. When you are farming, you are never conscious of whether or not there is a recession on — there is always the next job to do. How does a recession impact on you — except in the newspapers or listening to the politicians blaming each other? Times are never good or bad — it is only what you are doing that counts. Of course, if your neighbour gets laid off, it's a recession. If you get laid off, it's a depression. But, really, I was not concerned with whether the pundits thought we were in a recession, or coming out of one, or whether there was stagflation or what. Whatever I was doing had my total concentration and devotion.

In 1977, you were well into the early stages of the oil boom. But as early as June 1973, four months before the October War between Israel and Egypt, I wrote an article for *Business and Finance,* the sub-title of which was 'Oil, Arabs and the Next War'. Oil was desperately under-priced in the early 1970s. It was selling for less than milk, Coca-Cola or soda water. You could get a drum of it for two dollars. Everything else had escalated. The price of gold was leaping off the charts, yet oil was still selling at this ridiculous price. The United States, with six per cent of the population, was consuming thirty-three per cent of the energy in the world. It did not take a genius to see that this could not go on — the market would eventually assert itself and the oil price would rise. I thought the cutting edge would come with Gaddafi, who was just in power at the time. This was before all the hoopla that followed thereafter. Gaddafi put the first squeeze on the oil companies bringing the price up from two dollars to two dollars and thirty cents. He simply seized the production of companies who would not go along with him, like BP. Occidental came in and took over BP's production. Where the push came from, however, was not from Gaddafi, but from the quietest, most sedate of the oil producers, the Saudis, from Sheik Yamani, who learned his trade from the Texas Board of Railway Commissioners, the original pro-rationers. The Texas Railway Commission pro-rations the production of oil in Texas. When there is over-supply they order you to shut down your pumps. Now they let you produce flat-out, but it was not always like that.

Yamani wanted to introduce some form of pro-rationing. Of course the oil companies were against that. He was trying to get the oil price up and, as it turned out later from his writings, he was looking for three to three and a half dollars a barrel. He came over to the United States with his King, and Nixon let them sit for something like five days in a hotel. They went back without seeing Nixon and raised the price to five dollars a barrel. That was the beginning — it went from five dollars to eleven dollars to thirteen dollars to seventeen dollars, and then it took a huge jump after the Iranian revolution to forty-two dollars. Nobody in the business could have foreseen that enormous elasticity.

Aran-B.P. had made a strike in the Porcupine around 1977. Friends in the United States were saying, 'What the hell are you doing over there? You're paying $10 m. a hole to drill in 1,500 feet of water. That's really mainlining it.' The whole mid-continent section in America was wide open for leasing, so why not get an Irish group started in that basin? Nial O'Connor and I put together a project with seventeen original investors on the basis that the most efficacious way to get into the oil business was through land-leasing in the

United States. The whole mid-continent section has been prospected for seventy years and there are terrific records. There was oil in these areas, but it would not have been economic at a dollar sixty or two dollars a barrel.

Now, Ivor, it all comes down to a question of belief. There was a not very complimentary book about Bernie Cornfield. He used to bring his salesmen into the auditorium and the first and most important question he asked them was, 'Do you *sincerely* want to be rich? Do you really believe — or is it just a job? If it is just a job then you are not suitable.' If you *believed* that the oil price was going to stay high, then what you should do is go after the leases which were available for a dollar an acre and a dollar a year thereafter, ten year rentals. That was not the popular perception in the United States, I can tell you. I remember listening to the president of Winnebago, the manufacturer of these huge campers, saying that a dollar a gallon for gasoline was un-American. With that mental implant in the United States, the price of the leases had not escalated with the price of oil.

We put together an initial pool of £260,000. I went off to the United States to build up a block of leases. We worked mainly in Western Kansas. I had one of my near-misses there. I met up with an American company that had a board of directors that read like a who's-who of the business community in New York. Between them and us we put together over six hundred and fifty thousand acres. This would have been significant for Esso. OK, it was marginal land but, as I say, you had to believe that the oil price was going up. My idea was that we would sell the leases as they appreciated, but the American company said no, no, no. We are going to drill. Now drilling for oil at the best of times is a dangerous business, very speculative. This was a change in the game-plan that we had originally agreed with them. They said they knew about these things, they could raise the money and I was just over from Ireland, what would I know. I bowed to what I thought was their superior knowledge and they promptly raised $10 m. to drill the properties.

They drilled twenty-eight dry holes in a row. My friends here in Ireland would always say it was twenty-nine, but I know it was twenty-eight because the number is engraved on my soul. They were refusing to recognise a dry hole and believing their own propaganda, which is deadly.

In his early days, Mao Tse-tung sent a letter to his generals. It should be mandatory reading for every executive. In it he said that the Party was going to begin a big propaganda campaign about the inevitable success of communism, but his generals were not to believe this. He wrote, 'Remember that propaganda is meant for the other side.'

I spent the winter of '78 travelling in a pick-up truck in Western Kansas. It's as flat as the top of that table and the winds coming down from the north would skin you alive. I set out to find each one of those twenty-eight dry holes to find out what had happened to our money. I found them one after another. I found eight thousand dollars' worth of pipe lying on one site. I found a guy swabbing a well and he had been there for thirty days — swabbing means trying to pull the oil up by suction. You'd normally try it for two days at the most. I went back to New York and met our American partners in the Union Club on Park Avenue and asked them if any of them had ever been to Oklahoma City where they had an office. No. 'Anybody been to Western Kansas?' No, nobody's been to Western Kansas. I told them that somebody better get out there and see the twenty-eight dry holes.

I went back there and spent most of that winter in motels and the back of the pick-up truck trying to prevent the whole thing caving in completely. Finding that eight thousand dollars' worth of pipe under a snow-bank was like finding a gold mine, because we were able to sell it and hire in a contractor to complete one well or re-treat it or whatever. In the pits of all that, Jim Stafford, a difficult man, came out to see me. He found me in some motel and said, 'Come on. You can't go on like this. We are going out for a good meal and a good bottle of wine.' His money was in the deal too. I was furious about the whole lousy business — I was gritting my teeth. Jim had a chauffeur-driven car — in Western Kansas! We drove to the Town Hall and were directed to a restaurant that I never knew was there — a sort of plantation place with black-coated waiters and a big log fire. Jim insisted on seeing the wine list and, by God, he lifted me out of my depression. He stayed with me for two days and got me going on the road again. By spring, through various treatments, eight of those wells had been brought back into being producers. And then a stroke of luck.

Money was now pouring into the oil fields. Oil had risen to thirty dollars a barrel and the same pundits who told us the price would never rise were forecasting a hundred dollars a barrel. This famous promoter came along to us. He needed land-leases and he paid us ten dollars an acre plus a royalty. We got paid off by the American company we were working with — they went on to great things and became one of the biggest independents in Oklahoma City. We recovered our entire investment and came out of it smelling like roses. But it was a damn close thing.

I came back to Ireland vowing that never again would we work with an American company as the junior partner. If we were going to make mistakes, we would make them on our own.

One of the big changes in Ireland in the last ten years has been the change from traditional methods of financing — bank finance and government grants. The extraordinary generosity of the Exchequer through the IDA meant that there was a relatively low priority on raising new equity. Equity invariably carries with it outsiders' opinions and shareholders' votes, and management is not always comfortable with that. The existing structures in Ireland were being subsidised by taxpayers' money and relied overly on bank borrowings. We have seen a dramatic change even in the last five years in the use of equity to finance public ventures — that is what the stock exchange is, or should be, all about.

To understand the private limited company you have to go back about a thousand years — to China. At that time China had a very advanced court system with particularly effective tax collection. It was highly centralised and that gave it the leverage to do enormous public works like the Great Wall. Why was such a powerful civilisation overtaken by Europe which, at that time, was just a rump of Asia? Why did a small island country which was a rump of the rump succeed in colonising a great part of the known world? Western Europe had two things that China did not have. Firstly, it had a peasant society which used cattle as the accumulation of wealth rather than rice paddies. Secondly, it had forests. The forests meant that the peasant was able to accumulate cattle — capital — outside the reach of the central exchequer whereas, in China, the rice paddies were readily accessible. The cattle breed, so every year he has a few more. The forests give him a chance to hide them from the eyes of the tax inspector. In Western Europe, you had for the first time the accumulation of wealth in the hands of the individual. Even to this day, in China the individual is not able to accumulate wealth.

The accumulation of wealth in private hands meant that there was an alternative way to finance any ventures you might care to undertake. You did not have to go to the court, to the exchequer. This first came to fruition in the trading states of northern Italy, Genoa and Venice, from where caravans and fleets were sent out on great adventures. But these were essentially one-off programmes. There was no continuity to them. The great contribution the Anglo-Saxon genius has made is the divisible negotiable security certificate. That's what a share certificate is. Now many individuals could subscribe as much or as little as they liked to great ventures. Unlike the Italians, the Anglo-Saxons formed companies that had a continuing life. What's more, the individual subscriber need not stay with them forever — he could sell out with his negotiable certificate. That gave a great flexibility to financing. Wherever the English went in the world they brought with them the idea of the public limited company. You have the Singapore, Kuala Lumpur, Hong Kong, Toronto, Vancouver Stock Exchanges. You have them in South Africa, Australia, across the United States. They play a vibrant role in developing their economies. The other colonists did not do that — the Spaniards plundered their colonies. While there are stock exchanges in Latin America, they do not play a predominant role. The concept of the public limited company was missing in Ireland for years — it had been usurped by government grants and by over-reliance on bank borrowings. Only recently has the Irish Stock Exchange been coming into its own. It's no coincidence that this has happened while government grants are being cut back and the banks are looking for more equity to be put into companies to which they lend.

In Texas Continental we tried to do everything through the concept of the public limited company — no joint ventures, no shareholders' agreements, not trying to carve out little loopholes, not trying to protect ourselves from the ultimate decision of the market-place. The paradox is that if you go into the system believing that it will work, it very often does. Sometimes you have failures, but it's not because of the system, it's because of the individual enterprise. Though the exploration sector is seen as speculative, no Irish exploration company has gone bust. Irish exploration shares may have their ups and downs, but none of them has gone out of business and none receives government grants or rescue packages. The same cannot be said for banks or insurance companies or glass companies — all companies that we regard as mature and safe and respectable. They're the ones who have been relying on government rescues and grants and who, despite all that, have often gone wrong. The balance sheet of the exploration companies remains sound, provided there are no borrowings. Exploration should be funded only with equity.

The stock market is a reflection of individuals' judgments. When you are promoting a new company, you have got to

270

persuade the market that this is a fair deal. There are no certainties — there can be either success or failure, but you have got to convince the punter that he is going to get a run for his money, fair value. You have to state openly the risks. You have to abide by the decision of the market-place — you can't try and fix it. You should have nothing but an unvarnished risk-taking enterprise. The paradox is that if you lay it all out, all the risks, you will make it more attractive, not least because you enhance your credibility. Only a fool would believe that investing in a new venture is without risk.

I've never seen myself other than as a worker. I would like to consider myself a long-distance runner — staying with projects over a long period. That's not to say that I stick with every project — for example, my role in some is as a catalyst, putting deals together and bringing individuals into a structure where they can play out their parts. That means not always having to be a member of the cast. I tend to stay with companies where my personal credibility is at stake.

I don't see the rest of my life as a smooth progression from where I am. I see it rather as coming in bursts and one does not always follow from the other. For example, there are one or two books I'd like to write. The one guideline is, whatever you are doing, jump right into the middle of it and don't hold back.

15

Feargal Quinn

*One of the ways I measure success is to do things
that please people, that benefit people — and
that make good business sense as well.*

Feargal Quinn is Managing Director of Superquinn.

He was born in Dublin on 27 November 1936, the son of Eamonn Quinn, grocer, and Maureen Donnelly, a post office clerk. He was second in a family of two: one daughter and one son.

He was educated at:
Monkstown National School,
Koska College, Clontarf,
Newbridge Dominican College,
UCD (B.Comm.).

He is married to Denise Prendergast. They have five children: Eamonn (26); Gilliane (23); Stephen (19); Zoe (14) and Donal (12).

He opened his first shop in Dundalk in 1960 and his first Dublin shop in Finglas in 1965. In 1970 Quinn's Supermarket became Superquinn which has now twelve large stores and five shopping centres.

He has been:
Chairman of An Post,
President and Chairman of The Irish Management Institute,
President of the Irish Quality Association.

He is Chairman of the Finance Committee of The Dublin Archdiocese,
Member of the Board of the Centre Internationale des Enterprises du Secteur Alimentaire.
He is a founder and honorary treasurer of the Irish Grocers' Benevolent Fund.

He won the 'People of the Year' Award in 1984 and holds honorary doctorates from the National Council for Educational Awards and the University of Dublin. He is a Fellow of the Institute of Grocery Distribution (Britain) and a Life Fellow of the Irish Management Institute.

I would not mind at all being called a showman. I think there is showmanship in most entrepreneurs. There is probably a bit of theatre now in all businesses, not just grocery, but in banking, in packaging, even in the weather forecast.

A US company for which I have a lot of respect talks about 'theatre-in-the-store'. Shopping should be a pleasurable experience: you should entertain visually as well as excite the taste buds. People's enjoyment of shopping comes not just from things like a clean floor, but also from things that are almost theatre — the display of pineapples or fish, or the way the staff will mind your children or wheel your trolley or hold an umbrella over your head. There's a bit of showmanship about all that.

In 1960, when we opened our first shop in Dundalk, Brendan Rooney and I went to Dublin to Sound Systems and talked with the boss there, a Colonel Watchhorn. (He was the most important man I had ever met — I had never met a colonel before!) I explained to him that I wanted an amplification system for a shop. He was amazed, and he came all the way down to Dundalk to see a grocer's shop with music. I bought six Ray Conniffe records, and eventually the staff got so sick of them I had to go out and buy Johnny Mathis.

Our first Dublin shop was in Finglas. In 1965, Finglas had a large population, a lot of children, a population not used to supermarkets. Each week we aimed to have an event, so a customer walking home would stop a neighbour and say, 'Do you know what's going on in Quinn's?' (as it was then). You could win your weight in groceries or if you burst a balloon you won a prize.

I don't think being a showman comes easy to anyone — I know I have to work very hard at it. For me, a lot of it came from my father. He started Red Island Holiday Camp in 1947. As a result, all of us grew up with a microphone in our hands. I was one of the better bingo callers at the age of twelve. I was shy as a teenager, but not too shy to use a mike.

How I got into the supermarket business at all was like this. When I was a student in UCD, I was also working in the Co-op in Dun Laoghaire and enjoying it. But since I was an only son I assumed I would go into the holiday camp business. So when I finished college I decided to go to France to learn something about catering. This was 1958, the year of the World Fair in Brussels. I hitch-hiked to Brussels, toured the Exposition and since by now it was September, I thought I had better do a little work. I went to the station in Brussels: I remember standing in front of the ticket office and saying in my best school French, 'Could I have a ticket for France, please?' The man behind the counter said in somewhat lofty tones, *'La France est un grand pays, monsieur. Que voulez-vous?'* I said, *'La première gare après la frontière, s'il vous plaît, monsieur.'*

I got off at Metz with my little duffle bag and started looking for a job. I got one right there in the Buffet de la Gare. I worked in various places and came back to my father at the end of that winter. I told him that what had excited me was not catering but that, for the first time, I had really seen self-service.

There were three kinds: self-service shoes — in Ireland then, they did not sell shoes, they sold cardboard boxes; self-service sweets and self-service magazines and newspapers — all of which then in Ireland were sold from behind a counter. In France you picked them up and paid for them at the *caisse*. I told my father that it was great: people bought more and you didn't have the same wage costs.

It was my father who said, 'Whatever about sweets and magazines and shoes, people will always want to eat. I suggest that if you're going to get into self-service, you should get into grocery.' I spent the following winter working in self-service grocery shops in England.

Mine was by no means the first self-service shop in Ireland. John Quinn had taken over the H. Williams business, which had been around since the 1890s, and about 1949 opened a self-service shop in Henry Street. It was probably the first in

Europe. He closed it within a year, simply because products did not then come in packets. Butter was about the only thing that was packed — everything else came in big sacks. You had to pack everything in little brown bags and put them on the shelf and everything looked the same. But he still had the idea inside him and in 1957 opened the first H. Williams self-service and succeeded. In 1960, when we opened in Dundalk, we were the first *provincial* supermarket. Some time later, in 1961, the other Williams — D. E. Williams — opened in Limerick.

I was fortunate in my timing, and in the fact that I had a father who encouraged me and steered me in the right direction and was able to keep a watchful eye.

I must have been one of very few people who left university and went into the grocery business. In those days, if a farmer had four sons, one was going to become a doctor, one a vet, one a priest and the dumb one was going to mind the farm — or become a shopkeeper.

When I opened my first shop in Dundalk, I actually knew something about working capital from my accountancy lectures in UCD. We borrowed £14,000 from the bank and I calculated the interest on that overdraft to be about £30 per week. Allowing for that, I was conscious during our first six months that we were not quite coming up to our break-even point. So it was a pleasant surprise to find out after the six months that we had made a profit after all. The mistake I had made was in assuming that we owed the bank £30 each week, when in fact being in a cash business meant we did not have any overdraft at all after the first few weeks. At least I had erred on the right side. By the time Christmas came we had money sitting in the bank — we weren't even smart enough to put it on deposit.

I made exactly the same mistake five years later when we opened in Finglas. We borrowed £80,000 from the Provincial Bank. I calculated that at 10 per cent, to rent that money would cost me £160 a week. In the event, of course, we didn't need it after a very short while because of the cash-flow. So there are times when a little financial education can be dangerous. In my case it was beneficial because it made me somewhat conservative.

From the beginning, our thing was customer service. For me, that's what business is all about — giving superior customer service. It's what turns me on. An American friend of mine said to me that he can see the change in me when I step on to the shop floor. That's where I really get a kick — being among the customers, having held on to them, seeing them leaving the shop proud of their decision that they shopped with us.

I was giving a talk recently in one of the universities to marketing students. Afterwards, they gathered round for a cup of tea, and two of them said they had worked in Superquinn and found it dull. I said I was sorry about that: had we known they were marketing students we would have moved them around to different jobs. They said: 'Oh, you did do that, but we still did not find it very interesting.' I asked them what they had done. 'We just dealt with customers.' I was horrified at the fact that marketing students had found meeting customers *dull*. I think they expected to sit at a desk drawing up grandiose marketing plans.

I get more satisfaction out of properly packing a customer's bag or finding out if they see anything wrong with the shop than I do out of poring over balance sheets. Yet here were two young people going into marketing who did not get turned on by meeting customers. So one lesson I learned from that is that everybody isn't automatically turned on by customers, by the sense of service.

What customer service means is a whole host of things. Some of them are very small and seem insignificant in themselves. A smile is terribly important.

I was in the United States recently and we stayed in two different hotels — both very good and very expensive. The difference between the two was the people: the smile, the recognition, the calling you by name. Even more so, the fact of the employee greeting you *before* you greeted him or her — the person cleaning the floor having the time to take that split second to look up at you and say 'Hi!'

That does not come naturally. It comes from training, from a philosophy of how things should be done — and from example, from seeing the top people in the organisation do it.

There is a great rule in a supermarket company called Stew Leonard's in Connecticut: 'Rule Number 1 is that the customer is always right. Rule Number 2 is: if the customer is ever wrong, go back and re-read Rule Number 1.' It's very easy to say the customer is always right but to carry that through, you have to behave as if he is right even when he *is* wrong.

That doesn't mean you shouldn't stick up for what you believe in. In the early days we had a customer in Dundalk — she was used to bargaining and here we had opened a supermarket with fixed prices. We had a young fellow of sixteen whom she would single out and browbeat into giving her a lower price. She was a good customer and I did not want to lose her. Having been brought up in a business where the customer was always right, it went against the grain to have to go to her and say gently, 'I'm sorry but if you persist in this, we can't serve you any more.'

The best way of dealing with situations like that is to find a creative way around them. When my father was in the grocery business (before he became a hotelier), he wanted at one stage to move from the traditional way of doing business on credit to a system where all customers would pay cash. The way he approached this shift was to change the name of his business. He changed it from 'Quinn's' to 'Payantake'. The name said it all, and people accepted the change. He had changed their expectations. You can't change your customers, but sometimes you can change their expectations.

Another of those small things that go to make up superior customer service is using customers' names. In the days of the family grocer, the people in the shop always knew the customers' names, and used them. That's why, once a year, we get our customers to wear name badges: it helps us to get to know them.

There are other ways you can get to know a customer's name. One simple trick is to read it off the cheque-book or credit card when they use it. Mind you, my zeal in this direction has sometimes back-fired on me.

One day, I looked over a customer's shoulder as he was doing a Visa card. I went behind the customer service counter, took off my jacket and hung it on the chair on which the girl behind the counter was sitting and then said to the customer: 'Mr Butler, will you do me a favour? Will you see that Adrienne doesn't lean back and crease my jacket?'

Mr Butler didn't even look up: he totally ignored me. So I tried again with another silly remark — still no result. I eventually became aware that Adrienne was kicking me on the shins. What I didn't know was that she had identified the Visa card as a stolen one. She'd already pressed the alarm button under the desk and the security people were on their way to catch 'Mr Butler'. In the event they didn't get him, because my attempts to get his attention eventually frightened him off and he disappeared before he could be caught.

In the early days people would come to my mother and tell her that they had been in my shop and that it was very good value — thinking they were being nice to her. She, however, would immediately get worried that I was going out of business. If, on the other hand, someone were to come to her and say that I was not very good value, her relief would be mighty. The balance between my father and mother was very good. She was very conservative, he was the one who would take chances.

Unusually, I think, we own (rather than rent) eleven of our twelve sites. This was probably very wise in the early 1970s because, with high inflation, it was a good idea to buy a site on an overdraft; a few years later, it was worth much more than you had borrowed. Owning rather than renting the sites is a conservative approach and may very well have come from my streak of conservatism or fear of failure.

I *have* thought about failure. There is not a week goes by but I think about it and I am thankful that I am still in business. There have been nineteen supermarket chains in Dublin since we started in 1960, and now there are only three of us left. Some of these names were very familiar — Findlaters, Home & Colonial, Liptons, Monument Creamery. There were also more modern ones like Tesco, Albert Gubay and Pat Quinn — all of whom, like the most recent one H. Williams, have left the scene. I should write them up on the wall as a constant reminder that size is not the most important thing.

Sometimes people do say about our company that we are not big enough. It's true we have not concentrated on making the company bigger and bigger and bigger. Our development has been very regular: we have had a new shop every two years for the last twenty-four years. I sometimes find myself almost having to apologise that we are not trying to do more.

Our pace of development is influenced by a fear on my part that the company would change. If the company got much bigger it would probably need a hierarchical management structure, and I would become remote from what I regard as the centre of gravity — the shop manager. As it is, I have no difficulty talking with each of the shop managers at least once a week. That's with twelve shops and a staff of 2,000.

We have not grown through acquisition, though we have many times looked at the possibilities. I think the first time was back in 1966, just when Finglas was up and running: I heard that Findlaters might be closing. Finglas had only just become profitable and I didn't have enough money to start another shop, but I decided I would approach Mr Findlater. He told me that, in fact, they were opening a shop in the new shopping centre in Stillorgan, where Pat Quinn was opening up too. They opened a beautiful shop but, as we know, it didn't work out. That taught me a lesson: it's probably easier to start from scratch than to try to change the ways of an old established business.

That is why all our operations have been new, green-field, why we have not tried to take over other companies and change them. When we open a new shop, we start with a clean sheet — with new staff whom we train carefully in the way we do things.

Most of that training has to do with the philosophy, traditions and culture of the company rather than with saying this is how you do your particular job. It is about the way we deal with customers rather than about how you slice bacon. When I see people acquiring other companies and changing them around, I admire them no end — it's not easy. But we are unlikely to grow by acquisition.

Perhaps growth for growth's sake is a twentieth-century phenomenon with, particularly, institutional shareholders. A private company years ago would have measured itself in a different way. Growth is a great way to keep people on their toes, but it is not the only way. As well as growing, or instead of growing, you can get *better.* A good example is Marks & Spencer — they have 283 stores, exactly the same number they had in 1949.

The word 'best' is whatever the public recognises as best. With food it can be freshness and taste, with non-food things it can be price. You have to sell things that the public want to go out of their way to get, and subsequently to be proud of what they have bought. I would be as turned on by people saying, 'That company does things very well' as I would be by people saying that we were getting bigger or that we were the biggest. Maybe some day we will find that we have to grow much bigger to survive but, even then, I would like to do it the way *I* wanted to.

Our organic growth has not been without its adventures. In 1971 Pat Quinn was moving very fast and had opened seven or eight stores. At the time there was a fierce price war and our results were not great, but I had bought a site for a new shop in Walkinstown. As usual I went to our bank, the old Provincial, which by now had become AIB, and was told there was a new regime — I would now have to go to their merchant bank. The merchant bank told me that they would certainly advance the money but in three ways: part as a straight overdraft, which we wanted; part as a seven-year term loan (and we didn't want money for seven years); and part in exchange for shares in the company.

My heart sank. This was the first time I was faced with losing control of the business, and I simply did not know where to turn. I was already committed to the site.

My brother-in-law, Jack McCabe, who was a director of our company, told me that he did not think his bank, the Northern, would behave like that — and he introduced me to them. They advanced the money and, fifteen years later, I was talking to one of the senior people in AIB — we deal with them as well, now — and he told me that how they lost the Superquinn account had become part of their folk-lore.

To an extent I don't measure risk-taking in money. I came back from seeing my first Carrefour shop in 1973, excited about the fact that they had a bakery in the shop. I got the people who supplied the machines to Carrefour to do the sums for me and they did not really work out. It also meant opening up with a new union — the bakers' union had all sorts of rules that were very difficult for us to accept. We were going to have to take a chunk out of the shop and spend £10,000, which in 1973 was an awful lot of money. But really what I wanted was the smell of fresh baking in the shop. If you were to measure it purely in monetary terms, the risk for that was probably unwarranted. But if you're motivated by wanting to be better than anybody else, then the risk pales into insignificance. In fact it did raise the standards and made a profit as well.

The playhouses for customers' children were a bit like that. Isn't it great when you can do something that is worthy and gives people less pressure or takes stress off them — and is profitable, too? One of the ways I measure success is to do things that please people, that benefit people — and that make good business sense as well.

If you measure the supermarket business on the return
you get on every pound's worth of goods you sell, all around
the world you would get about twopence, which is a penny
in the pound after tax. Our profits are about 1.80, 1.90
pence in the pound before tax. I know that sounds very
small but I am not sure it is the best way to measure. Return
on investment might be a bit better — are you getting
enough out of the business to pay off your bank and to re-
invest so that you are healthy in the years ahead?

Sales per square metre of shop-space are critical, because
the overheads of that metre remain the same whether there
are 500 or 5,000 customers in the shop. So the idea is to get
as many people through as you can, and get your costs
down on that basis. With our margins you have to sell £1,000
worth to get £10 and that is a lot of selling in a very competitive market.

In business terms, I am not sure that I am ambitious
enough. There are no great unfulfilled ambitions out there.
I value family and home a great deal. I don't at all envy
those people whose positions take them away from home,
particularly when the children are growing up. I am lucky
to be a happy man. It's great to have a wife who is also your
best friend. We have a way of life in which our children are
close to us. I like to get home to lunch every day, at least in
theory. So not only am I happy but I regard myself as being
terribly lucky. Hardly a day goes by that I don't hear of
somebody with some trouble or other and I say, 'There but
for the grace of God go I.'

When I joined An Post as chairman I purposely stepped
down from other committees I was on, hospitals and things
like that. I felt I could only do one or two things well and, in
fact, I was involved as chairman of the IMI at that time also.
I prefer to take on a smaller number of challenges and get
closely involved — it's a hands-on thing. I have recently
joined two international boards and I find it fascinating to
sit with the best in our industry. I think I am more a focused
than a broad-spectrum guy.

John McCormack lived beside people I knew in Booterstown. He went into the newsagents one day. 'Why do you not sing any more, Count?' He said, 'Because I prefer to have people ask that rather than ask why *do* you sing any more!'

Well, I am still singing.

16

Martin Rafferty

A key thing is the capacity to grasp opportunities.
Along with that is the capacity to say no to an
opportunity which others may perceive but
which you do not.

Martin Rafferty is a banker and businessman. He was born in Glenamaddy on 22 February 1933. His father was Martin Rafferty, a grocer and publican. His mother was Mary Connolly, a housewife. He was the eldest in a family of six, three brothers and two sisters.

He was educated at:
The National School, Kilkerrin,
Castleknock College,
UCD (B.Comm.),
Institute of Chartered Accountants in Ireland,
Institute of Cost and Management Accountants,
University of California at Los Angeles.

He is married to Elizabeth Walsh, housewife. They have five boys: Jim (27), Kevin (26), Martin (24), Paul (22) and David (20).

He has held the following positions:
Cost Accountant with the Irish Sugar Co.,
Senior Finance Specialist with the Irish Management Institute,
Managing Director of Allied Irish Investment Bank.

He built up the BWG Group which was acquired in 1984 by Irish Distillers for £17 m.

He is now:
Chairman and a significant shareholder in Mahon and McPhillips and United Drug,
Chairman of Ulster Investment Bank and Lombard and Ulster Banking,
a director of Ulster Bank,
Chairman of Readymix plc,
Director of Aer Lingus, the IDA, Norish plc, Church and General Insurance plc and Lyons Irish Holdings plc.

He lectures on management programmes at European centres.

I was born and reared in Glenamaddy, a small town in the west of Ireland. My parents owned a pub and grocery business. From the earliest days I was influenced by the fact that we lived on the premises. I was expected to help out, something I gladly did and from the age of ten would spend quite a bit of time in the shop.

I was sent with my brothers to boarding school, Castleknock College, at a great sacrifice on the part of my parents. We had a family solicitor, Frank Meagher of Tuam, who had been to Castleknock and an uncle of mine was there for a brief period. It was an unusual choice for a family like ours. I enjoyed my time in Castleknock, particularly the chance for sport — an interest that has continued. There were relatively few opportunities in Glenamaddy for sport. When I finished in Castleknock, my first thought was to do engineering but the exposure to the small business eventually decided me to do commerce and then to go on to become a chartered accountant.

My father was in failing health and, during the university vacations or, indeed, any time I could spare from college, I was back helping in the business. Glenamaddy had a population of 150. There were twelve pubs of which we were one. The parish at large had about 500 households. For every one person living in the parish I would say there were three or four who were born there but were living abroad. There was tremendous migration to England, particularly Manchester and Birmingham, and to the United States, to the Bronx and Boston. One of the most revered and influential people from the village was a master ganger with McAlpines in England.

I found myself taking an increasing responsibility for the business. Then both my parents died within a very short time of one another in 1958. So as the eldest in the family — I was twenty-four then — it fell to my lot to take charge. I had just done my final accountancy exams. There were two choices before my parents' deaths: one was to inherit the business and live in Glenamaddy — I did not give that too much thought. The business was too small and that kind of life did not seem very attractive following an education which had given me wider horizons. My second choice was to go back and run the business, but only until the education of the rest of the family was completed. I spent three years running the business on my own. That was a very major influence on my later career. I was behind the counter in my white coat selling everything that would go on to the breakfast table. It was a classical country pub. We were also into provisions, things like pollard, bran, flour and we used to buy wool and we were undertakers — up in the loft there were always half a dozen coffins. We did not rise to a hearse, that was sub-contracted. I enjoyed it because there was always something happening. In small villages in County Galway in the 1950s the church and the pub were often the focal points of the local community. The pub was a place of relaxation for some, a place of escape for others. In some ways a kind of confessional — it taught me to be a good listener.

My father was a definite influence. He instinctively understood aspects of business for which I got the official names only in latter years: things like stock control, credit control and cash management. I remember standing behind the counter and being a little bit lax in my attention to a customer and getting a kick in the arse: I was quickly told that customers were my life blood and my job was to serve their needs and to do that better than anybody else in town. He left school at fourteen but he had an instinctive business flair. He was quite innovative. I use that word now. I would not have understood what it meant then. He opened an extension to the shop to sell sweets and ice-cream. It was really a separate profit centre to serve a different market. In those days the younger people would have been a little inhibited coming into the shop where the older people were. So having to take all the decisions about the business at age twenty-four or twenty-five was a major formative influence. I didn't feel any tremendous change or pressure — I had been well prepared for it from my previous involvement.

Inheriting the mantle was simply a progression. Indeed my father knew his life-span was short and in the last year did his best, through conversation and dialogue, to ensure that I had the benefit of his experience and thoughts about what I would now call strategic planning.

After growing up in a small community I now realise what kind of vision was needed by the founding fathers of Nestlé and Rothmans to grow their companies from Vevey and Stellenbosch, towns the size of Athlone and Maynooth respectively.

From my university and accountancy training, I knew there was no chance of building into a wider world from a small business in a small town. At the end of three years I sold the business for the princely sum of £7,000, having already got myself a job in industry. My first job was as a cost accountant with Gaeltarra Eireann where I spent three and a half years. That was followed by two years in the Sugar Company. My first five years in industry were spent working for two state-sponsored organisations. I learned how large organisations work. I saw organisations with twin objectives, social and economic. Particularly in Gaeltarra, you saw the tremendous difficulty of trying to marry those two. I also got, from my junior position, a view of the interrelationship between the organisation and the bureaucracy and the politicians. What hit me was the difficulty of trying to serve two masters: to try and produce a good bottom line and, at the same time, to meet social objectives. I very much enjoyed my time in those organisations. In Gaeltarra I spent a fair amount of time in the Gaeltacht areas and a lot of the work was done through Irish. The Sugar Company at that time was beginning to expand — it was the early days of Erin Foods. I spent three or four months — Monday to Friday — working as the office manager in Manchester. Looking back, it was pretty chaotic. There were many times we had product but we did not have orders and when we had orders we did not have product.

I was one of a number of people who were recruited at that time. In one room there were four accountants, one of whom was Vincent Ferguson. In another room there were three of our colleagues who were on planning: Brendan Halligan, Tony Brown and Willie Scally. It was interesting how all our careers developed.

I was offered a scholarship to an American university. I spent five months at the University of California at Los Angeles and another month visiting various businesses. It was a unique opportunity — there was no way you could pay for something like that yourself — I had got it through the Scholarship Exchange Board. What it did for me was to broaden totally my vision of the world, in particular the world of business. At UCLA my fellow students were all working for very large businesses and most of them inter-national. The fact that they were looking outside their own national boundaries at growing their businesses was a major influence. Secondly, this was at the time of the development of behaviouralism with, for example, sensitivity training with people like Tannenbaum and Weschler. I did a sensitivity training course myself. It started with a weekend up in the mountains at Lake Arrowhead. It was designed to sensitise you here and now to what people were really thinking and feeling. Then we had three sessions on campus for twenty weeks. That was a hell of a jump from a small town in the west of Ireland or even Dublin to the attitudes and thinking of the people of California at that time. I found the direct-ness of my classmates very hard to take at first. Even yet in Ireland there is often a tendency to fudge the direct question or avoid giving a direct answer. It was at times a painful but a useful experience to hear others tell you straight how they saw you.

Another major influence was the whole approach to the planning and organisation of a business. The best selling text of that era was *Principles of Management* by Harold Koontz and Cyril O'Donnell. George Steiner was a big name in the field of planning and a lecturer on campus. I did not have the experience to grasp all of what was being taught — a lot of it went over my head. But some of it stuck and made me stop and think. Now, many years after, when I look back, I can say that some of what passed for learning in the classroom was not that great. However, there were some techniques that I was introduced to for the first time, like discounted cash-flow or the evaluation of capital projects, the whole concept of the cost of capital, that were all very new to me. It was like being brought up to a very high hill to get a real view of what was down below. Those techniques, together with the behavioural area and also a basic approach to marketing, had a profound effect. In many ways it was my first exposure to breaking down the job of management into its component parts. But the real benefit of it all was the broadening of one's view.

When I came back from UCLA, I was doing much the same kind of job and I began to get impatient. I wanted to apply the new learning and an opportunity arose in the Irish Management Institute where I spent the next four years. It was a hell of a jump leaving a job in industry on Friday and finding yourself in a teaching job on Monday though, as I quickly found out, the IMI was not about teaching, it was about learning. I very much enjoyed my four years in the learning environment. The difference between teaching and learning was really the difference between putting the emphasis on the customer, by contrast with the university where the emphasis was on the professor. We were a very small team in the IMI at that stage and you worked closely with people from other disciplines, but we were beginning to make an impact and it was an exciting time. I spent about half my time in the finance area and the other half running courses for smaller businesses mainly in the distribution sector as well as making an overall contribution to general management courses.

There must be many people out there who can recall epic weeks in the Woodlands Hotel in Greystones on an IMI residential course. I was not too popular at home at the time because the courses used to start on a Sunday evening. I remember well one I ran with the late Eddie McDermott for electrical traders. On the last Friday of the course, the class spokesman stood up to thank Eddie and myself. He explained that, the night before, they had decided to have a collection for the hotel staff but, on second thoughts, had decided that the money should go to us. Eddie and myself divided £32. 9s. 6d. Eddie, however, had second thoughts too and said that, since it was my course, I should take the lot and, next time round, it would be my twist. About eighteen months later I had to pay a very sizeable bill for dinner for six in London.

That period gave me an opportunity to meet many lecturers from abroad and to see how their material could be adapted to the Irish scene.

During my fourth year with the IMI, the Institute was asked to make a contribution to some formal training for the banks. I had done a lot of work for the AIB Group and was approached. I was offered the job as general manager of their recently established merchant bank. I joined in 1968 with no knowledge of banking. I wasn't worried because up to that point when I had moved from job A to job B there was not much in common between the jobs.

Over the next four years we put together a team of very able people and, since the economy was beginning to move, it turned out to be an exciting time in merchant banking. One of the things I learned in the IMI was the need to have good people. I was lucky enough to be able to recruit people of the calibre of Tom Toner, Vincent Ferguson and Nicholas Leonard. Our aim was to create a merchant bank with a difference. The common denominator between us was that none of us had been in banking before. That helped us to look at the industry with a totally new view. It was during that time that many of the mergers and take-overs which were to form the basis of major Irish companies took place. Smurfit made their first four acquisitions in Ireland, CRH was formed through the merger of Cement Limited and Roadstone and the two major Irish banks began to move outside the domestic environment. The transition from teaching/learning to merchant banking was one of talking about money to actually lending it to develop businesses.

It was not then unusual that people who had moved into merchant banking should ultimately want to do their own thing — that was happening in London and New York. In 1972, with two of my colleagues from the merchant bank, John Harnett and Tom Toner, we decided to follow the path of Tony O'Reilly, Vincent Ferguson and Nicholas Leonard and to set up a company of our own. We started off by acquiring Joshua Watson, a malting company based in Carlow and employing 12 people. We picked it to start off with because it was a small business with few employees. That was built over the twelve years of our company into a fairly sizeable conglomerate by Irish standards with a turn-over of £140 m. and employing 1,200 people before it was sold to Irish Distillers in 1984. Along the way we acquired sixteen or seventeen companies and divested of five.

We had a lot of success and a number of real problems. With the benefit of hindsight, perhaps we went too far too fast and we were exposed to the change in oil prices in 1973. That had a severe and rapid effect on business conditions generally, and particularly on us as builders' suppliers and timber merchants. We found ourselves committed to forward orders with a price that was moving downwards at a pace. It was an extremely difficult period. It involved the reduction of the workforce in the builders' providers from 1,000 to 330. The fact that we were three people rather than one was certainly a help and Tom Toner had considerable industrial relations experience.

When in 1984 we sold what was then the BWG Group, I tried in a way to combine all the things that I had done previously: firstly, an involvement in the equity of companies; secondly, an involvement in banking; and thirdly, a little bit of teaching. Later, it followed that I would be invited to join the boards of a number of companies.

Those tough times in the timber business succinctly brought home the pluses and minuses of having a personal stake in the business. It was not just a question of your job being at risk but of your entire net worth — all was on the line.

There is no doubt but that I have arrived now at a more peaceful place. I have always been turned on by variety. I like now to be able to use, across a number of fields, the experience I have picked up along the way. Financial independence is a factor, but it is not the be-all and end-all. There are things I try to do now which are not made any harder or any easier by financial independence, though I suppose freedom consists in the ability to choose what you want to do, rather than be, for example, the chief executive of any particular company. I would not now be attracted to being chief executive of anything. That would be a limitation on the freedom I enjoy. I would not now choose to work within the confines of a single organisation. And it's not so much that I want to be on top, but that I want to be in control of what I do. The key thing is to be able to exercise a substantial amount of influence or control.

I like to do different things. I very much enjoy being involved in sport. I like all sport with the exception of two major ones: golf and racing — they give me no kicks. I get a lot of kicks from Gaelic football, soccer, rugby. I like major events like Wimbledon. Recently I have tended to go to the French Tennis Open which I enjoy more than Wimbledon because it's not so crowded. Participation in sports, both as an individual and part of a team, can not alone be enjoyable in itself but also sharpens the reactions and reflexes, necessitates thought, concentration and judgment, and you learn to live with victory and defeat. No bad training for a career in business, as long as one realises that dexterity with hands, limbs or body, does not easily translate into marketing, manufacturing and financial skills.

If friends were not important to me, I think I would have been more attracted to work outside Ireland. All my career, with the exception of the six months in business school, has been in this country. Now, as I travel more, I have begun to appreciate the quality of life here. With any reasonable standard of living, it would not be possible to get anywhere a better way of life.

I think I have the capacity to be cool in trying circumstances. In banking we used to lend a million pounds a day — I suppose that takes a certain amount of shrewdness and coolness. I think many people forget that money is somewhat different from other products. Other products you buy and use, money you lend and you want it back.

The classroom is a great learning experience — for the tutor. You have to combine a number of things. You've got to have some understanding of human behaviour, you learn how to deal with some difficult people, and, in the final analysis, you have to be able to communicate sufficiently with your audience so that they get a return on their investment of time and effort.

Growing up in a small town in the west of Ireland helps you not to have any notions about yourself. In ten seconds flat, the people you grew up with would have you back to where you should be. It distresses me to see people who want to flee from their background. I will always have a great feeling for the part of the country I was brought up in. A rural background can give one many advantages — life is fashioned often by events other than book learning. I can think immediately of one such experience and example. In the 1950s, during the days of the GAA ban, I was playing rugby with Galwegians and Gaelic football with my local parish. Having won our championship match, an objection was lodged against me as an illegal player and I feared I would be banned and the club suspended. Our club president and mentor drove me to the enquiry at the divisional board and, as we drove to the meeting, marked my cards. My name would be called in Irish and the charge would be read out in English. I was to respond for ten minutes in Irish, making sure not to make any long pauses. As the chairman did not understand Irish, he had two choices, either admit that fact or dismiss the case. We won our next round match the following Sunday.

I used to wonder how I came from Glenamaddy to where I am now, but I really feel that it is through your own volition that you get to where you are. A little bit of luck also helps. Luck is not something residing in a large tin and that is doled out on a day-to-day basis. You make an awful lot of your own luck. Opportunities come and go — some people take them and turn them into success. For other people, they just pass by. If you are entrepreneurial, some things you perceive as opportunities turn out in a way totally different from what you had anticipated. I have spent a lot of time trying to find out what makes very successful people. A key thing is the capacity to grasp opportunities. Along with that is the capacity to say no to an opportunity which others may perceive but which you do not. Success in business is a combination of flair, opportunism, vision, timing, leadership, management skills and luck. The successful entrepreneur will endeavour to complement his own skills by ensuring that those in which he is lacking reside elsewhere in the organisation. Most entrepreneurs at some stage feel like God, some tend to act the part as well.

I have faith in my own judgment but at various periods in my career that faith has been shaken. Anybody who says different is not seeing reality. What you've got to do when you make a poor judgment is to ask yourself why you did that and what you can learn from it. If you don't stop, think and consider, the likelihood is that you will just continue to repeat mistakes. But any entrepreneur will, along the way, put his faith in business ventures where it is misplaced. The entrepreneur has to look at himself — he can't blame the judgments of others.

Looking back, my career has had a logical pattern which was totally unplanned at the outset.

Informal and formal education, experience in industry, followed by learning and teaching, providing money for business and finally trying to do it oneself. Some people try and fly too far by the seat of their pants, others can over-rely on formal education and management courses. It's not what people say or do on courses that is important, it is what managers do or do not do as a result — that is the ultimate bottom line which determines whether they themselves and the company who finances their attendance get a reasonable return on their investment when they go back to the real world.

Business is no different from big game hunting. In hunting, as in business, you have to find your prey, follow it, outwit it, and pounce at the right time.

17

Geoff Read

*I don't ever get a sense of achievement because
I am never content with what we have got.
I guess that's my problem — I always
see more potential.*

Geoff Read is Managing Director of the Ballygowan Spring Water Co. Ltd. He was born in Dublin on 31 December 1954. His father is Gerald Edward Read, General Manager of Dictaphone (retired). His mother is Margaret Helen Oxer, housewife. He is the second child of two — one sister, Pauline.

He was educated at:
Monkstown Primary School,
Kill o' The Grange Primary School,
Sandford Park School,
The High School,
Ringsend Vocational School,
Kevin Street Technical College.

He is married to Wendy Mary Wolfe who worked in advertising. They have two sons: Alexander (3) and Christopher (16 months).

He was:
an electronics technician,
a shoe salesman,
shoe designer and manufacturer,
a male model,
a house refurbisher,
a landscape gardener.

He is a Patron of the Aids Trust.

My sister may have been an unconscious influence on me. She always had bright ideas. She is a radiographer and is married now with three children, but, at one time, she started a hat-hire service. It really took off. However, she tends to lose interest in things once they've been started. You can see from my background that I chopped and changed quite a bit. Male modelling and landscape gardening were a means to an end — to enable me to pursue the bottled water idea.

I was interested in sound engineering and when I left school I applied for a job with BBC Northern Ireland. They suggested I get some qualifications and come back to them in a year. The only place I could get the qualifications was in Kevin Street Technical College, but to get in there, I had to do a year in Ringsend Vocational School to get the right mix of subjects. After a year in Kevin Street, I decided I might as well go the course and get the full three-year qualification, which would lead ultimately to a more senior position.

About half the class stayed the course: one girl, the rest men. The oldest in the class was forty-six. Coming up towards the final exam everybody was furiously sending off about forty applications for jobs and, seemingly, getting nowhere. I decided not to send off any applications and to take a break of a year after qualifying.

There were seventeen papers in the final exam and I ended up having to repeat some. I'm not studious or academic. I found the subjects easy enough — what I found hard was to sit down and repeat, I did not like that at all. In any event, the whole subject was not what I expected it to be — it was dreary and the prospects were pretty poor. It was a means to an end, certainly not an end in itself. However, I stuck it out and, indeed, enjoyed bits of it — the logic and the mathematics. I have a reasonably logical mind.

I went to London and met a friend of mine who was working for somebody I knew who had set up a footwear business. He was making two or three hundred pounds a week, quite a lot in 1974. When I went for an interview, the guy who owned the company, Christopher Brooks, saw me and said, 'Give that guy a job.' I thought that this was great and would keep me going for the summer until I got something more permanent. I was managing a shop and was making three or four hundred pounds a week after a week there. The most I ever earned with that company was £500 a week on salary and commission, the least, £300. It was money for old rope. That gave me a terrific life-style, but there was more to it than that. I would get together with the managers of the other shops and we would design a shoe, send it off to the manufacturers, and then sell it when it came back. Business was good but, unfortunately, Christopher Brooks got some bad financial advice and was also very ambitious. Instead of ordering 20,000 pairs of shoes, he would order 200,000 and they would sit there on the docks until he could raise the money to get them out. He became a bit over-extended, flying private jets around India setting up factories there. But he was a great character and a great entrepreneur and would, I suppose, have been an influence on me.

I became more involved in the wholesale side of the business and then, probably inevitably, it was sold. The chap who bought it was an English aristocrat for whom it was a toy. He hired a New Zealand accountant called Biggs to run it for him. Biggs and I could not exist side by side in the same company. I decided to go out on my own. The business had stopped being exciting, it had become a chore. I joined up with one of our biggest customers. He had one footwear outlet and we quickly expanded until that became four. I ran virtually the whole business and that was exciting for a while as well. In 1979, VAT was brought in and the recession started to bite and I got fed up with the footwear business. It was a much drearier existence than it had been previously. Anyway, the set-up was never what I wanted to do — I wanted to have my own business, totally, something that was a bit more creative, a bit more original.

I went on a two-month break to Greece and decided that I would come back to Ireland and have a look around.

I have never liked working for people — that has probably been my most consistent thing. I don't like being told what to do.

Maybe it's a rebellious streak in me. I don't mind working *with* people at all. I don't mind taking decisions in business with people. I am very bad at taking decisions outside business — but in business I like to be in charge.

I remember well, even to the day, the origins of the idea for bottled water. It was in London and I was suffering from an extremely bad hangover. I had been at a party on the Friday night and I had to go to work on the Saturday in our shop in Oxford Street. I felt terrible and I sat around in the store for the morning feeling worse and worse and worse. A woman came in with a bottle of French mineral water in her bag and it struck me that what I was suffering from was dehydration. I went across to the local Underwood store and was amazed at the range of bottled waters on the shelf, something I had never noticed before. I picked a bottle and brought it back to the shop and drank it throughout the day. The taste was OK, nothing special, but not as good as spring water I remembered from Ireland in the Japanese Gardens when I was a kid. I thought the packaging was poor, the imagery was not there. I thought that this must be a great business to be in — I knew that tap water was recycled up to ten times. Even tea was a bit unpleasant in London because of the chlorination. I thought, well, that's a natural product for Ireland and I don't know of anybody doing it. I remember thinking that I would love to chase that up and see what the potential was. Every major city in the world is going to find its water supply getting worse. That was really the stimulus that started the whole idea.

I came back to Ireland in late 1979. I had a little money. I had sold off everything I had in the UK and was not in a hurry to rush into something. I was living at home with my parents when I got a call from a woman who ran a model agency, who had not met me but who said she heard I was presentable. I got what seemed an enormous sum of money for doing virtually nothing for a day. Then I had to go off to the Canaries for a week to make a commercial for a travel agency — terrific! Soon I realised that the money was great only because the job was so boring, hanging around all day grinning at a camera. I knew there was a stigma attached to male modelling, but if you were paid a lot for hanging around all day in the company of attractive women . . . And it was something I could do virtually at my leisure, a day here and a day there. You might work every day for a week and then not for six weeks. It made me very flexible.

The next thing, I was talking to a friend who was going on a start-your-own-business course run by the Irish Productivity Centre and AnCO. It was a five-month course, paid you forty pounds a week, and you had to do a feasibility study about starting your own business. I went into the interview for the course with the spring water idea on which I had already done some work. The Geological Survey had done some research and had found that there was an adequate supply of good quality spring water in Ireland. I told them at the interview that this was the coming thing, that soft drinks started as bottled water, then they added carbon dioxide, then they added bicarbonate of soda, then they added flavours, then they added preservatives. Now the wheel has turned full circle where you are getting away from heavily sweetened, additive-full drinks, back to pure spring water. Now you have caffeine-free diet Cokes, no artificial this or that. People are coming back to bottled water as the most natural product of all. I felt there were quite strong reasons for developing such an industry in Ireland. We had missed the industrial revolution, were not involved in intensive agriculture and had vast areas of land totally unpolluted. Ireland had all the environmental advantages together with a population that was not big enough to pollute the water sources. The people who ran the start-your-own-business course seemed to think it was a good idea — and they were short of people to put on the course.

The first two months consisted of lectures — people coming in and telling everyone who was on the course that they thought they were nuts. I think there was method in what they were doing: they were sorting out the men from the boys by saying, 'If you can't get through all these obstacles, then you are wasting your time.' I am not sure if this was entirely the right idea as there were some people there who needed nurturing, who needed their hand held. That was followed by a three-month period during which we had to do the feasibility study. We had access to a telephone and secretarial assistance and I was the only one who used them. There were seventeen people on the course. A few of them came in a few days, but I was the only one there every day. I used to ring C & C, who distributed Perrier, pretending I was a student doing a thesis, to get market information. I rang Highland Spring in Scotland which had only just been set up. I went into the CTT library and got as much information as I could. The CTT library was a bit out of date, but I could see the trends, that people were becoming more health-conscious, more concerned about additives in their food, more environmentally conscious. Since the information was out of date, it told me only that an explosion in sales of bottled water was inevitable. It did not tell me that the explosion had in fact happened in 1979.

I had just about finished the feasibility study when I read about this American guy down in Kilkenny who was going to start bottling water. I thought to myself I must give that guy a ring and see what he's got because all I had was the research and he must have had the source. His name was Francis Walsh, though in that part of the country they pronounce it Welsh. He had a spring source beside a disused garage. He had the water tested and it met the EC standards. I think, however, that what he was really trying to do was to exploit to the full the IDA grants. I had talks with them too and the upshot was that I took over the whole facility. Walsh did not own the land or the spring. It belonged to a local farmer. I wanted to set up a test market operation and

I agreed with the farmer that I would pay him a royalty on sales. I put in some pumps, tanks and filters. It really amounted to a row of taps on a wall. To be initially credible, one had to have a product and I started producing some samples. I wanted to see if people would actually buy an Irish product if they saw it on the shelf. We were the first people in the world to put bottled water in PET — plastic — and I had a special green label designed for it. In fact ICI used to take my bottle to seminars to show what PET could do — that was nice. Now approximately fifty per cent of bottled water sales in the UK and Ireland are in PET.

I had gone around some advertising agencies asking them for a name for the water and got some ridiculous answers. There was a townland near the source called Ballygown — and I added an 'a'. It was only afterwards when I went to register the trademark that I found there was actually a Ballygowan in Northern Ireland. Ballygowan has either of two meanings — either the town of the goat or the town of the smith — either way it's a one-horse town! I thought myself the name was right. I did not do any market research on it — I simply checked it out with my family. Then I went to a designer, Noel Hayes, and told him exactly what I wanted by way of imagery. I wanted it to be obviously Irish, but not shamrocks and leprechauns. I felt that Irish products had always foundered because they had gone the bog-Irish route by selling on this twee Irish image. I wanted a contemporary image, but one that was obviously Irish because there was great value in being Irish and that was what the product was all about. It had to be seen internationally as a high-quality, premium product. I designed a label which was not standard. It was a keyhole shape and could not be applied by machine — it had to be applied by hand because of the shape of it. I felt it was so unusual that it was worth the effort to do that. I had gone to PanPak and had the green bottle made. The sales manager there, Gerry McMahon, was very helpful. I used to hire a van at six o'clock in the evening. I timed it so that I could drive to PanPak at night and pick up a pallet

of bottles. At five or six in the morning I would drive to
Kilkenny, exactly 100 miles from my home where I would
sterilise and bottle and cap. Then I'd load the bottles in boxes
and put them into the van. As the demand grew, I started to
hire a couple of local people and would even bring down
some people from Dublin with me. At the weekend I would
bring down the family, my father and my fiancée, Wendy,
and a friend of mine, Pat. Every night of the week my
mother and father and Wendy would sit at the kitchen table
sticking labels on with gum and a brush. Every bottle was
checked visually and one out of every batch would be
analysed. It was a laborious activity. Then I would take them
out and sell them. I got agreement from Superquinn to list
Ballygowan and I did all the deliveries to them. I bought a
van because I was spending so much money hiring one. I
got one of these long wheelbase Datsun Urvans, but it was
getting really out of hand — I was driving up and down
every day bottling and labelling and selling.

At this time, I had gone to a neighbour who was a leading
accountant in Reynolds, Cooper, McCarron. He put me in
touch with a former colleague who had retired from the
accountancy practice while he was still in his thirties, had
gone to the US and had recently returned to Ireland. He
helped me set up the Ballygowan Spring Water Company
Limited and came with me to interview people who had
shown an interest in the company in the early days when
Frank Walsh had advertised for partners.

The one thing I was paranoid about from day one was
quality. One bad bottle could damage the whole thing. I still
believe that to this day. It's an absolute and the problems
Perrier have encountered have to an extent proved that.

Anyway talks were going on with several potential investors,
nobody was really biting, and we were becoming more and
more frustrated. People were saying they were interested all
right, but not when it came to stumping up the readies and
we were looking for a long-term commitment. We did not

want somebody who would just throw in a small amount of money, because we knew that when it took off, it would need proper financial backing. Eventually a business acquaintance put in £4,000 for an option on thirty-three per cent of the company. The accountant had sixteen per cent and I had fifty-one per cent. I would have a right to buy them both out if we did not go forward after the test-market phase. So, we were capitalised at about £10,000 — I had to put in all my savings at that time. All the capital that was invested went on putting the basic facilities in place and buying the raw materials, as, indeed, did all the income also. A friend of mine, John Kenny, who was then running Life Force Foods, very kindly allowed me to warehouse my product in his place. He did not charge me and he did some distribution of Ballygowan into the health food trade. When things started to develop, he took over the distribution into Superquinn and then I could concentrate more on production.

Up to now this was only still-water in one-and-a-half litre bottles. I was dealing with supermarkets, delicatessens, little family businesses, sandwich bars — just to see how the product would go in different places. I knew that if I could produce a sparkling water, I could have a go at Perrier. However, I was in a vicious spiral where I had to keep producing more to meet increasing demand, but I could not get outside the spiral to get more capital to automate the production so that I could spend more time on selling. At that time there was a VAT of eighteen per cent, and table water duty at a fixed price of 37.2 pence per gallon which I had not accrued. It's a duty which goes back over a hundred years and which applies to any product that's put in a package for sale except milk or fruit juices. I had decided to take the authorities on because pure spring water was more natural than milk or fruit juices. Pure spring water comes straight out of the ground — milk goes through a cow. It's processed to a degree. Pure fruit juice is processed. I felt I had a good case but the Customs and Excise wouldn't wear it and they hit me with a bill going back a year. I had to pay the duty bill, but I managed to get VAT zero-rated. The Coalition Government was in power at the time and I met with various politicians: Alan Dukes, Gemma Hussey and John Bruton. Gemma Hussey was very helpful and has since promoted the drink on many occasions as, indeed, have other politicians. Alan Dukes was Minister for Finance and he wrote to the Revenue Commissioners. The zero-rating was very helpful because it meant that Ballygowan could come in, in or around major branded soft drink prices.

I decided to stand back and see where I was going. I wrote to Superquinn and told them that they had sold 11,000 bottles and I never had a complaint on quality, but that I now wanted to reassess the situation, was withdrawing from the market but I would be back. They did not complain — they have always supported Irish enterprise.

What I needed was a production facility. I knew there was spare or even unused bottling capacity around. After a search, I heard of Richard Nash in Newcastle West, who had apparently shown an interest in bottled water. I suggested to him that rather than have several little spring water companies, we should get together to make an impact on the market, a market I had thoroughly researched and now knew pretty well. I found that he had a source which dated back to A.D. 1184. The Knights Templar had built a castle at the source. It had become the property of the Earls of Desmond who were pretty colourful figures in Irish history. It was well protected: it was on the flow side of the town. There was no industry and no agriculture. There were 400 acres of parkland. Another thing was that the western prevailing winds were coming in off the Atlantic, ensuring that there was no acid rain pollution. These were unique attributes and the source tested really well. I got a hydro-geologist from Trinity, David Ball, to make sure that there was an adequate supply of high-quality water to meet foreseeable demand. I also got him to train in the people in Nash's on water, as distinct from bottling soft drinks. It was one of the most sensible things I ever did. I had, up to then, been producing a fine product, but really going along in blissful ignorance of all the pitfalls.

So, in 1984, we launched into still water with a fifty-fifty stand-alone company. The Ballygowan company now had exclusive rights to the source and also the option to buy land surrounding it. We had a separate, commercial agreement with Nash's for bottling. At this point, I had bought out my other two shareholders and passed on fifty per cent to Nash, so that the ownership of the company was vested in just myself and Nash's. I had all sorts of tax guys advising me on putting the structure properly in place.

We launched the still water in March 1984. Now that it was being produced for me, I could devote my time to selling it. I flogged around in my van. I got it back into Superquinn, into Quinnsworth and into several other outlets.

About three months later, we introduced a sparkling water. It was an excellent product and, by now, we had got distributors to carry the product with their other wares. In September of that year, we introduced a small, 250ml bottle. I had originally wanted a green bottle to represent Ireland, but we could not get one, so we designed a green sleeve. It was something that had never been done before in Ireland. The sleeve comes down over the bottle in a tube and is then cut by a laser. It was very attractive, gave protection for the bottle, you get very attractive print and it was not that much more expensive than the normal label.

I started to do some promotions and sampling at places like the Spring Show, but I was still the only employee in the company. I only took on a girl in 1985 as a second employee, and up until the time we did the deal with Anheuser Busch, three young girls and myself were the only employees in the company. It was a very lean organisation — I did not pay myself any salary until 1 January 1985. Since I couldn't afford to pay for advertising, I went in for a lot of the public relations stuff myself. I had this obsession with quality and with the image that came from that. A product could succeed in the international market only if it maintained its quality and its quality image, but with no shamrockery. A mistake that a lot of Irish people have fallen into is the American Paddywhackery image of Ireland as opposed to creating your own image for them.

Then the product started to take off and to attract a bit of attention. I decided to do a bit of advertising, so I got some people from advertising agencies to do nixers for me. We did a series of five ads humourously knocking the French: 'Eau dear', etc. Then, when I had a regular advertising agency, I used them to finance the extra sales they created by not paying them until the money from the sales had come in. I could do this because I had total control of the company: finance and marketing and also, really, the production. I had my finger on every single pulse and I had taken the thing from first principles — I knew it inside out.

I think everybody in Ireland had the idea of bottling water once they had seen Perrier, but nobody had actually done it. And it had a clean wholesome image — there was nothing bad about it. John Fanning of McConnells wrote an article called 'The Ballygowan Factor' at the time, a time when people were not buying Irish. I believe people should not buy Irish unless the product is of at least equal value or quality to the imported product. A few people along the way have said to me, 'I buy Ballygowan because it's Irish' and I tell them that they are not doing me any favour: the only reason to buy it is because it is better than anything else available. Don't buy it because it's Irish, buy it because it's best. The fact that it is Irish is a plus.

I still like to see it displayed at political and trade union and management conferences. It wasn't difficult to get them to display it — it always looked benign — the difference now is that they actually drink it. People are no longer embarrassed to be seen drinking bottled water. It also came at a time when people were beginning to move away from alcohol, especially hard liquor. They wanted to be able to go out to the pub and not drink. Bottled water could be a gin and tonic or a vodka. There was no social stigma attached to it as there was attached to asking for a Club Orange and people would say, 'Are you not having a real drink?' Ballygowan said all sorts of healthy things about the people who were drinking it. So the timing was right.

The image of this upstart taking on Perrier was attractive to journalists. Then it began to create its own momentum — it became more credible, more plausible. But I realised that it was something that had to be kept all the time in the public eye. The more sales grew, the more money I would take out to invest in advertising. I grew it to a £1 m. turnover with a £10,000 overdraft. I was using whatever mechanisms I could to generate cash-flow.

In 1985, companies like Gilbeys and Irish Distillers started to show an interest in us. I was concerned that the thing would grow too fast and that I could not keep up with it. Though Nash's were responsible for the production, it was a one-man band and I felt a bit vulnerable to competition. If any of the multinationals had come in at that time, they could have bought the market. I also felt that since it was going so fast, it would out-grow Nash's facilities and we would need a spanking new factory. We would also need that to be credible internationally. Nash's plant was not up to the efficiency standards you would need to compete internationally.

We had discussions with Gilbeys and Irish Distillers, both of which came to nothing. I think they were more interested in developing a local brand with a little exporting while we were interested in developing an international brand. Also, perhaps, they were cautious — it is hard for big multinationals to relate to one guy, albeit one with a contract bottler. While the profile then was high, the market was too small. In retrospect, I was probably being patronised a bit: 'Be a good boy and you'll go far.' I have had that since, too, and I don't like it one bit. Myself and Richard Nash always had the same view, that Ballygowan could be a major international brand. I'm great friends with David Dand of Gilbeys and I have a great respect for Richard Burrows of Irish Distillers but, at the time, they were not suited to what Richard Nash and I wanted to do. I don't think they fully recognised the potential of our company.

Around that time we had heard that Anheuser Busch were interested in getting into the bottled water business. We had been selling a bit in the States, the response had been very good and we had every lunatic there chasing us for exclusive rights. I even had one guy purporting to be from the IRA telling me that if I did not give him exclusive rights, there'd be trouble. I told him where to go.

In May 1985, Anheuser Busch asked us to send them some samples. After some investigation, they decided that they liked the product — they were interested in an imported bottled water. In November 1985, Richard Nash and I decided to go to a soft-drink conference in Anaheim in California, to see what the trends were and we would stop off in St Louis on the way back to see if Anheuser Busch were really interested. En route, we met some multibillionaires who were interested in getting into Ballygowan and they introduced us to major soft-drink figures in the US. They felt there was tremendous potential for it — it was all very exciting. People were looking at this small Irish company and saying that it had the potential to be a major brand in America. I was still a bit cautious not wanting to get wound up too much in the hysteria.

We had some discussions with Anheuser Busch senior managers. We told them we would have an interest in a relationship, but that we were a very small, young, Irish company and that our bottling facilities were not suitable for long-term development, but we had the land and we had the source and we intended to build a new plant.

I should say here that I got on very well with Richard Nash. While he was a director of the Ballygowan company, I was the only executive director and he let me get on with the job. I had needed some grey hairs around me both for credibility *vis-à-vis* Gilbeys and Irish Distillers and the banks and for advice. Billy Sutherland was chairman. He is an old family friend and father of Peter, the former EC commissioner. With Paddy Kevans, a solicitor, Brian O'Connor, a former SKC partner, together with Richard Nash and Bill Wilmot, we had a board of directors with plenty of wise heads. They backed me in everything I did. Billy is a very statesmanlike figure (you can see where Peter got some of it) and he was particularly helpful in negotiations. Paddy Kevans was my major supporter and is one of the best businessmen I have ever met.

In January 1986, a team of three came from Anheuser Busch to inspect our facilities and the source: their financial woman and two technical people. They offered us a deal through which they wanted to take an equity participation in the company and distribute the product in the States. We were going to build the new facility and we showed them the drawings. It was very exciting. Here was the biggest brewery in the world and I was effectively the only employee in the company.

We negotiated a deal, and ten days later we were to have a meeting with the top financial guy in Anheuser Busch. He flew into Shannon and essentially told us that we would not be ready in time to meet their requirements and that they would have to put it on the shelf. They were ready to sell millions and millions of bottles of Ballygowan in the States and we were not ready to produce them. The upshot was that I had three months to produce a business plan. I did and it was as thick as a telephone directory. I did a number of pricing and volume scenarios. Then I did work on sourcing materials and the legal and tax implications. It was a very comprehensive document that we couriered to them. They responded positively. They thought it was a good plan. We met with them and they said that the higher projections we had put in would be the ones that they would go for and that we would tie up a deal in the summer of 1986 before the Derby. It was now well over a year since they first tested the product. In the pre-Derby negotiations, they decided they were going to be conservative and they cut the volumes and the advertising spend in half. The financials still looked good and they made us an offer to acquire a controlling interest in the company and to acquire the trademark for the US. Their equity would help set up the new facilities. They also lent us a couple of technical people. They wanted me to be available in the States to help with the sales and promotion there and also to run the marketing programmes elsewhere. I agreed to move from being managing director to being marketing director worldwide, but with the same reporting responsibilities.

We started building the new plant in November 1986. We had it up and running in July 1987. We moved our production from Nash's but continued to use the same source. All this time we had been doubling our sales every year. We were doing well in Northern Ireland and starting to do well in the UK.

The Americans had planned to take quite a considerable amount of product. This did not happen, for reasons which had nothing to do with us — their own beverage division started to fall apart. Denis Long, the president, left, and new products had a low priority. So almost immediately we signed the deal with them, they started backing down on their commitments. They were going through terrible internal traumas. The new plant needed volume to go straight into it because it was quite a liability. They were not putting any prospect of volume in there. They kept putting the plans out and out and out. The very first board meeting took place nearly nine months after they got involved with us. The balance was now 50 per cent Anheuser Busch and the rest divided between Richard Nash and myself. The new board of directors was five Anheuser Busch and two each for Richard and myself. I had Paddy Kevans and Richard had Bill Wilmot, the manager of the new facility. Denis Long was still president, even though technically he had resigned, with Michael Roarty, a senior vice-president and the second-in-line in the company, and Terry Poulos, the head of the beverage division, i.e. all the non-beer products, and Larry

Lentz who had been sent to Ireland as our liaison man. Technically, if we needed anything we were supposed to relay it through him. It was a very heavyweight board but they had made Lentz chairman which went down very badly because he was very much a junior. I felt the Americans were back-tracking on their commitments because of their own problems in the beverage division. They were losing $100 m. a year. They just couldn't get it to work. They had promoted people into jobs that they weren't capable for. Top management were saying that they were not to do anything until they got that right. We were such a small piece in their corporate jigsaw that we were certainly not getting top priority. I felt that unless we got top priority, we were going to get into financial difficulties: the brand new plant and facilities were a big liability. Our volumes in Ireland and elsewhere at the time did not justify their existence. We entered a period where Richard Nash and I decided that we were going to put pressure on them to meet their commitments. Anheuser Busch were treating the company as if they owned 100 per cent of it: they really were not used to having other shareholders. It was all sweetness and light at the beginning, but as we got into it, there was a lot of arse-protecting. We entered a very difficult period. Sales were still growing dramatically, particularly in Ireland, but in the States, they had put it into test-marketing which was really only a holding operation so that we would not be suing them for breach of contract. It was unfortunate because I think it was the best deal ever, if they had done what they could have done. They had enough muscle to create the brand, for sure, in the States, if they had the will to do it.

We had to take them to court under Section 205, where we claimed they were using their majority shareholding to oppress the minority shareholders, basically for not carrying on the business of the company in a proper manner. Fortunately we settled the case after three ten-minute court appearances. I was prepared to lose everything, but in the end I got what I was seeking.

It had been two and a half years of turmoil and hassle with them. It's one thing doing a deal with the biggest brewer in the world, it's another when you sue them. We were right to do it. They were prepared just to sit on the company and see it lose money. For them it would just be a tax write-off. Originally, they were prepared to spend $19 m. over the first five years advertising Ballygowan in the States. They did not know how to launch a totally new product. They had formulae and the formulae did not fit. The problem was that they were professionals, not entrepreneurs. Promoters — entrepreneurs — don't fit easily within a corporate structure, a structure that has 40,000 employees and turns over $10 b. a year. A big company like that can't relate to one like ours which needs to be dynamic.

What we are doing is selling water and that is basically a marketing exercise. You have got to communicate the benefits of your product and your raw materials over those of everybody else. For many people, there is a perception that one is equal to the other. We have to communicate with the consumer, make the package look attractive and then get the product to where it can be sold, which is the key thing. You have to get into a position where people will aspire to buy your product out of all the range of products available. I believe we have been particularly good at that. I think we'll get better because we have a unique proposition. So it was not an easy fit for us with a big company which wanted to retrench. Retrenchment was not what we wanted.

It was all very frustrating for me — I could see the opportunities we were missing. I could also see this corporate mentality — people writing memos to protect themselves, not to inform. There were sheets of paper with fifteen people copied on every sheet.

If I did not sit easily with them, there was no reason why they should sit easily with me: we were the only company in their group where they just barely had majority control. So they had this bunch of minority shareholders sitting there griping at the senior management of their company, at four vice-presidents and the president of this mega-corporation, aggressive Irishmen telling them that they had made commitments and that they had better keep to them — or else.

It was an incredible experience. In a very short time I'd come from a one-man company to sitting on a board with four or five of the top management of one of the fifty biggest companies in the United States. To put it delicately, I feel their contribution was bureaucratic rather than dynamic. It was both weird and enlightening. I suppose I enjoyed the experience because I realised that if you try hard enough, things are achievable. It also had the side-benefit of teaching me how to structure a formal board meeting. I learned how to communicate through the layers of bureaucracy of a huge multinational corporation.

The experience convinced me that that was not what I wanted to do — and it was not going to make the company successful. That's why we had to extricate ourselves from the situation. If we hadn't extricated ourselves, I would have had to go because they would not have continued to sit with me. I would not fit. As the promoter of the product, I had a deep desire to see it succeed, more than anybody else could have.

Now, having got back in the driving seat, I feel the challenge is there again. It had been subsumed in conflict for a while. We moved very quickly and brought a few people on board with the result that the work-rate expanded rapidly. More people create more work. We are growing at a pace with which we can just cope and we are now turning away business. We could not service properly new business other than that which we have strictly planned out for the next two to three years.

It's very difficult to build a brand in an international market. It's easy if you have money to throw at it. The first thing in a branded product is that the quality has to be right, because the consumer is both fickle and discriminating, and poor quality will soon be exposed. The trade is becoming quite discerning as well and, after the problems with Perrier, is becoming more educated. All that suits us.

I work on building credibility, building relationships, so that you are familiar to people before you start doing business with them. They have got to know that you know what you are talking about and that you won't make commitments that you cannot honour. We could have serviced the UK supermarket business much earlier, but I felt that we did not have the infrastructure and we would make mistakes. We built our credibilities slowly — we took our time. We are very loyal to our customers and they become very loyal to us. We go to a lot of trouble to support the brand. When you build a base like that, you are building a platform from which to grow. Then you start to get to the consumer through advertising, communication, in-store development. Then you are building a consumer franchise, so you have got a solid proposition to go to the next customer with. You can then go and tell them that a UK multiple has fifty-seven brands of bottled water and that we are in the top three or four. We work on the basis of mutual trust and commercial reality. We build the relationships brick by brick. It's the only way, because we are coming from a market of 3.50 m. people in Ireland to a market in the UK of well over 50 m. We don't have the financial resources to go on TV the first couple of years.

If we are to be a major brand in the market, we need to be in all sectors, so I was three years negotiating with Grand Metropolitan brewing. We were in the supermarkets, but Perrier were really the only mineral water in the pubs, which they dominated and, because they dominated, they were not very good: they were arrogant, they were not giving good margins and people were apathetic towards them. Eventually I persuaded Grand Met that they could support other brands in that sector. Grand Met was the first link in the chain. We've done well with them. They have access to 15,000 pubs and also to hotels. We had to pull our launch with Grand Met forward a month when Perrier had their troubles. That was fortunate timing for us but, in fact, it was the result of three years of negotiation. Grand Met just did not pull us in overnight to substitute for Perrier. We're also beginning to do very well in the US again and we sell successfully in a number of different countries.

I get disappointed if somebody chooses another product instead of ours — something that rarely happens. But even if it does, I never give up. I always believe that we are much better. It's not arrogance, I just have confidence in the organisation and in the product, and I suppose I've confidence in myself — I know my business now. That is not to say that I am the world's best businessman. Maybe in some areas I'd be weak. I might agree too readily to something to make progress instead of standing back and playing hard ball. I think, at the end of the day, you have to strike a balance between being expedient and being dull.

I don't have time to ask myself what drives me, we are so busy. Every day is like panic stations. Maybe that's the wrong way. Maybe it should be nice and organised — I don't know any other organisation that works as hard to a man or a woman as this one does. The reps are out building this business till eleven o'clock at night. We are operating three eight-hour shifts, six days a week. It seems to be a continuing thing that everybody is working extended time and nobody complains.

Maybe it's paranoia, the feeling that it might all be snatched away. But, what is true is, the minute you take it easy, there is somebody out there ready to screw you. There are now fifteen people bottling Irish water. You take your eye off the ball and somebody is in doing something else. For some of them, it is not their primary product and they will cut a deal with the customer, give him an inferior product at a low price — and then we get compared with that — and that's business.

I don't ever get a sense of achievement because I am never content with what we have got. I guess that's my problem — I always see more potential.

18

Tom Roche

*I feel very happy when I stand back and look at
that bridge — but then I recall the very first
gravel-washing plant we put up in 1944.
I suppose what we work for is this sense of
achievement. You just go on building and building.*

Tom Roche was born in Limerick on 4 April 1916, the fourth child in a family of five of Thomas Roche, a civil servant and Kathleen O'Halloran, of peasant stock.

He was educated at The Star of the Sea National School in Sandymount, at the Christian Brothers School in Westland Row and at Blackrock College.

He is married to Florence McAvoy of Belfast, who was a school secretary. Their children are Maura, Eleanor, Tom and Claire.

He has been self-employed since the age of sixteen. Tried sitting on various boards but was never easy at board meetings.

Managing Director, in chronological order, of:
Roche Brothers,
Castle Sand,
Roadstone Limited,
CRH plc.

He is a recipient of the President's Award of the Association of Consulting Engineers of Ireland.

When my father died, my mother got a little shop in Inchicore. I was then fourteen. When I was sixteen, she realised that I was interested more in practical things than in school. The man who had sold us the shop had a small coal and concrete block business opposite. My mother decided that my eldest brother, who was four years older than me, and I, should go into it as a business.

I think that you're born with a temperament and it's an accident. The temperament I was born with was to do things with my hands. From the earliest I can remember, I was belting away with a hammer, making wheelbarrows or chairs.

I was ambitious, even as a youngster. I wanted to build something, no matter what. The trigger for all that was that small business. It seems incredible now — my mother paid £250 for it. It consisted of a yard where we stored coal and a block machine with which we made concrete blocks. My brother, Donal, who joined me in the business, left school even earlier than I, at age fifteen. He's been the steadying influence when I strayed too far from the sensible path.

We had lived first in Sandymount, but when we moved to Inchicore, which was an industrial district, I got to know working people well.

1932 was the year we started with a truck that carried a ton and a half. By the year the war came, we had four trucks, each of which carried six tons. Donal did more of the bookkeeping and general administration, I was more on the practical side. I kept the trucks going and made bodies for them. I was blessed with the people that were working with me. Of course, I had some unhappy experiences with men, which I now regret, as I should not have been so hard or, at times, so indifferent or callous. It's only when you look back that you realise that.

My mother was the practical one when my father died. He left only a few hundred pounds. We were very fortunate in meeting a man called Kirkham who had a cinema in Inchicore. Beside it was the shop he sold us for £800. Whatever arrangements he and my mother made, he gave us time to pay it off. Kirkham was a lovely old man, a Quaker. He had great sympathy with my mother. His nick-name was 'Daddy' Kirkham. He was also a builder.

I was just about old enough to feel my father's death, but it was shattering for my mother. The only thing she knew how to do well was to bake, so she started a little bakery, as well as the sweets and cigarettes. When we opened first, we used to take in £20 a week. If you were to convert that now, it would be £600 a week. It grew and we managed to make a living. Unfortunately, my oldest brother, William, died in 1934 from TB. My second brother, Desmond, nearly died with it — one of his lungs was taken out. TB was a frightful scourge in those days. Desmond was bookish and scholarly and wound up in the civil service.

You could put it this way: one day I was at school, and the next, I had a shovel in my hand and I was delighted. My mother set an example. I think that may be common in Irish mothers. My father really died too soon to have influence. But mother was not strict. She was the opposite.

We used to get clinker or breeze from the railway and make lightweight blocks as well as sand and cement blocks with one of these old hand machines. It was our introduction to the building side. Later, we dropped the coal because an accountant told us we were not making any money. Before that, we'd go down to the docks with a little truck, load it up, put the coal in bags and go round selling it to friends of my father who wanted to help us. I came in touch with the dockers of Dublin. They were a tough lot. That was one of the ways I got to know workmen. I enjoyed the freedom physical work gave.

There was some feeling that we had come down socially, from Sandymount to Inchicore. I avoided the Blackrock College people. I knew I was now cut off from that. But the fact that I went to Blackrock has always been a great sheet-anchor or point of achievement. I'd often used it when I was young: when I'd meet people on building sites, I'd casually mention that I went to Blackrock. Ah, it was great to have gone there, although at times I was not very happy. I was bright enough, but I was a bad pupil. I did not take to learning. My eldest brother was such a good student that he was held up as an example to me. I left after the Inter Cert. Looking back, I can only remember that the results were kind of middling. Funnily enough, the only prize I ever got was for French. Maybe that was because we had a very good French teacher, Fr Joe Butler. The little bit of geometry I learned was useful later in building. I had a few pet hates and one of them was Irish. When I think of all the hours wasted, cramming Irish, a tragic waste for the whole country, especially for poorer youngsters. This god-damned Irish was foisted on them. They were proficient neither in English nor in Irish. I think that was one of the worst things de Valera could have done for this country, whatever idealism he had. The other was religious instruction, which I detested. Apart from that, school was not bad at all. The priests of the older regime in Blackrock were tough, but then I was not a very good pupil. And I got a surfeit of religion. Now that I'm over seventy, I really think a lot about the mystery of why we're here. Undoubtedly, there has been some extra-ordinary Creator — you only have to look at the complexity of living things.

What I look to in times of trial is a depth of inner strength that I can call on. I think it originated in my mother. Fortunately, I can call on mental reserves: I don't need alcohol or pills. I think it also had its origin in the fact that I was grubbing for pennies when I was young. When you start from such a low base, it must condition you afterwards. As you know, we've had rough times in this Bula Mines thing financially so I've had to accept the worst that can happen and learn to live with it.

Bula Mines was a mistake. I was tempted by the piratical aspect and the romance of it. There were a few times when I could have got out, but I hadn't the final say. All the assets that I had were sucked into it.

One morning I was half-shaving and half-reading Shake-speare. I hadn't studied Hamlet's famous soliloquy at school and I was really gripped by it. I think that Shakespeare was one of the outstanding fellows who really understood what life was all about. In that soliloquy, he sums up the dilemma of all of us.

I am a loner, with some exceptions. I had one very good friend, Dan Herlihy, who is dead now, and he was very supportive.

Position for position's sake never seemed to register with me. I remember when we were living in Woodlands Park, in a very nice house I built there, I was driving in one Saturday in my Buick car and I was very depressed. This was long before Bula, and I thought to myself, here I am, with a beautiful house, a Buick car, a good business, and I'm in the depths of depression. My depression had nothing to do with the business. It was a very personal thing. Looking back now, I could say that I had everything and I could be just as dejected then as I could be now, when I have relatively nothing. No, I don't miss Roadstone. I look back in a kind of wonderment sometimes that I was head of it and built it up. I have no regrets. It was a marvellous life. In fact, it was unique, because I had absolute freedom in the business, something that's given to very few.

In a way, it's like setting out for a walk. The first step is the hardest. Then you take a second step and a third and it becomes easier. The hardest thing of all was to establish the base of the business. And my mother, God bless her, pro-vided the base in that tiny little business. I learned an awful lot from the three workmen who came with the business. They were nice people. They showed me the ropes. You have five or six days in the week; you do a little every day and try to build on what was done the previous day. I think it goes back to temperament. You just go on building and building.

Before the war, with our four trucks, we used to carry sand and gravel — and bricks and tiles — for people called

Concrete Products, who are now Chadwicks. They were very good to us. In that way, I got to know the building side of things very well.

During the war, we had plenty of time to think what we would do after it. I was always interested in trucks, the bigger the better. It was natural to get in on this washed gravel business. There was practically no washed gravel in Dublin, but there were two good plants in Cork. I went down to have a look and was very taken with them. When you're making concrete blocks, you get to know the best kind of gravel. We formed a little company. My older brother was friendly with Joe Kidney, an architect. Joe's father was an accountant and they were mixed up in Jury's Hotel and were quite well-to-do. I was introduced to the Kidney family and I explained to them that I would like to put up a gravel washing plant after the war and buy some more trucks. They were very helpful.

Also, during the war, we got into the demolition business. We made more money pulling things down than putting them up. We knocked down things like jails and workhouses. You then sold the material by auction. It was quite profitable and we accumulated enough capital to go into the Castle Sand business with the Kidneys. It took off. It was very timely. One of our first jobs was Dublin Airport with T. J. Moran & Co. This was followed by the Leixlip Hydroelectric Scheme, then the Bus Station in Dublin and a few others. We put up our first plant at Kill, near Naas, a part of the country where there was a lot of gravel.

In or about that time, I met John Wood from Cork. He owned one of the washing plants down there. He had been working in the North of Ireland. He was a remarkably far-seeing man. He was going to put up a quarry at the Hill of Allen, about thirty miles from Dublin. We thought this would interfere with our business and suggested that we get together, but he was not forthcoming. We decided to go ahead anyway and put a quarry up in the Dublin mountains. When he saw this, he agreed to come in with us and so

Roadstone was founded. We merged Castle Sand with Road-stone and formed a public company.

We lived at the time in Mount Merrion near Con Creedon, with whom I became very friendly, and who was in the gypsum business. I asked him how you formed a public company and he told me there was a solicitor called Dillon in Suffolk Street who managed his affairs. Dr Beddy of the Industrial Credit Company helped us. The issue would be called a flop now because the Industrial Credit Company were left with a lot of the shares. That was about 1948 and few people had any faith in the stone or gravel business. Dr Beddy was one of the most perceptive characters I've met in my life. He could say more with fewer words than any man I've ever met. To the day he retired, he was always supportive.

My way of going for the next ten years was to spend too much money and then we would have to go to the public for more. My unfortunate brother, Donal, had to worry about it. The business was centred around John Wood's site at the Hill of Allen, a beautiful site, a perfect hill of basalt in the middle of a bog.

In 1949, I went to the States to see what they were doing there. That trip was worth three years at a university. When I saw the scale of their operations and their approach to quarrying, I knew exactly what we wanted. We put up this whopping plant — it was one of the biggest in the British Isles at that time. Stone comes out in big lumps and the bigger the first crusher is, the more economic everything else is. We put up a crusher which was five feet wide and three and a half feet the other way. Previously, the little crushers had been maybe two feet wide and one foot the other way. That quarry was quite successful and, being the restless kind, I looked around for number two. I got a set of geological maps and I used to look for lumps of basalt. One of them that stood out was at Slane. The Marquis of Conyngham of Slane Castle owned it. We bought a couple of hundred acres from him for £10,000. One of the high points was having lunch with him in his castle to celebrate.

The butler stood behind my chair and I was very impressed. He was talking about his salmon and he used an expression I had never heard before. He said the salmon 'ate very well'.

That quarry was also successful and it led to our first export venture. About two years after it started in 1955, a chap called Van Neerbos arrived from Holland. He wanted tons and tons of a particular kind of basalt which was about the size of wheat. We put up a set of export bins on the quayside in Drogheda. When a ship would come in, we could load it quickly. We then looked to England which was a hell of a lot nearer than Holland. In Liverpool, they were already importing stone by ship from Wales, but I got a very frosty reception from the Docks Board. I met the whole board, all fifteen of them. When they said no, I said, 'Thank you very much, gentlemen', and walked out. However, we got around that by buying a little business there that was importing tin ore for smelting. It gave us a quayside. We bought the Forticrete Company and started to make concrete blocks on American Besser machines. Eventually, it developed into quite a good business and spread to other places, Somerset, Leicester and Buxton.

Meanwhile, back home, we had taken over Clondalkin Concrete. It did well and the next place we looked for a quarry was near Limerick. We put one up near Bunratty, where there was very hard limestone. It only broke even for a while, but eventually became profitable because it was near Shannon Airport and there was a good deal of road activity. After that we went to Castlebar, Castleblaney and Kilkenny. Eventually, John Wood sold out to us for shares. That was very successful because John Wood was a great businessman and had good reserves of gravel. Somehow, we always seemed to be able to raise the money. Dr Beddy was a calm, resourceful man in this. He was succeeded by Frank Casey, who was equally nice.

We also put up a machine shop in Inchicore, where we would design and make a lot of our own plants. That was one of the things I'm glad about because, years after they might have left us, workmen would come back to me and say, 'You know, we got a great training in your place.' I didn't realise it at the time but we were acquiring a lot of know-how. I thought this was great for Irish people — we were so behind in these things. We became less and less dependent on English suppliers. I was always very conscious of the fact that the Irish were so low in the industrial scene. We first bought our plant from Goodwin Barsby. The people who came over from them were very superior, very English. I went out to see one of them who was staying at Ross's Hotel. He was at breakfast and asked me, 'Who are these Walsh brothers?' I told him the name was Roche and that I was one of them. He didn't suggest coffee. Later on they could not have been more helpful.

Behind a lot of what I've done was to show that the Irish can do it — and we now know that they can.

I'm an engineer at heart, a builder at heart. I was very interested in houses and built six very nice ones at Woodlands Park. I'd say a builder would define the kind of person I happen to be.

Anyway, the business was expanding and I was managing it in a very personal way, down in the workshops, interested in everything. I would ask the quarry managers what their biggest problem was. We'd start at the biggest one and work back. I would note everything and I would always see that it was done. Donal was getting a bit worried that the business was becoming too big for my style of management and it was he, around 1965, who got in Bill Murray as a consultant. Bill had a profound influence. He set up an organisation and it was no longer a personal business. He said we were selling material too cheaply. Regretfully, when we put our prices up in later years, it brought in a lot of competition. The most valuable thing that Bill Murray did was to recognise the kind of people who would be needed to succeed me. He brought in young men like Henry Lund, Don Godson and Jack Hayes. Jack Hayes is now the number two in the outfit and Don Godson pioneered all the work in America.

For six months after they came, I didn't know what to do with them.

Don Godson came up to my office one day and sat down. He's very quiet. He said, 'I've been here six months and you won't let me in on what you're doing.' I said, 'I don't see the necessity, Don.' He said, 'The trouble with you is that nobody ever told you to fuck off.' That was a small remark, but it had a big consequence. As you know, Don grew — he's a remarkable fellow and a great personal friend. It was an organisation now. I also thought that at the age of fifty, which coincided with that time, I had passed my peak. Maybe it was all the influence of these new-style managers.

The next big event was the long cement strike which meant we were nearly out of business. Then there was the attempted take-over of Cement Ltd, which resulted in the merger. That had a fair amount of difficulty because of personalities. There was a very strong character in Cement, Anker Lund. I got on well with him and with Gunnar Larsen, the chairman, but they did not really want to be taken over, or merge, or have anything to do with us. They had an absolutely beautiful monopoly business going. Let me give you an example. John Wood was doing business with them from the time they started in 1930. Once, a cheque of his got lost in the post. They immediately stopped supplying him with cement. He had to go down to the Post Office and send off a series of forty-pound drafts — you couldn't send more than forty pounds at a time — until his account was cleared. A few days later, he got a letter saying that they had found his cheque in their office, that it had been mislaid, but there was no apology.

The merger would never have succeeded except that, in the middle of the negotiations, Readymix tried to take us over. Cement decided that they would be better to tie up with us, people they knew, than allow Readymix to assume a dominant position in Ireland. The negotiations were difficult and it meant a complete change of style for them. Even still at that time, I was accustomed to running the place as a boss. Once the merger was in place, it became a corporation and had to be run on formal lines and that did not suit me at all. We didn't think much of some of the things they were doing, and I suppose they didn't think much of some of the things we were doing. The two companies continued to be run separately but, in time, Anker Lund and I became joint managing directors of both companies. Funnily enough, we got on very well and he's still a good friend. When Anker retired, I became sole managing director. It didn't suit my style and I stayed only nine months. I was succeeded by Jim Culliton. Jim started out in Bray with us when he was eighteen, selling gravel to builders. He was one of those fellows who, when an opportunity came, would say, 'I think I can do that.' One of the things he did was to go to Clondalkin Concrete and make it more efficient. He was a natural successor. Jimmy was the best thing that ever happened to that merger, because his personality is so calm and he's so steady and so clever. And he knew the business very well. He was the correct man at the correct time. Things settled down once he came in.

Jimmy Culliton and I were talking one day about who might fill the bill as his number two and I had met Tony Barry in Cork. He seemed to me a very solid, efficient man. I suggested to Jimmy that he bring him up from Cork. He has since proved himself. He is all the things I thought he was at the time: solid and reliable and clever. Thank goodness that worked out very well.

Looking back, it was great fun building up Roadstone. I think the merger had one virtue that I used to harp on. Cement sat on their monopoly and did nothing about going abroad. They made little use of the money they generated. They had a very strong link with Denmark which, of course, I resented, being so Irish. With the financial strength of both companies, we could really go abroad and do things. That's the way the British Empire was built. We took over Van Neerbos, expanded in England and, of course, in America, under Don Godson. You see, Cement was a very respected company and we were slightly piratical. I don't think I was well regarded by the establishment. Bobby Kidney was much more acceptable. So, the merger was a good thing in that it enabled us to expand abroad.

When Jimmy became MD, I stayed on for a while, I'm not sure in what capacity. It did not work because you're inclined to give advice, and Jimmy had to say a few times, 'We'll have to decide who's running this place.' Finally, I thought it would be better to leave.

At this stage, I was getting interested in the toll bridge across the Liffey. I started to work from my home here. It took me about a year to adjust. I was quite wealthy. I had a million shares in Roadstone. Again, this was before Bula.

I had always been poring over the map of Dublin because we wanted to locate plants in strategic positions. It struck me, if you could jump across the Liffey, at the place where the toll bridge is now, it would be a hell of a short-cut. Very early on, I got young Tom, who was only seventeen at the time, to stand on Butt Bridge and count the traffic. My first thought was a drive-on, drive-off ship that would shuttle across the river. I had been very much involved in hydraulic hoists because of the big dumper trucks we had. Wouldn't it be nice if you could put a bridge there and shove up the middle of it with hydraulic hoists? I started working on it, reinventing the wheel, designing a lifting bridge. When I went to look at actual bridges, I saw they were very sophisticated. They were far in advance of anything I could conceive.

I started knocking on the doors of the Corporation and the Port and Docks Board to see if they would approve. The Port and Docks Board were initially afraid it would interfere with shipping, but they came around. The Corporation were neutral. They had advanced plans for the Eastern By-Pass, an eight-lane highway going over the Liffey where the Gas Company is. But people objected a lot to this and eventually it was shot down. It took me about seven or eight years and involved an act of parliament to enable us to charge tolls. It took an awful lot of foot-slogging, knocking on doors, and walking into rooms when you were not expected. I don't think I ever envisaged that it would not get done. I would ask myself every day, what can I do now to promote this venture? I would go down and visit people in Ringsend or call into the Corporation and annoy them again. About half my effort went into persuading the local people who were worried about what the traffic might do to their houses. As part of the community effort, we built forty-five porches on houses, two boat clubs, nine bathrooms added on to houses. By this means, we got permission, so to speak, from the people to carry on with the bridge. In the event, the bridge has added to the place. It has certainly improved the river along that stretch. I must say the bridge was a marvellous thing to latch on to once I retired from Roadstone, apart from a couple of black spots along the way. It gave me something to strive for. If I could have, I would have called it Sinn Fein Bridge. It expresses what I've always felt most deeply — as an Irish person, to do it yourself.

Now, the West Link is up and running, opened in 1990. It, too, took a long time. I began it in August 1979. It is a very big viaduct across the Liffey valley, between Palmerstown and Castleknock.

These two bridges were a life-saver both for myself and my family because of the overshadowing disaster of the Bula Mines affair.

We had an opening day for the West Link the Saturday before the formal opening. It was an extraordinary sight to see 10/15,000 people strolling along the bridge, drinking Coke and admiring the view. We had a little fun-park for the children — it was a heart-warming sight. It was the culmination of ten years of trying — not very hard, but in an interesting way — to get this thing going. The western bridge was easier than the East Link because we had the considerable help of the authorities who were building a motorway and have great powers of land acquisition. They were also satisfied with the financial arrangements: that they would participate in the income from the bridge generated above a certain traffic level. It was nice that the public perception of the bridge was good.

I feel very happy when I stand back and look at that bridge — but then I recall the very first washing plant we put up in 1944. I actually began that with a spade in my hand cutting sods for the foundations for a little workshop. When the plant was finished, Bobby Kidney came down and said to me, 'You must feel a great sense of achievement.' Now, this plant cost under £10,000. So my sense of achievement dates from a very long time back! Really, it goes back even farther when I used to make chairs for the kitchen and my mother would say, 'That's a grand chair.' Maybe I've been used to getting pats on the back but, like politicians, you never tire of it. I suppose what we work for is this sense of achievement.

However, so far as the West Link is concerned, my sense of achievement has to be shared with the very many people who had a part in it even before I came along. But, having said that, it was lovely to see, literally in concrete, something the way you had envisaged it.

I think it's fair to say that the East Link had bridged the gulf between the public and the private sectors. The politicians were uncertain — they were not sure how it would work and they thought people would resent tolls. An advantage we had as a small company was that we could approach the community in a very personal way and show them how the bridge would ultimately be to their advantage. Yes, the East Link was a break-through — once it was going, people accepted it. It's amazing the amount of compliments we get from people who use it because it is such an amazing short cut. Michael O'Halloran, a member of the City Council, said to me that it would be known as the Dick Turpin bridge: 'Stand and deliver!' We became good friends after — in fact he opened the bridge as Mayor at the time.

It has been successful financially, even though we have paid no dividends until this, the fifth year, when we shall pay dividends for the first time. But then it was started almost on a shoe-string. We had to borrow most of the money and it was very sticky at times dealing with the Allied Irish Bank. It was like the dance of the seven veils. I said to them, 'When we've just agreed to one of your conditions, you whip the veil aside and there's another one.' I am grateful to Bob Hayes and the Dublin Port and Docks Board who came in at the end when we were stuck for the last piece of money.

I think that in this country we have come to expect too much to be given to us by government. A man who begets twelve children gets help for all of them from the state — I wonder if that's right. If we were rational about these things, we would have said long ago that we can't afford them. It may be easy for me to talk like that, but I don't think we're earning what we're paying ourselves. We simply don't work as hard as they do in other countries. We have not created the wealth that can generate taxes, so we tax what is there and it's not enough. We're trying to emulate immensely wealthy countries like Britain and America. We speak English and we think we should have the same as them. Then, the political system is one of promises: 'Put me into the Dáil and I'll get you such and such.'

I have always had an intense interest and a concentration of effort in whatever I take up. I try to do well whatever I'm doing. One of the reasons we were so successful at exporting stone was that we met the needs of very discriminating German customers. I went to an immense amount of trouble to produce for them cubical stone instead of slivers. Whatever you're doing you've got to concentrate on it and do it better than anybody. As a nation, we're inclined to be a bit slipshod: 'Ah, sure that'll do.' The Americans have that ability to become intensely concentrated on a single small facet: who would think you could build an empire on chickens or Coca-Cola? I suppose one of the things I could tell managers would be really to concentrate, not to get distracted, and to do things by *international* standards. I used to have Irishmen coming in selling me machinery. They would have a leaflet with them and they could not get

beyond that. If an American were to come to sell you crushing machinery, by God, he knew about crushing. He knew
his job. Think of the sort of experiences you have here getting
your car serviced. If you go into a garage in France, it's
spotless. One of our failings here is simple cleanliness and
good housekeeping. We tend to put in three-quarters of the
effort and we end up with three-quarters of everything, not
ninety-five per cent.

I have been very fortunate that I was able to express the
kind of person that I was.

19

John Teeling

Risk is the greatest of all aphrodisiacs. I like the feeling that you can be wrong but I like the odds to be in my favour even if ever so slightly. Once the risk goes out of a project, I lose interest. Risk is not a philosophy, it's an addiction.

John Teeling is Chairman of Cooley Distillery plc and CountyGlen plc.

He was born in Dublin on 7 January 1946, the eldest of four children — two brothers and one sister. His father was James Teeling, an insurance salesman. His mother is Emily Kinsella, a housewife and retired insurance saleswoman.

He was educated at:
St Joseph's Christian Brothers School, Fairview, Dublin,
UCD (B.Comm. and M.Econ.Sc.),
Wharton School of Finance, University of Pennsylvania (M.B.A.),
Harvard Business School (D.B.A.).

He is married to Deirdre Shaw, a guidance counsellor. They have three children: Emma (17), Jack (14) and Stephen (10).

He was a lecturer in Business Administration in UCD from 1966 to 1968.

He was a feasibility consultant to the Irish mining industry from 1969 to 1981 and a consultant with Colin McIver Associates from 1972 to 1985.

He began to take equity stakes in various businesses in 1972 beginning with Leixlip Clothing and running through seven Stock Exchange quoted companies, all of which have now been sold.

He currently holds executive positions as Chairman of Cooley Distillery plc, CountyGlen plc and African Gold plc.

Since 1981 he has been active in the establishment of a series of mineral exploration companies and he holds equity stakes in a number of them and is a director of three.

He is an active member of Clontarf Football and Cricket Clubs and a member of the Friends of the Rotunda Hospital.

I am very clear about when it all started — 2 October 1960, when my father died. I was fourteen, my father was forty-four and my mother was only thirty-seven. He had been an insurance salesman and had a small money-lending business. It was left in chaos. Two things: first, my mother placed a lot of trust in me — which was great for a fourteen-year-old; and second, there was a lot of work to be done. So, even before I did my Inter, I ended up collecting insurance premia on a daily basis for the Royal Liver Friendly Society in Marino, Cabra and Donnycarney. That lasted for about a year until the commission-book was sold off, something you could do then. My mother also had to begin to collect, but it was more difficult for her: she knew nothing at all about the business, had come from a country background, had married when she was twenty-one and had never subsequently worked outside the home. She had a hell of a job adapting.

There are a few crystal-clear memories of that time. One was having to cycle up Griffith Avenue on a November evening, cold and wet and the wind coming down. Oddly enough, I don't think I have had to do anything as hard since. It was two miles up and it was all up — it was great when you were finished, coming down on the bike. But it had to be done and there was a lesson there for me — if something has to be done, it gets done. I now have no trouble making decisions, none at all.

Neither my father nor my mother had any secondary education. When my father died, the only one who knew anything about the family business was me. I had been giving my father a hand for two years. There was nobody else, so I ran it for ten years. Money-lending should not exist in a modern society, but I am afraid it does. It was there for people who were uneducated and poor. The two are important: if you are poor you can still have access to money. But if you are uneducated as well, you don't know how to go about it: you can't talk to a bank or a building society or a finance house. You go to the fellow who gives you cash money. My mother really disliked the business, but she had to feed her kids. It lasted until the early eighties, but it was not the most successful business venture. After I gave up, my two brothers and my sister worked it a bit. I was MD at age fifteen — nothing like that to boost your confidence! When I was doing Commerce in school at seventeen, I knew as much as the teacher did about practical matters such as bank accounts, books of account and company law matters.

It was only after the Inter that I took Commerce, a course which is, much to my disgust, badly taught and is deemed suitable for weaker students. I got 97 per cent in the Leaving Cert in Commerce. I still don't know how I lost nine marks out of three hundred. One paper was an hour and a half. I finished it in forty-five minutes and got thumped by the teacher when I came out. I got a good Leaving, but so did a lot of people at that time, and then the second element came into play — I am lucky. There is this notion that you make your own luck. I don't believe it. I have friends who are cleverer and more able than I am, but they are not lucky and nothing works for them.

There used to be sixteen Dublin Corporation scholarships to university. The year I got my Leaving, there were, for the first time, forty-eight — and I got the forty-eighth. But there had to be eight girls and there were only seven, and I got a note saying, sorry, there has to be a girl and the girl who got fifty-first place got it. But then somebody dropped out, so I got the scholarship. The scholarship was fees plus £160 — I was living at home. Sure I was rich. Still I worked that summer — I drove a van.

Like many people, I did not know what I was going to do. I had no family professional background. I had thought of Commerce because I had done well, but I also thought of Medicine or Arts. I remember there were queues where the various faculties were recruiting and I rambled over to Economics and met Louis Smith. I was fierce impressed with Louis so I signed up for Economics and Commerce — something you could do at that time. I came home and told

344

my mother what I was going to do. She thought I had been going to do Medicine and I suppose I might have. The thing that put me off Medicine was the seven years' study — I ended up spending eleven years studying business.

My mother had made me apply for all the 'good' jobs. I got called to the ESB. Early the first morning they handed me forms to sign up for the pension scheme. I was seventeen. I walked out. I would have been a grade 18C clerk — £6. 10s a week — good money. My mother nearly had a heart attack. This was just before I went into college. I think, in fact, I had really made my mind up that I was going to college. With the ESB I was just having a look.

Mind you, we weren't poor. We weren't wealthy either but there was enough for the family. We did not have many holidays or anything like that. Perhaps the best holiday we had was a caravan in Skerries.

I would be embarrassed now to go back to the ESB. I wonder where they thought I went. I am still not in a pension scheme. Pension to me signifies end-of-life. I am either going to be very rich when I am sixty-five or very poor, and in neither case is a pension going to matter. Or dead! If I have plenty of money I am not going to need a pension, and if I have no money the pension is not going to let me live the life-style I would want anyway. I have no life assurance — I don't believe in those things at all. Anyway, I was quite sure I was going to succeed at something — damn it, at age seventeen I was running a company, I had cycled up Griffith Avenue, I had been through the fire.

I have never had a job where I had to go in at a fixed time as I would have to have done in the ESB. In UCD, for example, you had a lot of flexibility, you could control your own time. My God, I used to think of my poor friends who used to have to sign on in the bank before a quarter past nine when the manager drew a line underneath. I still like the flexibility. I love the idea that I can get up late in the morning and go to work when the traffic has gone. I think I have the freedom. I believe I have it, but I suppose I don't.

But if there is a morning I don't feel like going in then I don't. But of course, that never happens.

The big thing was that I was my own man at seventeen. Most people don't get that chance. And my mother was great. The night I was seventeen — that very night — she let me drive the car. God help the woman, she really had confidence in me.

UCD was fabulous — I thoroughly enjoyed it. I did not do at all well in the first year because I discovered the joys of being free out of the Christian Brothers and out of a rigid home-life. My mother and father never went out and all of a sudden I was into parties and college societies, things I had thought of but had never seen. I did a bit better the second year, and by the third year I had enough sense and worked very hard. I got second in the class behind Breffni Byrne who was light years ahead of us all. He is now a partner in Arthur Andersen and still a good friend of mine. There were only three of us on Corporation scholarships doing the B.Comm. because the Christian Brothers thought that if you were good enough to get a scholarship you should do something decent like engineering. The three of us got first, second and fourth: Breffni Byrne from Monkstown CBS, myself from Fairview and John Hogan from Coláiste Mhuire. John Hogan joined me later in UCD teaching finance. He is now a partner in Riada but still involved in UCD. Incidentally, I have the highest of regard and respect for the Christian Brothers. Everyone was pushed to realise their potential. Apart from the strong grounding in the 3 Rs, 'the Brothers' forced you to do as well as you could. That approach is sadly lacking in most schools today.

When I took the B.Comm. I did not really know what I wanted to do. James Meenan, the Professor of Economics, told me I should join the Investment Bank of Ireland. Brian Gregory, a Business Administration lecturer, told me that I didn't want to leave UCD because I was afraid to go out into the world. Maybe he was right. Anyway, I had done well in James Meenan's subject, National Economics, and I got a tutorial fellowship, very prestigious, £680 a year. That was a lot of money, as much as my friends were earning in the bank. I did the M.Econ.Sc. and got a 2.1 — did not do all that well, made a mistake in one of the papers. It was during that year that I became interested in an academic career and particularly in studying business in the States. That was almost an alien idea twenty-two or twenty-three years ago. I applied for the Boston College Scholarship which I should have got, but I blew the interview. It was not the first time I blew an interview. I came second — to John Hogan, in fact, who went on to Boston College. This was 1967 and, though I was upset at not getting the scholarship, there was no problem in getting a job with an M.Econ.Sc. However I came second in a national fellowship offered by the Friendly Sons of St Patrick. I got a personal call from Jeremiah Hogan, the then President of UCD — I was very impressed. He told me that the chap who came first in the scholarship had dropped out and asked me if I would go to Philadelphia. So off I went to the University of Pennsylvania, Wharton School of Finance, to take a two-year M.B.A. in Finance, all expenses paid.

I am just naturally good at finance. A balance sheet holds no terrors for me, something which has been very useful in later life, thank God.

I finished the two-year course in Wharton in a year and a half — I am always in a hurry. I took six courses a semester — I had to work very hard. But how could an Irish student not do well at the Wharton School? Twenty to a class, superb professors, *seventy* copies of a book on the open shelves, where in UCD there would have been one with the pages torn out, and six hundred students in James Meenan's class doing national economics, playing cards or reading the newspaper at the back. I did not find the M.B.A. at Wharton difficult at all.

In the third semester, Michael MacCormac, the new professor of Business in UCD, arrived out and took me to lunch and asked me to come back to UCD. Michael had decided that he was going to set up a business school and staff it with people with American degrees. He hired five of us. I sent in a scruffy, hand-written application — I don't know why I do these things to myself. Michael himself wrote out the application, got me to check it and got Marguerite Flanagan to type it out. I got the job. I must have a death-wish. I started in UCD in January 1969 and taught a whole pile of things, finance, marketing, planning, control — there was nobody else to teach them. I was a twenty-one year old teaching Business Policy to M.B.A. students. That's not right.

UCD paid £920 a year at that time. To survive I needed another job. Noel Mulcahy, then of the IMI, now in the University of Limerick, got me an interview with the Smelter Corporation of Ireland, part of Northgate/Tara. I got a part-time job based in Clontarf at twice my UCD salary. The office I got in 1969 I'm still in today.

Michael MacCormac had decided that if the school was to be of international standard, it had to have Ph.D.s and, in any event, UCD had brought in a rule that if you wanted to get promotion to college lecturer, you had to have a Ph.D. The rule was OK so long as it was applied to all but, of course, you couldn't do that because there were some guys in UCD who could not do a Ph.D. and some who would not get it even if they tried. A bunch of us came under the rule. In 1970 the president, Tom Murphy at that stage, and Michael MacCormac nominated me for a Ford Fellowship, a very prestigious thing at that time. There were a set of hurdles that you had to cross which I was ideally suited for crossing. You had to be teaching in a business school somewhere outside the States; secondly, you had to be accepted by five of eight business schools in America, and there was some other minor one. I had a good American M.B.A. and I also knew the system which 99 per cent of European applicants hadn't a clue about. I picked five schools. I did not pick Carnegie-Mellon or Chicago, but I picked five schools who would accept me and they did, of course. I went to Harvard because it had always seemed the top school. I went out to

do a Doctorate of Business Administration in International
Finance and the day I arrived the professor left. So I did
International Business/Economics with Ray Vernon. It took
me a long time to finish. I was getting old. It is hard for
students in their twenties and I was getting married and
sundry other things. The D.B.A. was a four-year programme:
course-work, teaching method, research, a thesis. It was not as
intellectually rigorous as the Ph.D. but it was longer. It was
really designed to teach you how to teach business. It failed
miserably in that objective. Nobody went into teaching business. They all went into business. One way or the other, I
spent from 1970 to the end of 1972 in Boston, but took a
further two and a half years to complete my thesis.

If there is anything Harvard teaches you, it is an appreciation of wealth. There are no poor people at Harvard. I did
not find it a very difficult school, not as difficult as Wharton.
But it just has to be the basilica of capitalism. It's a physically beautiful place and it's all big money. You can't go
through that without absorbing some of it through your
pores. It doesn't surprise me one bit that Wharton and
Harvard lead the field in financial engineering and money
manipulation. If there is anything they *must* be good at, it's
making money. Going through Harvard, you just knew that
you were going to be in a position to make a lot of money.
None of the people there was ever going to be poor. The
guys going through are given the keys to the kingdom.
Getting through is not the problem, getting in is, and when
you come out the other end, you get the passport to riches.
I don't know anybody who has not done very well out of it. I
know people who have done strange things and not made
money, but that was their choice.

When I came back to UCD I was still a bit greedy and
hungry so I continued consulting with Tara Mines and did
some jobs for Colin McIver consulting with Bord Failte and
Guinness and people like that. I ran three jobs for about
four years. I put the pressure on myself deliberately. I have
never had a mortgage in my life — I bought my house on a

term loan. I had to work to pay it off and did. Twenty-year money is long-term — I am not into that scene at all. I am really quite short-term. I needed to build a nest-egg as quickly as possible and there is no better way to do that than to have to meet heavy repayments every month. You can't start without a nest-egg.

Stock market speculation began in the early 1970s for two reasons: one, to see if it would work; and secondly, to build money. There were three of us Irish guys at Harvard, Brendan Hynes of Tara and David Doran who did his B.Comm. with me, both of them doing the M.B.A., and myself who was doing the D.B.A. We used to sit up late at night plotting how to make money. I identified eleven companies on the Irish Stock Exchange that I thought were suitable shells. I put together a plan to buy them and to create a conglomerate. The first on the list was Crowe-Wilson, but Tony O'Reilly and Nicholas Leonard saw that. The second was Joshua Watson which Martin Rafferty took up. But there were still a few around when I came home. David Doran and Brendan Hynes went to work for W. R. Grace so our plans to create a conglomerate died.

To keep the students in UCD interested, I used to run mythical portfolios, investing very small amounts. I have terrible trouble with the book theory in this area — the theory says you should spread your risk. But one investment is clearly better than another so, despite the theory, I am not sure that you shouldn't spend all your money on one investment. What I used to do was to take my money, gear it up as much as possible and invest it all in one company — I have about six roofs on my house. I have a good bank manager. Anyway the equities thing built up quickly. I did well on two ventures, but the first beauty was Irish Oil and Cake Mills in 1977. I have a standard model for buying shares. Very simple, not complicated at all, at all. I use a thing called net-net assets: i.e. the net assets per share and I write off all long-term debt per share. If the net-net assets are greater than the price per share, I buy, and that's it.

People say there couldn't be shares like that and there are. Irish Oil and Cake had net-net assets per share of 50p but was selling at l9p. I put everything I had into buying shares, intending to get at least a strategic stake which, at worst, I could sell on to other investors.

At first in 1977 I was on my own with Irish Oil and Cake and then Donal Kinsella came along. He is very different from me. He was and is a risk-seeker. He genuinely likes the high from taking risks. When you're dealing in shares, you have to be able to take the stress when something goes wrong because you're usually dealing with borrowed money and something always goes wrong.

There was a lot of shenanigans with Irish Oil and Cake — a very high profile in the press, all sorts of accusations flying, mainly because share raiding had never happened before in Ireland. So, to an extent, Kinsella's name and mine were made, though in fact it was only share-trading. We got out of it in 1979 at a profit, but not without stress and court cases. Donal Kinsella had got the bug at this stage — it was his first attempt.

In 1979, Donal and I and some friends went after, in rapid succession, three well-known public companies. In a short space of time we built up large stakes in Seafield Gen-tex, Glen Abbey and Dublin Gas. All three were selling at a fraction of their asset worth but, as I had time to regret with hindsight, only Glen Abbey met the criteria of my net-net model.

The strategy did not work. It was like Napoleon's or Hitler's wars — we overstretched the supply lines. We were up to our tonsils in debt. Our partners lost faith and had to be bought out. The directors of all three companies refused our requests to join their boards. The banks got nervous. Then the directors of Seafield informed us that they were going into receivership. Had this happened we would have lost everything, as the banks would have called their loans. I offered to run Seafield. I took two years off college (1979–1981). I succeeded in rescuing it almost at the cost of the patient's life. The cure was almost terminal but the alternative was worse. I went into a company with seven plants and closed five in the first six weeks, for the simple reason that AIB threatened, 'You are going to see Laurence Crowley next Friday.' Each Friday I had to go to AIB to give an account of my stewardship — I hated that. Eventually the plants were closed, all £3.90 m. of debt cleared and the quotation preserved. I sold out at break-even in 1981. Seafield is now a Joe Moran/IWP shell.

In the meantime, I was negotiating my way out of Glen Abbey and Dublin Gas. By 1981 I was out of both at little or no profit.

The 1979–1981 experience was fantastic. I learned so much. It became obvious that manufacturing investment in Ireland was not great. I also came across a bit of political pressure in Seafield. I am not political in any shape or form. It was interesting to learn how managers are circumscribed by the political environment in this country. A decision to fire an employee or close a plant can bring the most amazing pressure. Everybody is just a phone-call away from the Prime Minister.

Donal Kinsella was incredible in this period. He seemed to have no nerves. It was all right for me, I was making the plays and could see the strategy and the game, but he largely invested on my say-so. He could take a much higher level of uncertainty than I could — at least I thought I knew what I was doing. He had to believe! He was the pillion-passenger. In this period he put up all of his assets, including some he had not got. One morning he called me up at eight o'clock to tell me that he had been sitting on the edge of the bed since half past four. It was then that I realised that he was human like the rest of us. If you are going to go in for a high-risk strategy, it means that you will wake up at night. High-risk means exactly that — it does not necessarily mean high-return. By the end of 1981, I had sold out of all three companies. Donal had decided to stay in Seafield and Dublin Gas. He eventually made money in Seafield and had a glorious battle with Dublin Gas.

By 1981 I had made a bit of money. I had learned two things: I was confident in my own abilities, not that I had ever many doubts, and also that the techniques I had learned worked. The future became very clear — it did not lie in my speculating on the stock exchange all the time. The Irish Stock Exchange is too small. I thought there were also opportunities to set up things. These were speculative opportunities. I read a lot now about people who have created things and I wonder about the fact that those who stuck it out are now seen as great entrepreneurs. Those who sold out after a couple of years, took the money and ran (which is probably what all entrepreneurs want to do in the first place) are seen as having failed. The difference is those who stay the course.

After Seafield and Dublin Gas, I decided my next play was going to be the shell, the vehicle to build a conglomerate. Glen Abbey was the obvious one — I had been there twice before and got out of it with a profit though not much. I bought Glen Abbey according to my model, the assets were worth infinitely more than I paid, so I took no risk i.e. net-net assets of over 50p, market price 18p. Liam Jones of Good-body stockbrokers negotiated the purchase from the Barnes brothers who had founded Glen Abbey. This gave me control as executive chairman. Liam joined me on the board.

I made a decision that we would try and run Glen Abbey as a textile company. I ran it for eighteen very hard months: a lot of aggro, a lot of change, a lot of travelling. The losses were £10,000 a week when I went in. I cut it down to £114,000 a year of which £70,000 was theft by my own workers. It was an inside job so there was no insurance claim. I am not able to handle that kind of stuff at all. I had 830 employees and they just did not care. They knew who was responsible for the robberies but they closed ranks. We could identify the people but the police were not interested.

At that stage I said, to hell with it, why was I breaking my backside for them when I could sell it off and make five times the money, six times the money — the Glen Abbey shares were at 20p after two years' really hard work and me paying excessive interest on my borrowings. I just don't believe that the workers in Ireland care a hell of a lot about the future of their enterprises and that colours what I do. I think a lot of them want to commit hara-kiri. It's not like that in the States, where there is a lot of loyalty to the company. I think workers in Ireland *feel* that they are loyal — but not to the extent of really helping or co-operating.

Maybe I think that because I have never worked in a good company — why would I buy a good company? There would be nothing in it for me. I had expanded sales in Glen Abbey from £11 m. to £16 m. and had made no profits, so my working capital needs had expanded considerably. The Bank of Ireland were now owed £4 m.

The call came one day to go down to Baggot Street to talk to Corporate. I did something that's in the books: I called a strategy meeting. I got the four divisional managers each to do a strategy paper according to a model I gave them. We spent two days in the Killiney Court Hotel with the board of directors looking at each division in turn, half a day each. The board as usual had not read the papers — boards don't. But it was good for the management in that it forced them to think through where they were going to be in two years' time, how they were going to get there and how they were going to finance it. Up to then, it was central finance for everything. They got their money from the parent company. It became perfectly clear during the exercise that there was not enough money to finance the development of each division. It was easy to decide to sell off one or more divisions. Eventually I sold all four divisions. By the end of 1986 Glen Abbey share price had gone from 22p to £1.06. Every time I sold assets, the price went up. The Glen Abbey shell which I bought back in 1989 has two employees, a financial controller and a secretary. There are £4 m. in assets. I was cute. I sold the businesses and kept the buildings — Glen Abbey is now a property company. I am not in the least worried about having had to sell off the divisions. It was the right thing to do. The workers had taken one leg from under me and the other was that I just hadn't enough money to run it as one company. Now that the divisions are sold off as separate businesses, some of them are making money and some are not. In 1987, I sold control of Glen Abbey to UK property developers. A series of owners did little, and in 1989, after great hassle, I bought back control.

Business is not, in the slightest, a personal thing to me.

One of the problems I have is a surplus of opportunities. There are always things and I just can't handle them. The distilling one is something I'm doing for enjoyment. The fact that I shall make money out of it is secondary. In 1986 we were offered an opportunity to buy out Irish Distillers in a leveraged buy-out with the Bond Corporation using Glen Abbey as a front. The buy-out would have been financed with $176 m. debt, $22 m. equity. I hadn't the heart to take on the whole country as we would have asset-stripped Irish Distillers. Bond Corporation was going to take the international marketing of the whiskey and I was going to be left with Ireland. Can you imagine me taking on Jack Lynch, who was then chairman? What hope would I have had? But we had spent four months researching the whole thing and I felt there was an opportunity for an alternative, for another Irish whiskey.

When Ceimici Teo was liquidated by the state, an opportunity arose to buy a chemical plant — I had been watching it for a year. I bought it in 1987 without seeing it, which was probably a good idea because, if I had seen it, I would not have bought it. Nobody else would buy it. Ceimici made alcohol originally from potatoes and then from molasses — in fact the quality of its alcohol was very good. They made alcohol for Gilbeys, for gin and vodka. I applied my net-net model to the plant again: twenty-five acres, a pile of property, stainless steel. I offered £100,000 and was laughed at. The word went from the liquidator to the Department that there were a couple of eejits prepared to buy this thing. Departments can behave very sensibly at times. They sent me out a letter saying that they would sell it to me at scrap value provided I would attempt to 'rescue and resuscitate' it. I said I would try and if I failed I could flog the land and sell the plant to Brazil. I bought it for £106,000. It must have cost millions but, of course, if you are not going to replace it, it has no value. Over two years, some £5 m. was raised and pumped in. Donal Kinsella, Liam Jones and Paul Power have supported the project all the way. We are now up and running — it's probably worth about £15 m. We have bought Lockes distillery in Kilbeggan as well. I am currently acting chief executive — I am now back in management which is where I do not want to be. I'm making decisions on advertising campaigns, employees, wage rates — all the things I don't want to do, so I shall have to get out very fast. Of course, we shall eventually joint-venture it. There is absolutely no future for Irish whiskey trying to survive on its own in the international market-place. It needs a big, powerful, world-wide partner. But that partner needs a product — a distinctively Irish product. There is now only one way they can get it: buy it from us or make it themselves. If they want to make it themselves, they are two to three years behind us.

The other major strand in my investment activities is mineral exploration. Working with Pat Hughes in Tara, and people like that, I developed an understanding of mining. Firstly, there is a lot of psychology involved. Secondly, a lot of very bright young geologists had gone to work for Northgate and Tara and had developed 1970's and 1980's techniques, unlike almost anybody in Europe. The third critical factor was that there was a group of Irish investors willing to invest in mining. I have been involved in six or seven companies: Minquest which was the first, then Conroy, then Burmin, then Kenmare, the most successful to date, African Gold and Pan Andean, which is the latest. What you do is this: you put together a very focused strategy; you select a mineral; you select a country; you select a body — and you finance. You say, 'Right. Go look for gold in Zimbabwe, Joe Soap.' You back him for a year or two. We started off with about £15,000 and were hard-pressed to get that. Now we're dealing with a group of people who would put up maybe £5 m. So far, these are all mainly exploration companies — they have not become mining companies, but everybody has got more than their money back. Kenmare is almost a mining company. Conroy will be a mining company, and Burmin I don't know. African Gold has two small mines in Zimbabwe. Pan Andean, in Bolivia, is drilling for silver.

The 'we' in the exploration companies is a small group of like-minded people whom you hit for money first and, possibly, second time round and who make a bit. I now have a group of ten to twenty people whom I can ring up and say, 'Look, I have this project. It's going to cost £300,000. I want £15,000 from each of you.' They would not ask me any questions. They would send me that money. If £300,000 wasn't enough, I then have a list of twenty or so more people to whom I would send a note asking them to put up what they could. I then have another group which would be up to 500 people who might put in £1,000 each. They'll all stay in it so long as they make money, and so far we have had a fabulous run. To my mind, the exploration companies have been the most exciting ventures, not so much that you have ended up in the mountains of Bolivia or in the deserts of Sudan where we have one of the Pharaonic gold mines (5,800 years old — it isn't profitable, it wasn't a good decision), but the ventures are fascinating. The people who do it are fascinating — there are now five Irishmen working out in the middle of the Nubian desert. It's 145 degrees. There is nothing more satisfying than taking the *concept* of a gold mine in the Sudan and turning it into a gold mine — the money now is secondary. I have to say, however, not much secondary — very nearly primary!

My job in the exploration companies is to get the money, the people and the projects, manage it for a while, then hire professional managers and get a public quotation for the shares.

I don't think I will do much more stock market speculation unless the stock market collapses and a lot of intrinsic
value appears. I think, though, we will develop the mining
companies where I have a very clear objective. I would like
to be known as somebody who actually developed a mining
business. My model for that is Pat Hughes, who has almost
no profile in Ireland, but who is known in Canada and who
developed Northgate Exploration. Northgate is still the
only Irish company with a full big board quote — which it
has had since 1965: it's quoted in Toronto, New York and
London. It's not quoted in Ireland because it is too big. Pat
Hughes lost some battles with the multinationals, but he
can look back on a lot of success and is a wealthy man, and
to me, is the epitome of the absolute risk-taker. For him,
management was secondary. I think the group of us who are
now involved in mineral exploration companies have a very
good level of sophistication by international standards. We
have the ability to raise money and to get geologists and
metallurgists and hydrologists in the twenty-five Irish exploration companies: these are people who are on a par with
anybody in Canada and Australia. Of the 120 Irish-Canadian
exploration companies who explored in Ireland, only four
found mines. These were the companies that explored in
Ireland in the fifties, sixties and seventies and three of those
came from the Hughes stable. So over 99 per cent of the
companies lost their entire investment. The same is going
to happen among the twenty-five Irish-based companies. I
hope that I am in the lucky one.

The question now is, 'Where do I go for my next venture?' The excitement for me in ventures is in setting them
up: seeing the opportunity, gathering together the people
who believe in them — in other words, the money, and the
human resources where I don't think I'm good, and getting
them off the ground. I have no interest in running things
and I don't think I'm a good manager. I spent many years
learning management up as far as the D.B.A., and I think
it taught me that I can't do it because I've come to the

absolute conclusion that it's a people business. I am not at all a people person. I suffer from the appalling problem that I know that nobody can do the job as well as I can do it. It's not that I believe it, I know it. I delegate a lot and then I abuse the people when they don't do it my way. Also, the idea that the manager should work his eight- or nine-hour day and leave something for tomorrow is beyond me.

I think manufacturing industry in Ireland is one of the most difficult tasks that any human being could take on. It's a thankless task with international competition and we have so many disadvantages.

What I do is, I trade money. That's all I do. What do I make? I make money. My entire activities are financially orientated. There is a present value in a project for me. If a man came through that door today and said I'll give you £5 a share for Cooley, it's sold. The fact that I may have broken my ass for four years to build it means nothing. I have no emotional ties to any of my projects. Sure, it's nice to think you have built something, but there is always another one over the hill. Is this entrepreneurial? It depends on how you define it. Ability to take risk? Yes — very much so, it's the greatest of all aphrodisiacs. I don't drink, I don't smoke, I don't gamble. But I like risk. I like the feeling that you can be wrong, but I like the odds to be in my favour even if ever so slightly. Once the risk goes out of a project, I lose interest — it just becomes work. This is the old ESB pension problem coming back.

I don't see any point of arrival. It's like the horizon. It just keeps disappearing. I do, however, have the niggling feeling that I would like to concentrate all the effort into one big one and build an entrepreneurial organisation, in other words, to have something there that would take bigger risks. I think I'll keep stakes in all the companies I'm connected with. It's very hard for the entrepreneur to get out — he is usually the last one out the door.

One of the difficulties I have is that I feel very self-sufficient, so I don't work with a lot of people. I read in your previous book that entrepreneurs are loners — that's absolutely true. I'm not a joiner — of any organisation. I am very happy with my own decision-making ability. A lot of that can be attributed to the education I got. If I can't make the right decision with four business degrees, who can? I am happy with my own judgment and I think that is the greatest strength I have.

Of course, I have self-doubt. There are times I wake up and say, 'I should not have done that.' It's always at three or four o'clock in the morning, when your wife is asleep and it's dark and it looks awful. But it always looks better in the morning. When I make a mistake, I give out to myself. I very rarely think about what other people may say about me. I live with my own decisions and I have made some horrendous ones, usually where I have sold too soon. My epitaph on my tombstone will be 'He sold too soon.' If it's not put on, I'll leave all my money to the Cats and Dogs Home. I nearly always sell early. I have friends who were too greedy and have gone bust. I'm a good seller, not a great seller, but I still hold some stocks that should have been sold.

An awful lot of things can be *made* work. If I go into something and it turns out to be a fundamental error — and that has been very seldom — I cut my losses. Otherwise you stick with it and just make it work. Then, once it's working, somebody else can run with it. I have had a fair modicum of success in a fair number of ventures and a lot of that is because you know what you're doing and you go at it. I have seen people fail who need not have. I'm committed, bull-headed, stubborn, thick. Risk is at its highest level at the conceptual stage, not so high when you're getting the resources, not so high again when you're putting together a prototype. Then you get into venture capital rather than seed capital — the level of risk is falling all the time. Once it's in place, then it's a business, then it is for professional managers to run it.

How does my family put up with me? I do a lot of business from home, either in meetings or on the telephone.

I'm lucky I met Deirdre when we were both seventeen. She has been with me all the way both in education and business. This helps. The fact that her father was active in his own small business until he was seventy-six also helped. Deirdre knows that business can be stressful and take time. I have to say that when the house was being put up as security for bank loans to buy speculative shares, it never occurred to me that my wife and family might object. I do not understand businessmen who say that they leave their business in the office. They are not committed. Business is my life. My home life is peppered with deals, callers, papers. If I have to see someone at 10 o'clock on a Sunday morning or midnight during the week, they will be well received and given hospitality.

Deirdre earned her spurs on one occasion where I reached an agreement at 1 a.m. in a restaurant to sell a stake in a company at a good time. The buyer was under the weather. I brought him home, woke her up and we fed him coffee and sandwiches all night until he was sober enough next morning to sign a legally binding agreement.

I won't leave Clontarf. If I had to go to the southside, I would take off instead for America. I'm comfortable in this place and with my family. When I leave you now I'll go down and meet my mother and then have a cheese sandwich with my brothers. You can be certain that we'll discuss Clontarf Rugby Club. I might even see my sister because she's a doctor over here. I am perfectly happy with that. I never ever wanted to work outside Ireland. I admire the successful international Irish businessmen and don't envy them in the slightest. I think most Irish people have a strong homing instinct.

If you offered me $50 m. to go and live for a year in Pittsburgh, I wouldn't go. Well, perhaps for fifty million . . . but it would have to be of that order.

My main purpose — objective — is to be happy within myself. I think you can see that I'm not too worried about publicity, good, bad or indifferent. It doesn't worry me when people write peculiar things about me. The idea of providing for my family was paramount — thank God, that is now fixed and I am most unlikely to lose everything. In terms of the amount of money I possess — it's a score-card and only a score-card. I have to keep feeding this internal monster that keeps asking me if I can do it again. I am competing only with myself. I don't feel the need to compete internationally at all. I have no great use for the trappings of wealth. I like comfort and good holidays, but I can eat only two or three meals a day and then I get fat and I'm on a diet for a month. Risk is not a philosophy, it's an addiction.

Index

MENS

Dry Cutting	*from*	£9.50
Wash and Cut	*from*	£11.00
Wash, Cut and Blow Dry	*from*	£12.50
Restyle and Blow Dry	*from*	£11.00
Beard Trim		£6.00

SENIOR CITIZEN'S

Shampoo and Set	£6.00
Cut, Shampoo and Set	£10.00
Dry Cut	£6.50
Blow Dry	£8.00
Cut and Blow Dry	£11.50

NG

	from	£23.50
	from	£23.50
		£18.50
	from	£41.50
		£12.00
		£41.50

	£23.50
	£34.00
	£38.00
	£41.00
	£47.00

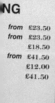

& Blow Drys
nclusive
et

Hairbrained

Charles Glover

Hairbrained

BLOOMSBURY

First published in Great Britain 2005

Copyright © 2005 by Charles Glover

Grateful thanks to Paula Cocozza and to the *Guardian*,
which first published a selection of these images in 2004.

The moral right of the author has been asserted

Bloomsbury Publishing Plc, 36 Soho Square, London W1D 3QY

A CIP catalogue record for this book is available from the British
Library

ISBN 0 7475 7748 X
ISBN-13 9780747577485

10 9 8 7 6 5 4 3 2 1

Printed by Tien Wah Press Ltd, Singapore
Designed by Jo Walker

All papers used by Bloomsbury Publishing are natural, recyclable
products made from wood grown in well-managed forests. The
manufacturing processes conform to the environmental regulations
of the country of origin.

www.bloomsbury.com/hairbrained

For Miranda

I would like to thank Charlie Viney for coercing me into
making something of my obsession, Rosemary Davidson and
Mary Davis, my editors, and designer Jo Walker, who has shown
great patience as I've found yet more salons. To Steve Harrison,
who had a mutual obsession and was happy to share it,
and to all at Bare Films, especially Alistair, Helen and Sue –
see www.bloomsbury.com/hairbrained for their masterpiece.
To Lisa, Laura and Peter at Flash Photodigital, and David at
Hi-Speed for all those scans. Special thanks go to all the salon
staff up and down the country, whose creativity and love of
life have made this book what it is. Finally thanks to Paul, my
long-suffering hairdresser.

Charles Glover, thirty-eight, is a portrait photographer who
divides his time between west London and south Oxfordshire.
He's married to an author and they have two children.

Hairbrained

There's a thin line between interest and obsession. I don't know when I crossed it, but I have done. But the embarrassing part of my admission is that the objects of my obsession are hairdressing salons and their punning names. Like all obsessions I'm not sure when it began. I do know that in 1990 I started to frequent a salon simply on the basis that it was called **The Hairport**. Since then I have always noted salons with appalling names. I felt fortunate to live near one called **Have it Off**, and work near another called **Man Streaks Woman**. Sadly, both have since closed.

Although I'm a photographer, this book, essentially, is not about an aesthetic. I'm using my skills merely to record what I find. There are no rules, I have taken the shot to best convey each shop's name, despite the numerous obstacles found on the high street: delivery vans, schoolkids and my reflection! My reward over the last two years journeying around the length and breadth of Britain has been to see the fantastically disparate means by which hairdressers present themselves to the public, usually with a level of optimism that their location, scale, graphic design and, of course, names, singularly fail to meet.

In this book I've collected together what I consider to be the hundred best examples. However, they're simply displayed randomly to let you decide for yourself which is funniest.

What is conveyed is that this is more than just a group of photos of funnily named shops. I hope that, as a collection, there is a depth of creativity that allows you to wallow in the 'hairbrained' culture of it all and, at the very least, ensure that a journey down the high street will never be the same again.

Enjoy.

'We were in Vegas in the mid-seventies and it was pretty glamorous. I knew people round here would know of **Caesar's Palace** so I decided to go for it'

'A lot of people smile as they go by, and we have had
customers refusing to write out cheques for us because they
weren't sure what to write. But on the whole the reaction is
very positive'

'We had a shop in the town first and that was a sports shop
with a hairdresser's in the back which is where the name
came from, because it was to do with running'

'It was called **Hair by Richard**, but I wanted something catchy and memorable'

TRIMMINDALES
HAIR SALON

8802 3316

www.trimmindales.

'I had a few names like **Barber King** etc. But when I found this place in Station Road and the railway station was at the top of the hill I just thought **Railway Cuttings**'

'There was a book, a Glasgow book, we got the idea
from a book'

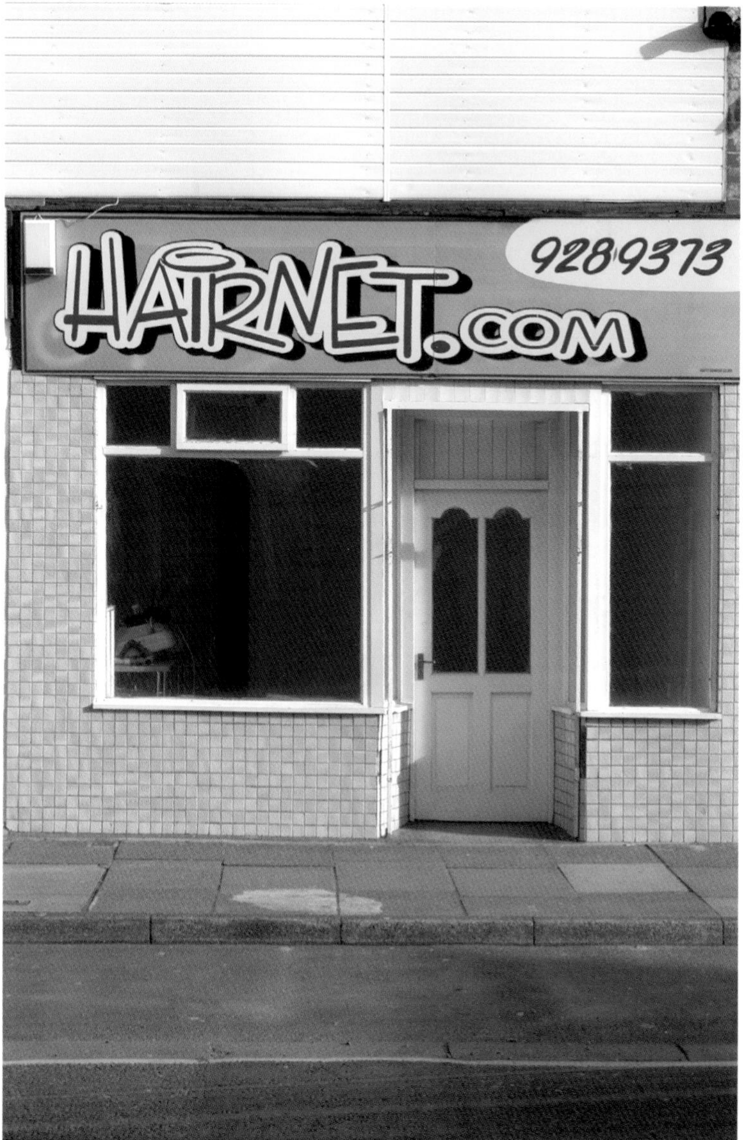
HAIRNET.COM
928 9373

'My husband thought of it; he's a solicitor. I loved it'

'We came up with **Hair and Rabbit**, because a lot of talking goes on here. But that sounded like a pub so we changed it to **Hairs and Graces** because we don't have any airs and graces. We're very down to earth, it's like a social club really'

Inhairitance

Ladies Hair Designers

'We opened the salon in 1996. We called it **Shearers** because Alan Shearer was still so popular round here at that time and we liked the double meaning'

'We do highlights, flashes, easy mesh, boils, colour correction and most things to do with colour'

'I was working at an airline so I always had the name, but when I bought the shop and it was in Terminus Road that was when I added the **Beauty Terminal**'

'We got the name from, err, I can't remember what his name is. He had a programme on TV. He wasn't a celebrity … Alan Bennett – it was Alan Bennett. He had a series on TV called **Talking Heads** and we liked the name'

'We knew about the comedy **Smith and Jones** but we didn't know about the cowboys. Only the other day my mum called up and told us to turn on the telly to watch the cowboys'

Hairwaves Beauty Centre
AFRO UNISEX HAIRDRESSING SALON

TEL:0181 809 1843

- PLAITING
- WEAVE - ON
- BONDING
- CURLY - PERM
- RELAXER
- PONY T
- CUT & T
- HAIR TREATMENT
- CORNROW
- WASH & SET

EXPERIENCES
STYLIST
REQUIRED
APPLY WITHIN
NOW!

'I was inspired by a documentary on hedonism in Jamaica. I looked it up in the dictionary and it said, "total fulfilment" and I thought that was pretty good for a hairdresser's'

You'll be having it off with . . . .

HAve it Off

178 Field End Road
Eastcote
HA5 1RF

you'll be off it

Telephone:
020 8426 2040

'Before I opened the salon I was looking through magazines trying to get inspiration and my daughter was watching **The Jungle Book**, then that song came on!'

'Our mum made up the name. "Herr" being German for mister
and we're a gents' barber'

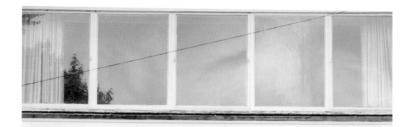

HEADS OF STATE

Tel: 01628 627243

UNISEX SALON

'My sister wanted to work with me so we went for something
with a feminine touch'

Alive &

☎ 01792 830973 | UNISEX HAIRDRI

HAIR &
BEAUTY.
CAMDEN LOCKS
BODY
PIERCIN
020-7284 4
DREADLOCKS
SUNBEDS
TATTOOS
10AM – 7PM
OPEN

'I was a big Pink Floyd fan and Roger Waters
had an album of that name'

tel. 01926 337766

BLONDE

'I made a list of about one hundred names then pretended to answer the phone using each name until I came to the one I liked, and that was **Chop & Change**'

'My name is William Burns, my son stopped me from calling it **Clippers** saying to call it **Sideburns**. When I heard that, that was it'

'It's something to do with a fella's hair, that the bosses used to do, and it was a perfect flick'

blade

ADT

hair

- european & afro caribbean
- cutting/styling
- colouring
- highlights
- relaxers/perms
- hair conditioning
- human hair extensions
- braids

quality products

kerastase

redken

fudge

PUSH

MOUNTGRANGE

unners"

beauty

facials
body treatments
self tanning
waxing
electrolysis
manicures & pedicures
body massage

quality products
md formulation

Salon
2255

7.00pm
8.00pm
6.00pm
5.00pm

hill.com
beauty)

md formulations

ST.TROPEZ
Air

Airbrush Tanning from
the celebrities favourite

1
CLEANSE

2
CARE

st tropez

jessica

KÉRASTASE
PARIS

'We've always been into gangster films and we wanted to have something no one else had got. We were looking at the poster by the door, so we just took the 'f' off and put on the 'b' to get the name. The locals love it'

'I bought the shop and hadn't got a clue what to call it. I was sat here all ready to open and the guy next door, he has an electronics shop, he came up with it, and we thought it was great. He also suggested **Captain Ceranium** and **Halo Halo**'

HAIR RAZIN

TEL: 01702 461678

UNISEX STUDIO

Ahead 4 Hair
☎ 724080

HAIRDRESSERS ☎ 724080

'My wife and I named it, we liked the play on words, it's also nice and near the beginning of the phone book'

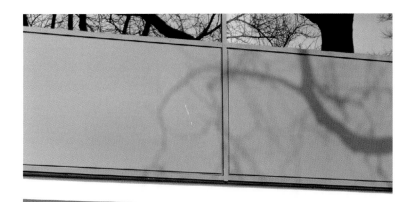

'I took the salon over seven years ago. It was already called **Public Hair**, I revamped it and someone stole the 'l' so I replaced it and it was stolen again. That happened again and again for about a year so I've left it'

Hair we all are ...

Ahead 4 Hair . . . . Eastbourne
Alias Quiff & Combs. Stoke-on-
. . . . Trent
Alive & Klippin' . . . . . Pontardwe
Alley Barber . . . . Basildon
Barbarama . . . . Hastings
Barber Blacksheep. . Brighton
Beauty & the
Beast. . . . . London
. . . . SW13
The Best Little Hair
House . . . . Belfast
blade runners . . . . . . London W1D
Blonde Ambition. . . . Leamington
. . . . Spa
Blonde Dye Bleach. . Southend-on-
. . . . Sea
Bobs & Croppers . . . London SE18
Bright 'n' Bleach. . . . Brighton
British Hairways . . . . Sheffield
Camden Locks . . . . . London NW1
Chepstow Choppers London W2
Chop . . . . Cheddar
Chop & Change. . . . . Addlestone
Clear Cut . . . . Glasgow
Curling U Softley . . . Southport
Curl Up And Dye. . . . New Malden
Cut'N'Run. . . . . Glasgow
The Cutting Corner. . Bletchley
Cutting Remarks. . . . Bromley
The Directors Cut . . . Ealing
expHAIRtease . . . . . . Huddersfield
Fat Boy Trims . . . . . . Brighton
The Final Cut . . . . Belfast
Fort Locks . . . . Little
. . . . Wavering
Fresh Hair . . . . Hastings
fringe.comb . . . . London
. . . . SW19
The Godbarber . . . . . Hanley

Grateful Heads . . . . . Southend-on-
. . . . Sea
Hackers . . . . Hanley
Hair & Now. . . . . London W10
Hair Apparent, ... London W6
Hair Base . . . . Hanley
Hair Expectations . . London N8
Hairlennium . . . . Keighley
Hairloom . . . . London W4
Hairnet.com . . . . Liverpool
Hair Necessities . . . . Stoke-on-
. . . . Trent
Hairods of Skipton . . Skipton
Hairoglyphics . . . . . . Brighton
Hairport . . . . Eastbourne
Hair Razin. . . . . Basildon
Hairs & Graces . . . . . London SE21
Hairs & Sirs . . . . Liverpool
Hair Say . . . . Warrington
Hairwaves Beauty
Centre . . . . London N9
Have It Off . . . . Pinner
The Head Gardener . London SW1
Headmasters. . . . . . . London W4
Headnizm. . . . . London SE22
Heads of State . . . . . Maidenhead
Heads-U-Win . . . . Aintree
Herr Flick . . . . Bilston
Herr Kutz . . . . Warsash
Illegally Blonde . . . . . Leamington
. . . . Spa
In Fringe. . . . . Bootle
Inhairitance . . . . Clydach
It Will Grow Back . . . London E8
Mane Event . . . . London SE1
March Hair . . . . Chandlers
. . . . Ford
Max Headroom . . . . . Hastings
Ministry of Hair . . . . . Eastbourne
The Nut House . . . . . Benfleet

LADIES

Shampoo and Set		£8.50
Cut, Shampoo and Set		£12.00
Blow Dry	*from*	£10.00
Cut and Blow Dry	*from*	£14.50
Restyle and Blow Dry	*from*	£18.00
Dry Cutting	*from*	£10.50
Wash and Cut	*from*	£12.00
Hair Up	*from*	£12.00
Tong Up		£8.50

CHILDREN'S

Dry Cut (under 4 yrs)	*from*	£5.00
Dry Cut (up to 10 yrs)	*from*	£6.00
Cut and Blow Dry		£11.00
Restyle and Blow Dry		£13.00
Blow Dry		£7.00
Hair Up	*from*	£8.50
Wash and Cut	*from*	£7.00

Tintin
Hi Lig
Semi
Natura
Toner
Easi M

Senior
Logic
Goldw
Goldw
All acid

All Pe
Se